```
PS        Vanden Heuvel,
3535        Michael, 1956-
.I224     Elmer Rice
Z93
1996         JUL 2 5 2000
```

ELMER RICE

Photo courtesy of The Billy Rose Theatre Collection, The New York Library for the Performing Arts, Astor, Lenox and Tilden Foundations.

ELMER RICE

A Research and Production Sourcebook

Michael Vanden Heuvel

Modern Dramatists Research and Production Sourcebooks,
Number 9
William W. Demastes, Series Adviser

GREENWOOD PRESS
Westport, Connecticut • London

Library of Congress Cataloging-in-Publication Data

Vanden Heuvel, Michael.
   Elmer Rice : a research and production sourcebook / Michael Vanden Heuvel.
     p.   cm.—(Modern dramatists research and production sourcebooks, ISSN 1055–999X ; no. 9)
   Includes bibliographical references and indexes.
   ISBN 0–313–27431–2 (alk. paper)
   1. Rice, Elmer, 1892–1967—Criticism and interpretation. 2. Rice, Elmer, 1892–1967—Dramatic production. 3. Rice, Elmer, 1892–1967—Stage history. 4. Rice, Elmer, 1892–1967—Bibliography.
I. Title. II. Series.
PS3535.I224Z93   1996
812′.52—dc20   95–39030

British Library Cataloguing in Publication Data is available.

Copyright © 1996 by Michael Vanden Heuvel

All rights reserved. No portion of this book may be reproduced, by any process or technique, without the express written consent of the publisher.

Library of Congress Catalog Card Number: 95-39030
ISBN: 0-313-27431-2
ISSN: 1055-999X

First published in 1996

Greenwood Press, 88 Post Road West, Westport, CT 06881
An imprint of Greenwood Publishing Group, Inc.

Printed in the United States of America

The paper used in this book complies with the
Permanent Paper Standard issued by the National
Information Standards Organization (Z39.48–1984).

10 9 8 7 6 5 4 3 2 1

Contents

Preface	vii
Acknowledgments	ix
A Note on Codes and Numbering	xi
Chronology	1
Elmer Rice: Life and Career	5
The Plays: Summaries and Critical Overviews	9
On Trial (1914)	9
The Iron Cross (1915)	12
The House in Blind Alley (1916)	13
Home of the Free (1917)	16
A Diadem of Snow (1918)	17
Help! Help! (1919)	19
Wake Up, Jonathan (1921)	19
It Is the Law (1922)	22
The Adding Machine (1923)	23
Black Sheep (1923)	26
Close Harmony (1924)	30
The Subway (1924)	32
The Gay White Way (1925)	35
The Passing of Chow-Chow (1925)	36
The Sidewalks of New York (1925)	36
Cock Robin (1928)	37
Street Scene (1929)	40
See Naples and Die (1929)	43
The Left Bank (1931)	46
Counsellor-at-Law (1931)	47

We, the People (1933)	51
Judgment Day (1934)	57
Between Two Worlds (1934)]	61
Not for Children (1935)	64
American Landscape (1938)	67
Two on an Island (1940)	70
Flight to the West (1940)	74
A New Life (1943)	78
Dream Girl (1945)	82
Street Scene (musical) (1947)	85
The Grand Tour (1951)	86
Love Among the Ruins (1951)	88
The Winner (1954)	91
Cue for Passion (1958)	94
Court of Last Resort (1965)	95
Primary Bibliography	99
Non-Dramatic Primary Works	99
Dramatic Publications	114
Unpublished Collected Materials	
(Archival Sources)	123
Annotated Secondary Bibliography: Reviews	129
Annotated Secondary Bibliography: Books, Articles, Sections	179
Productions and Credits	209
Author Index	233
General Index	237

Preface

Elmer Rice: A Research and Production Sourcebook is intended to make Rice's writings accessible to as wide an audience as possible. Rice was a voluminous writer of letters, articles, and diatribes as well as plays, memoirs and novels, and for this reason an exhaustive bibliography placing his significant writing in some relational context has been difficult to achieve. For readers coming to Rice for the first time, the present text provides a chronology of his achievements, as well as plot synopses and critical overviews of each produced or published play. Theatre researchers will find cast lists and an exhaustive bibliography of reviews of productions, while the listing of archival sources should be of help to those wishing to pursue more focused study of Rice's substantial canon. The short biography illuminates Rice's involvement at all levels of cultural production, as a playwright, producer, director, teacher and polemicist for various theatrical and political causes. The two indexes which close the volume will provide a resource for those seeking the names of those involved in the production of Rice's plays and the critical reception of them.

Acknowledgments

I have benefitted from the help and patience of library staff from around the country. I am grateful to those who helped me at each of the following: Hayden Library, Arizona State University; the Performing Arts Library, Lincoln Center, particularly those in the Billy Rose Collection; the Harry Ransom Humanities Research Center at the University of Texas at Austin; and the Library of Congress.

The Office for Research and Strategic Initiatives at Arizona State University supported me with two faculty grants which allowed summer research and travel. My stays on the East Coast were made considerably easier and more pleasurable by conversations and hospitality offered by Chris Wheatley and Ernest Suarez of Catholic University, Washington D. C. Bill Demastes receives thanks for exhibiting more patience than editors are known to possess, as well as for his foresight in initiating this project with Greenwood Press. Dundea Krebs and Isabelle Rucks provided useful translations, for which I am grateful. I thank Marilyn Benedict for the formatting of the manuscript. In addition, I thank Maureen Melino and George Butler at Greenwood for helping to see the project through.

Scholars never create their books in a vacuum, though they sometimes leave one as they spend considerable time away from their loved ones to conduct research. So for the time that's gone and for the time I hope now to have, this book is dedicated to Tracy.

A Note on Codes and Numbering

"A" – A prefix identifying primary, non-dramatic references alphabetically and annotated in the "Primary Bibliography"

"P" – A prefix identifying productions of plays listed in "Productions and Credits"

"R" and "S" – Descriptive prefixes identifying reviews ("R") and other secondary materials ("S"). These references and annotations are chronologically combined and are located in numerical sequence in the "Secondary Bibliography"

Chronology

1892 Elmer Leopold Reizenstein is born 28 September on Ninetieth Street in New York City to Jacob and Fanny (Lion).

1912 Graduates cum laude from New York Law School (LL.B.).

1913 Admitted to the New York bar in December. Collaborates with Frank Harris on two unpublished plays, *A Defection from Grace* and *The Seventh Commandment*. Also writes *The Passing of Chow-Chow* (published 1925).

1914 *On Trial* opens at Candler Theatre on 19 August 1914 and runs for more than 350 performances.

1915 Marries Hazel Levy in June. Studies drama and directing at Columbia University, becoming involved with the Morningside Players. *The Iron Cross* is produced there non-professionally (February 1917), along with *Home of the Free* (April 1917), the first American plays opposing WWI.

1916 Witnesses child work law violations in the South and writes *The House in Blind Alley* (pub. 1932).

1921 The farce *Wake Up, Jonathan* (written with Hatcher Hughes) opens 19 January. Changes name to Rice in time to be noted as such in program.

1923 *The Adding Machine* premieres. Writes *Black Sheep* (produced 1932).

1924 Collaboration with Dorothy Parker on *Close Harmony*. Rice also works on two adaptations of German plays, Herman Bahr's *The Mongrel* (produced December) and Rudolph Lothar's *The Blue Hawaii* (unpublished, produced in Boston). Writes *The Subway*, which does not see production until 1929.

1925 Writes *The Sidewalks of New York*, which contains the genesis of *Street*

Scene. Portions of the former are published as *The Gay White Way* and *Three Plays Without Words* in 1934. Also finishes *Life Is Real* (unpublished in America), which is published and produced in Germany as *Wir in Amerika* (1929).

1928 Collaboration with Philip Barry on *Cock Robin*.

1929 Rice's most productive year opens with *Street Scene*, which premieres on 10 January. After many difficulties, *The Subway* opens in Greenwich Village. *Street Scene* earns Rice his only Pulitzer Prize. In September, *See Naples and Die* is produced.

1930 *A Voyage to Purilia*, Rice's first novel, is published.

1931 *The Left Bank* premieres on 5 October. It is followed by *Counsellor-at-Law* which opens 6 November.

1932 Rice's shortest-running produced play, *Black Sheep*, opens and closes after just four performances.

1933 *We, the People* opens at the Empire Theatre on 21 January.

1934 Opening of *Judgment Day* on 12 September at the Belasco Theatre. Also, *Between Two Worlds* premieres on 25 October at the same site. Both plays meet little success, and Rice "resigns" from the stage with a passionate outburst against commercial interests in theatre in a speech given at Columbia University.

1935 The satiric parody of Broadway, *Not for Children*, opens in London and California. Rice writes to Harry Hopkins proposing formation of what will become the Federal Theatre Project, with Rice as a regional director. Initiates the Theatre Alliance in order to "put theatre in the hands of those who work creatively in it."

1936 Citing the censorship of the Living Newspaper's *Ethiopia*, Rice resigns as regional director of the Federal Theatre Project.

1937 Rice's second novel, *Imperial City* is published.

1938 Along with Robert Sherwood, Sidney Howard, Maxwell Anderson. and S. N. Berhman, Rice forms the Playwright's Company. Directs Sherwood's Pulitzer-Prize winner, *Abe Lincoln in Illinois*, in New York. In December, *American Landscape* opens at the Cort Theatre, marking Rice's return to playwriting.

1940 *Two on an Island*, starring Betty Field, opens at the Broadhurst Theatre in January.

1942 Divorces Hazel Levy and marries Betty Field.

Chronology

1943	*A New Life* opens on 9 September.
1945	*Dream Girl*, written for Betty Field, opens at the Coronet Theatre for almost 350 performances.
1946	The musical version of *Street Scene*, with book by Rice, music by Kurt Weill and lyrics by Langston Hughes, opens in January.
1949	*The Show Must Go On*, Rice's third and last novel, is published.
1951	*The Grand Tour* premieres and Rice finishes *Love Among the Ruins* (prod. 1963).
1958	*Cue for Passion*, Rice's last New York play, opens. Divorced from Betty Field.
1959	Rice's critical study of international theatre as a social institution, *The Living Theatre*, is published. He resigns his directorship of the Playwright's Company.
1961	Receives honorary doctorate of letters from the University of Michigan-Ann Arbor.
1963	Publishes his autobiography, *Minority Report*. Robert Hogan produces the 1951 play *Love Among the Ruins* non-professionally at the University of Rochester, with Rice in attendance.
1966	Marries Barbara Marshall.
1967	Rice dies on 8 May en route to Southampton, England, of pneumonia at the age of seventy-four.

Elmer Rice:
Life and Career

We may find it hard to imagine today that, when critics of the mid-twentieth century ranked American playwrights, they sometimes had to pause before promoting O'Neill over Elmer Rice as first among his peers (Hogan [S9]; Lewis [S96]; Chametzky [S148]). Rice, like O'Neill, had an astoundingly long and productive life in the American theatre. He made and sustained his reputation with a series of hit plays, potboilers and provocative experimental work which, next to the output of O'Neill, remains the most varied canon of dramatic literature produced by an American playwright. Moreover, unlike the reticent O'Neill, Rice was a true public man of letters and of the theatre, having worked, in addition to playwriting, as a Pulitzer-Prize winning director, theatre owner, producer, and tireless and vocal advocate for (as well as critic of) the popular American theatre.

Born Elmer Reizenstein on 28 September 1892 in New York, Rice grew up in Manhattan and lived most of his life in proximity to it. He was educated in the New York public school system and New York University, where he went to study law. After taking a job as a law clerk while awaiting his bar exam, Rice began to write plays for local competitions. His first plays, written with Frank Harris, were *A Defection from Grace* and *The Seventh Commandment*, the former winning a second prize from the Century Theatre Club. His first solo effort, *The Passing of Chow-Chow*, was produced non-professionally at Columbia University and won him a silver cup.

Rice burst onto Broadway in 1914 with one of the legendary first-nighters of all time, *On Trial*. This potboiler created a sensation because it used the cinematic technique of flashback to tell its crime detection story backward. Rice was lauded by the critics for the innovation and offered the amazing sum of $30,000 for the rights to the play the night of its first performance. He declined the offer and made over $100,000 from the play. Rice married his first wife, Hazel Levy in 1915, and spent the next several years studying drama at Columbia and writing more plays. *The Iron Cross*, a pacifist indictment of war, was his first attempt at the social drama which remained his primary metier. It was followed by plays expressing Rice's outrage at child labor (*The House in Blind Alley*), his suspicions of ultra-liberal social theory (*The Home of the Free*), and his humorous take on the Bolshevik revolution (*A Diadem of Snow*). Not coincidentally, Rice was by 1917 working in a rough neighborhood, New York's University Settlement, learning the experiences and the speech idioms of both slum dwellers and social workers. None of the plays written during the period, however, saw professional production.

While tinkering with other crime dramas (*Find the Woman* [adapted and produced in 1919 as *For the Defense*], and *It Is the Law* [prod. 1922]), Rice collaborated with his Columbia drama professor, Hatcher Hughes, to produce *Wake Up, Jonathan* (1921). He returned to serious Broadway fare in 1923 with *The Adding Machine*, a quasi-expressionistic satire against mass culture and technology. Though poorly received, the play remains one of the most anthologized works in the repertory: in 1995, a virtual reality-based production of the play was mounted at the University of Kansas. After more collaborations (*Close Harmony* with Dorothy Parker [1924] and *Cock Robin* with Philip Barry [1927]) and extensive overseas travel over the next three years, Rice returned to Broadway in 1929 with the solo effort, *Street Scene*, which won him his only Pulitzer Prize. Almost unnoticed the same year, *The Subway*, a more intensive realization of expressionist techniques, opened and quickly closed. The rest of the decade was devoted to several plays (*See Naples and Die* [1929], *The Left Bank* [1931] and *Counsellor-at-Law* [1931]) which ranged from moderate to significant successes. He also published his first novel in 1930, a satire of Hollywood entitled *A Voyage to Purilia*.

In the thirties Rice produced a series of plays dealing with the Depression and the rise of fascism. *We, the People* (1933), *Judgment Day* (which dealt with the Reichstag fire which brought Hitler to prominence [1934]) and *Between Two Worlds* (1934) all attacked complacency and privilege while suggesting avenues of hope and rapprochement between America's isolated past and the more complex present. While the plays were uniformly rejected by audiences, they kept Rice's name alive by the critical debates and contention they spawned. These led eventually to Rice's well-publicized "retirement" from the theatre in October of 1934.

After an absence of four years, during which he wrote his second novel (*Imperial City*, 1937) and helped organize and administer the Federal Theatre Project, Rice returned to Broadway as a founding member of the Playwrights' Company. He first directed Robert Sherwood's Pulitzer-winning *Abe Lincoln in Illinois* and then produced his own *American Landscape* (1938). This was followed by the comedy *Two on an Island* (1940), a vehicle for Rice's new love interest, the actress Betty Field. Rice renewed his attack on fascism with *Flight to the West* (1940). Meanwhile, he had resigned his position with the Federal Theatre Project over issues of censorship.

After divorcing Hazel Levy, Rice married Field in 1942. In 1943 she starred in *A New Life*. Following several unproduced plays, Rice created the very popular *Dream Girl*, also starring Field and later made into a film.

After the mid-1940s Rice's dramatic output waned as he increasingly turned to other forms of writing: a third novel, *The Show Must Go On* (1949); a collection of theatre essays, *The Living Theatre* (1959); and his autobiography, *Minority Report* (1963). An earlier metatheatrical satire, *Not for Children*, was revised and produced in 1951, as was *The Grand Tour*. Both were shunned by critics and theatregoers. He wrote *Love Among the Ruins* the same year, though the play did not see production until 1963. 1954 brought another failure, *The Winner*, and Rice produced his last play, *Cue for Passion*, a modern adaptation of *Hamlet*, in 1958. He divorced Betty Field in 1955 and married again, to Barbara Marshall, in 1966. At the time of his death in 1967, he was circulating two new manuscripts, *Slaves of the Lamp* and *Court of Last Resort*. The former was never published and neither has been produced.

Elmer Rice died of complications from a heart attack while en route to Southampton, England, on 8 May 1967.

Several factors make an overall assessment of Rice's career difficult. First, as one would expect in the case of a playwright whose career spanned more than forty years and over fifty written plays, the quality of Rice's work varied widely from time to time. Second, his willingness to experiment with a variety of dramatic forms makes it impossible to characterize his output in any one category. Finally, as Robert Hogan (S98) suggested nearly three decades ago, one cannot separate Rice's career as a playwright from his very active public life.

Rice was first recognized as an ingenious adaptor of melodramatic form to new theatrical techniques. The tendency is obvious in *On Trial*, but appears as a common denominator in most of Rice's plays. As Wright (R53) notes, even *The Adding Machine*'s expressionism is a continuance of melodramatic styles. Rice never strayed far from the traditions of melodrama, but could as easily be betrayed as enriched by them. In *Street Scene*, for instance, the melodramatic love plot is revivified by its ironic juxtaposition to the debilitating conditions of tenement life. In other plays (*Two on an Island*, *Dream Girl*, and, to contrary effect, *The Subway*) Rice utilizes melodrama to counterpoint comic and tragic effects. More often, however, Rice was susceptible to a too heavy dependence on simple melodramatic plots, stereotyped characterizations, and heightened language, and this often weakened his plays and nettled his critics. The problem is especially apparent in the plays of social commentary and in the anti-fascism plays of the early thirties. Atkinson (R164, R201, R239) was almost alone in noting, but forgiving, Rice's intemperate use of highly-charged rhetoric and plot coincidences to achieve a polemical edge in these plays. More common are the charges by Garland (R135, R159, R261) and Brown (R134, R157, S48) that Rice was sacrificing artistic polish in order to preach stridently to already-converted audiences.

Rice's dramaturgy was eclectic, but thematically there exists a common denominator linking all but a few of his plays. As Rice himself stated several times, his work dramatizes the various threats that exist to the idea of personal freedom ("Apologia Pro Vita Sua" [A47]). He promoted in his plays and other writings a philosophy based in an amalgam of democratic, mildly socialist, and liberal traditions (Mendelsohn [S92]) that in their own time were susceptible to attack from both the Right (Brown [S48]) and the Left (Himelstein [S91], Miller and Frazer [S158]). Palmieri (S141) argues that, like Shaw, Rice used the stage as a platform for social reform. One might add that Rice also resembles his British forbearer in his rigorous quest for new forms through which to express his desire for reform, although according to Greenfield (S147) Rice often let the experimentation draw attention from the overall social impact of the plays. Despite attempts by Levin (S19), Lewis (S96) and others to categorize the work into fixed "phases," however, the fact is that Rice often wrote almost simultaneously in melodramatic, realist, expressionist and agit-prop form, sometimes collapsing them into the same play. Therefore, while the consensus view that Rice's work diminished after *Dream Girl* in 1945 seems valid, this cannot be traced to his preference for one form or another of dramatic expression. More likely it is cultural and historical factors, such as the diminishing role of the Old Left as a viable perspective from which to critique American culture, that make Rice's plays often appear dated.

A more inclusive approach to Rice would analyze his career as a network or system of various historical confluences that as a whole represent American theatre and culture from World War I to the beginnings of the counterculture movements of the early sixties (Hogan [S98]). This would allow a study of the texts while also taking into account Rice's activities as a forceful cultural agent: his involvement with, and later critique of, the Theatre Guild; his tireless battle in the press against censorship; the debates spawned by his plays regarding the viability of drama dealing critically with topical social themes; his long career as a distinguished director and theatre owner; his short but significant role as administrator of the WPA Theatre Project and his perhaps even more significant resignation from the post; his status as a founding member of the Playwrights' Company and subsequent championing of repertory theatre, lower ticket prices, and university-produced drama; and, finally, his consistent quest to reveal Broadway theatre as mendacious by bringing traditions of non-Western theatre to light for American readers. Within such a broad context Rice's career could be assessed not solely by the longevity or significance of his dramatic texts alone, but by his position in relation a number of important foci in the history of American theatre and culture in general. The study of a man so imbedded in the civic and artistic life of the nation that, when his play *Flight to the West* faltered among the critics, Albert Einstein wrote to encourage him, should not be isolated to few dramatic texts.

The Plays: Summaries and Critical Overviews

The following is a collection of summaries and overviews of Rice's dramatic canon, including significant unproduced and/or unpublished plays. The summaries provide descriptions of central characters and outlines of significant events in the plot. Each overview includes sketches of the play's stage history, critical responses to it, and ensuing scholarly assessments. Full discussion of Rice's collaborations and adaptations of other artists' work is included. Important musical adaptations of Rice's work are also covered. A list of reviews follows each critical summary, keyed to the numbers assigned to the assessments in the Secondary Bibliography. Unless otherwise noted, dates are for premieres.

On Trial (1914)

Characters — ROBERT STRICKLAND: the defendant; DORIS: his daughter; MAY STRICKLAND: his wife; MR. DEANE: May's father, now deceased; GERALD TRASK: a business associate of Strickland's, killed by Strickland; MRS. TRASK: his wife; GLOVER: Trask's personal secretary; GRAY: the district attorney; ARBUCKLE: Strickland's defense counsel; JUDGE DINSMORE: presiding over the Trask murder case; DR. MORGAN: a court physician; RUSSELL: a hotel manager; TRUMBLE: foreman of the jury.

Plot Summary — PROLOGUE: After finishing jury selection, Gray gives the opening argument for prosecution. He reports that Strickland had borrowed $10,000 from Trask, and paid it back in cash on June 24. Later that evening, two men broke into Trask's house, robbed the safe containing the money, and shot Trask to death. Gray reports that Strickland has plead guilty and has asked not to have a trial. Arbuckle opens his defense by telling the jury that May Strickland has mysteriously disappeared after the murder, moving him to become suspicious of Strickland's guilty plea. He tells the jury he intends to call nine-year old Doris Strickland to the stand. Strickland interrupts his counsel, saying he does not want to traumatize his child. The trial begins with Mrs. trask taking the stand.

ACT I, Scene 1: Flashback to Trask's library, evening. Mrs. Trask and Glover are conversing when the phone rings. Mrs. Trask answers and finds it is a woman calling for her husband. She responds angrily, noting that she has had to deal with his infidelities for many years. Trask arrives and asks Glover to open his safe, but cannot produce the combination. He notes that he had inadvertently given the business card with the combination on it to Strickland. Trask succeeds in remembering the combination, and opens the safe. He tells Glover that Strickland paid off a $10,000 note in cash that day, and instructs Glover to put the money into the safe. After Glover leaves, the Trasks argue over Gerald's womanizing, with Mrs. Trask threatening a divorce. At first Gerald is compliant, but when Mrs. Trask threatens to bring up a thirteen-year old story about Gerald's seduction of a "Miss Deane," Trask changes tactics and convinces his wife that he has put the past behind him and wants to start anew with her. She succumbs, and both retire to their rooms. In the darkness, a figure goes to the safe, opens it, removes the money, and drops the cash box. Mrs. Trask arrives to investigate, and is thrown down and choked by the assailant. Strickland arrives at the French doors, and the burglar flees. As Strickland bends down to her aid, the phone rings and Gerald re-enters to answer. Strickland sees him, fires a revolver twice, and kills Trask. Glover appears, and subdues Strickland with a heavy cane.

ACT I, Scene 2: Back in the courtroom, Dr. Morgan has taken the stand to report on Trask's autopsy. Gray rests his case. Arbuckle calls Doris Strickland to the stand over her father's protests. She begins to testify.

ACT II, Scene 1: Flashback to June 24, early evening at the Strickland home. May is calling the railroad to report a lost purse. When Doris overhears and asks her mother about it, May tries to cover up the story. Strickland arrives and greets his daughter until Trask arrives. The two men resolve the issue of the note, and Trask gives Strickland the business card which also has his safe combination written on the back. Strickland offers to introduce Trask to May. He declines, but runs into her when he departs, leaving May nonplussed. May and Strickland then discuss their plans for moving west, until they are interrupted by Burke, who arrives to report he has found May's purse at the Long Branch station. May at first denies it is hers, but eventually must own up to it. Strickland questions her behavior, forcing May to prevaricate, until she finally is caught up in her story. Strickland surmises that May has been to Trask's home, and suspects she has been unfaithful. May tells him she wants to tell the truth, but is constrained by something she must conceal. He grabs his revolver and dashes out. May tries to call Trask, but gets Mrs. Trask instead.

ACT II, Scene 2: Back in the courtroom, Doris is finishing her story. She says that when May called Trask a second time, she heard a loud report over the phone. Her mother then said goodbye, and disappeared.

ACT III, Scene 1: The next day in the courtroom. Arbuckle arrives late, explaining that Mrs. Strickland had come to him the prior evening to tell her story. He calls her as his next witness. May reveals she is the former Miss Deane, and that she had met Gerald Trask two years before marrying Strickland.

ACT III, Scene 2: Flashback to 1900, where May is preparing breakfast in a hotel room she shares with Trask. Gerald has been proposing to her for some months, and she has finally agreed to say yes. Trask says they must wed secretly because of family concerns. They have traveled to the resort to be married by a clergyman friend of Trask's. Because the minister had not arrived on schedule, May has consented to share her bed with her presumed husband-to-be. Russell, the hotel manager, arrives with a telegram from May's father, saying he is arriving soon and would like Trask detained. By now, everyone but May realizes that Trask has seduced her. Mr. Deane arrives with Mrs. Trask, but Gerald has escaped in a waiting car.

ACT III, Scene 3: Back in the courtroom, May finishes her testimony. She reports that she married Robert for love, and had managed to put Trask out of her mind. She was troubled when Trask became a business associate of Strickland's, but hoped the impending move west would resolve the problem. But Trask arrived at her home on June 23, recognized her, and pressured her into coming to his home by threatening to reveal her past to Robert.

EPILOGUE, Scene 1: In the jury room there is a vote of 11 to 1 for acquittal. Trumble still feels Strickland may have been coming to Trask's home to rob the safe. The jury asks to hear Glover's testimony again.

EPILOGUE, Scene 2: Back in the courtroom, Glover's earlier testimony reveals he was the actual burglar. The jury proclaims Strickland innocent of murder.

Reviews — R01, R02, R03, R04, R05, R06, R07, R08, R09, R10, R11, R12, R13, R14, R15, R16, R17, R87, R267

Critical Overview — *On Trial* opened 19 August 1914 at the Candler Theatre and ran for 365 performances.

Rice's first important play garnered almost universally favorable reviews, many of which commented on the brilliance of his concept in joining cinematic techniques to dramatic writing. Hamilton (R7) even went so far as to claim that a recent article of his own had probably given Rice the idea for using the flashback. Price (R1) argues that the play's violation of all dramatic principles will free Rice to experiment for the rest of his career. He also suggests, anticipating Brecht, that the flashback technique will bring greater objectivity in the playwright's delineation of character because it frees it from sequence. Many critics (the anonymous reviewers of R3, R12) pointed out that, without the use of flashback, the play would devolve into hackneyed melodrama. An exception is the reviewer for *The Dramatist* (R6), who says the play fails when it attempts innovation but succeeds at conventional melodrama. Willa Cather (R14) provided the most negative review, saying the play was purely conventional and flawed despite the cinematic flourishes.

The Iron Cross (1915; produced 1917; published 1965)

Characters — WILLIAM: husband of Margaret and a patriot; MARGARET: wife of William, who suffers deprivations during the war; KARL SCHILLING: close friend of William and Margaret; FRIEDA: Margaret's sister, a refugee; ROSA: a war widow.

Plot Summary — ACT I: In their East Prussian farmhouse, William and Margaret stand over the body of Paul, a relative killed in the war. William is preparing to go to the front, as is his friend Karl. A Postman arrives to say that Paul has been given the Iron Cross posthumously. Marie, Paul's girlfriend, arrives and weeps at the bier. When it is revealed she is carrying Paul's child, Karl throws her out of the house. Captain Hable arrives to present the medal, while Karl makes sardonic comments about the morality of war. Margaret's sister Frieda arrives with a third sister's children, whose mother has been raped and murdered by Cossacks. William prepares to leave, giving Margaret a pistol to use on herself if the Cossacks threaten her honor.

ACT II: Karl is seen working on a clock, having returned from the war blind. Margaret's brother-in-law, Heinrich lies on the couch wounded. Margaret worries that she has not heard from William recently, but receives a letter this day. As she reads about William's heroic adventures at the front, Captain Halbe arrives to report that the Cossacks are entering the town. Frieda enters in a panic running from the soldiers. Margaret takes out her pistol, but is distracted for a moment. Frieda sees the soldiers in the window, and shoots herself. The Cossacks storm in and abduct Margaret.

ACT III: Margaret and Heinrich sit discussing the recent peace signing. Since William has not returned, Heinrich asks if she will marry him to help raise her nieces and nephews. She refuses to believe William is dead, and rejects him. He leaves with the children. Rosa arrives, another potential war widow who was raped by the Cossacks and has delivered a child. As they speak, William arrives amid great fanfare. He has lost an arm, but is covered with medals. After a joyous greeting, he discovers that Margaret was raped by the Cossacks. He asks why she did not commit suicide and calls her a coward. She explains that she survived in order to help the others, but he is not satisfied and leaves her.

ACT IV: Three months later, Karl and Margaret have restored the farm to some of its former prosperity. Karl tells her why there is no religious justification for war. William stumbles in while Margaret is out, and tells Karl how he has been rejected and forgotten by the country for which he done service. Karl tells him that he should beg for Margaret's forgiveness and ask her to take him back. When she returns, he kneels at her feet and begs for her compassion as she takes him in her arms.

Review — R19

Critical Overview — *The Iron Cross* opened in repertory at the Comedy Theatre on 13 February 1917.
Theatre Magazine (R19) called the play a "conventional peace tract" that lacked dramatic action. While the actors were praised the playwright was taken to task for being "perhaps too compassionate" to the Austrians.

The House in Blind Alley (1916; published 1932; unproduced)

Characters — GRANDMOTHER/MOTHER GOOSE; JOHN/JANFIRST; JACK THE GIANT KILLER; JULES/JULFIRST; CINDERELLA/LITTLE GIRL; GANDER; VARIOUS FAIRYTALE AND NURSERY-RHYME CHARACTERS

Plot Summary — ACT I: The stage curtain appears in the form of a book cover of Mother Goose tales. A modernized Mother Goose appears astride her gander, and discovers a newspaper. She is shocked to discover stories about child laborers, and resolves to do something about her children. She calls behind the curtain, and a variety of fairytale characters — Cinderella, Little Bo-Peep, Peter Piper, Jack Horner, etc. — appear. Mother Goose whispers to each of them, until the shadow of a large hand appears across the curtain and "opens" the page. We see John Furst reading from the fairytale book. His son Jack appears, dressed as the Giant Killer, and asks his father to help him enact a scene from the story. They are interrupted by Grandmother, who announces that John's brother Jules has arrived. Jules, a brusque businessman, enters and encourages John to buy shares in a coal mine. John balks at the offer, citing the terrible working conditions at the mine. Jules stalks out, and Grandmother enters to report that a waif has been discovered in the alley behind the house. The girl describes her terrible life as an oyster-shucker, until she tires and is brought to bed. A blackout follows, and when the lights come up we see Jack, now appearing as the actual Giant Killer, entering on a fantastic steed. An Old Woman (looking like Grandmother and Mother Goose) flies in on Gander, and tests Jack's kindness, wisdom, and courage. Satisfied he is a hero, she asks him to kill the last remaining giants, Janfirst and Julfirst, who enslave small children and then devour them at a special feast each year. She gives Jack three gifts, including magic spectacles and flashlight, along with the Gander. She also tells Jack that Cinderella is about to arrive, and suggests he offer himself as her champion. After she leaves, Jack falls asleep and the two giants enter (they look like John and Jules). One is cunning and duplicitous, the other a thing of brute force. As they discuss their means of acquiring wealth they enact an allegory of capitalism, which in their world depends upon the union of mystification and force. While Julfirst goes to round up the children in the village, Julfirst waits for Cinderella. Jack awaits and threatens to kill the giant, but Janfirst uses cunning rhetoric to convince Jack that he is actually a social reformer, and that Mother Goose is mad. As evidence of his work, Janfirst points to a line of children — the storybook characters who appeared earlier — and details their crimes and appropriate reforms. As each child passes by, the Gander sings a short ditty that explains what sort of labor the children are actually being forced into by the giants. When Cinderella appears, Jack is convinced she cannot be a miscreant because she is so beautiful. Over Janfirst's protests, he swears fealty to her. Janfirst tries to attack Jack, but is foiled by the Gander. Janfirst signals for Julfirst, who appears and runs off with Cinderella, Jack in pursuit.

ACT II: Outside the Furst house in Blind Alley, Janfirst races into a doorway, preceded by all the fairytale children. Jack arrives too late to enter, and casts about for help in knocking down the door. A stream of adult characters from various nursery rhymes — Peter White, Doctor Fell, Man in the Moon, Tweedle-Dee and Tweedle-Dum — appear in the guise of politicians, priests, teachers, doctors, scientists, and so on. Each provides Jack with a self-serving excuse or rationalization for not helping him rescue the children. Finally, Janfirst catches up to Jack, and again convinces him not to believe what he has seen, and to enter the house with him as his friend. First, however, he insists that Jack be blindfolded to protect his eyes from the bright and beautiful light in which the children inside play. Jack acquiesces, and is led inside. Cinderella is imprisoned in a cage, and the other children are at work in monotonous, grinding labor. Jack of course is blind to their suffering, and allows Janfirst to describe the splendid conditions of their existence. Eventually Jack insists on seeing for himself, but as he removes his wrap Janfirst switches on a bright shining light to blind him. Jack mistakes the light for reality, and remarks on its beauty. However, the Gander arrives and gives Jack the magic spectacles, which allow him to see things as they really are. Shocked at the real conditions, Jack charges Janfirst, but is intercepted by Julfirst. The two do battle, and Jack slays Julfirst. Janfirst strikes him from behind with a bag of gold, and imprisons him in the cage with Cinderella.

ACT III: In a fantastic feudal dining hall in Blind Alley, Janfirst leads his prisoners, including Jack. The giant leads them to a conveyor system, and locks them inside. Janfirst's retainers — the adults who refused Jack help earlier — enter, each carrying a stake which is attached to a noose around their necks. As they sit at Janfirst's table, they secure their respective stakes into the ground. Janfirst addresses them in a florid speech, informing them that Julfirst has been killed by an "agitator." At the end of the speech, Janfirst announces that they will now begin their feast. He engages the conveyor, which drags the silent children into a grinder and turns them into golden bread, loaves of which begin to appear off a ramp leading to the dining table. The retainers all scramble for the golden crumbs that are siphoned off to another quarter. Jack breaks his chain and makes for Janfirst, but catches himself on a stake and is immobilized. He appeals to the retainers to do something to save the children, but they respond by calling him a "socialist," "muckraker," and "revolutionist." They insist they do not want to know the source of the bread. When he continues to urge them to look, some of them begin to be swayed, but Janfirst convinces them to fall back. As Jack despairs of saving the day, the Gander flies in and drops him the magic flashlight. When Jack turns it on, a blinding flash occurs. Once it dims, the operations of the infernal machine are exposed, and the retainers see what is actually happening. They rush Janfirst, but it is too late; the last group of children, including Cinderella, are swallowed up by the grinder. Furious, the retainers beat Janfirst insensible. Jack suggests they check the "Refuse" bin of the machine to see if anyone survived. Several of the children come out, although transformed: one is a beggar, another a prostitute, a third a consumptive. All are taken in by the retainers, though their motivation sometimes seems questionable. Jack crawls into the machine to look for Cinderella, but when he emerges he brings only her corpse. Jack swoons over her body, just as Mother Goose appears on Gander and in a terrible wrath. She accuses the retainers of killing the "twin spirits of childhood," Jack and Cinderella, and she begins to weep. Janfirst rises from his stupor. A blackout is followed by the lights coming up once again in John Furst's study, where he is seen asleep in his chair. Grandmother wakes him, and John cries out that he has killed his own son. Grandmother calms him, but delivers the news that both the waif and Jack are missing. As they prepare to call the authorities a rough-featured man appears at the door with both children. He tells John that Jack had appeared at the oyster stalls with the waif, talking "nonsense" and asking for the giant of labor so that he might slay him. John pays off the man, and promises Jack that tomorrow they will go to seek this giant and to put an end to him. The curtain closes, and Mother Goose appears on the outside of the "book cover," smiling and waving to the audience.

Critical Overview — The play was never produced.

Home of the Free (1917)

Characters — JOHN CALVIN BURKE: a liberal-thinker; FELICIA HEMANS BURKE: his seemingly conventional wife; ROBERT INGERSOLL BURKE: their son, who has taken his father's precepts to heart; GENEVIEVE SWEET: his fiance, a "New Woman."

Plot Summary — In the Burke's spare living room, Mrs. Burke is observed darning and humming "The Rosary" while Robert listlessly reads "The Masses." He announces that Genevieve will soon visit, but chastises Mrs. Burke for being excited at the prospect. He asks that they be left alone when she arrives, explaining that he must speak to her about things his mother could not hope to understand (owing to her "unfortunate hereditary and environmental background"). He speaks of Genevieve as a "New Woman" and claims he has made her so. When Mrs. Burke asks if he intends to marry Genevieve, Robert dismisses the idea as Victorian and bourgeois, complaining that the idea infringes upon his liberty. He then admits he had intended to ask her just this question, but now will not because it is no longer a free choice. When Genevieve arrives, Mrs. Burke impulsively greets her, but is rebuffed by her guest's suspicion that she may be carrying the bubonic plague. Genevieve is reading a sociological tract for a seminar, and sees Robert's mother as a female neanderthal preceding the evolution of the New Woman. Mrs. Burke leaves and Robert asks Genevieve if she will "be the mother of [his] children." She agrees perfunctorily, mainly in order to pay heed to the Shavian Life Force about which they both have been reading. When Genevieve asks Robert if he loves her, be begins a disquisition on the social construction of love by sentimental poets, before indulging in a kiss. John Burke arrives, and as Genevieve prepares to leave they agree to "a maximum of five" children. She leaves as Robert's father enters. The two men argue about whose freedom to speak has precedence in the house. After compromising on the matter, John asks Robert if he had been kissing Genevieve. Robert refuses

A Diadem of Snow 17

"either to challenge or corroborate the testimony of [John's] senses," but finally tells his father that he has proposed to her. John tells him marriage between the two of them is impossible without explaining why. Robert threatens to marry her that night, so his father explains his reasons for opposing the marriage: Genevieve is actually Robert's half-sister. After agreeing he now cannot marry her, Robert tells his father that the "old-fashioned" Mrs. Burke must be told the truth. When she enters, John leaves and Robert tells her the story of her husband's infidelity. Surprisingly, she takes this calmly, and tells Robert he may still marry Genevieve because he, in fact, is not John Burke's child. She claims this is the result of her education, which taught her to "live up to her husband's principles."

Reviews — R18, R20

Critical Overview — *Home of the Free* was produced non-professionally at the Comedy Theatre at Columbia University on 22 April 1917 (directed by Rice), and later saw production by the Washington Square Players on 31 October, 1917.

Hogan (S95) reported in 1965 that the play still held the boards, having been produced five times in America over the past five years and once in Europe. The single extant review of the original performance in *Theatre Magazine* (R20) praises the bright and satiric style of the play, while also noting the startling final curtain. Palmieri (S141) comments on the topicality of the play's theme, while Hogan (S95) appreciatively comments on the play's droll depiction of liberalism.

A Diadem of Snow (published 1918)

Characters — NICHOLAS ROMANOFF: the deposed Czar of Russia, now living and working in exile in Tobolsk, Siberia; MRS. ROMANOFF: his wife, still infatuated with the memory of Rasputin; ALIOSHA: their son, heir to the Russian throne; VON BERNSTORFF: German envoy from Wilhem I; MRS. OSHINSKY: the Romanoff's neighbor, a shrill housewife.

Plot Summary — In an execrably furnished room dominated by an icon of Rasputin, Mrs. Oshinsky and Von Bernstorff (in disguise) appear. When Mrs. Romanoff appears, she and Mrs. Olshinsky exchange insults over the portrait of Rapsutin. After Mrs. Oshinsky leaves, the old man doffs his disguise and reveals his true identity, bowing before Mrs. Romanoff and calling her "your majesty." They discuss the post-revolutionary government now in power, and lament life in a democracy. She seems, however, relieved to be away from Petrograd and the burden of being in power. She tells Bernstorff that her husband has accepted democratic values to the extent that he no longer keeps any servants, and his reading now includes Tolstoi and Gorki. When she begins to grieve for Rasputin, Bernstorff tells her that the monk's actions were misdirected, claiming that only German politics represent the "political manifestation of the Will of God." He then informs her that he has come in order to restore the Romanoffs to power. At first Mrs. Romanoff balks, but when she considers that it is her son, Aliosha's, natural destiny, she agrees to support the effort. However, when Nicholas is heard at the door, Bernstorff hides.

Nicholas now returns from his job as a snow shoveller, lauding the benefits of hard work. He tries to convince his wife to accompany him to a Chaplin film, which has been highly recommended by a cab driver. Mrs. Olshinsky interrupts, dragging in Aliosha, whom she claims has assaulted her son. When the two women go at one another, Nicholas calms them with Christian sentiments. After dismissing Mrs. Olshinsky, Nicholas asks Aliosha what caused the brawl, and the boy explains that it was the result of playing "revolution." He reports that he is always forced to play the role of Nicholas, which entails abdicating his throne and giving the other boys all his money. On this day, Mrs. Olshinsky's son wanted to play "counter-revolution," and, disconcerted by this thought, Aliosha struck the boy. Nicholas is saddened by the story, but joyful at the outcome and proud of his son for denying the counter-revolution.

At this moment Bernstorff reveals himself, and tries to pay obeisance to the former Czar. Disdaining such attention, Nicholas claims he should not be treated differently than any other free man. He goes on to tell Bernstorff that his cousin, Wilhelm I of Germany, should also try hard work and exercise. Bernstorff, aghast at Nicholas's behavior, reveals what his true mission is. Nicholas is first frightened, then amused by the idea. Bernstorff mistakes this as interest, and details the planned counter-revolution, which includes blowing up the provisional government and enforcing order with the use of German troops dressed up as Cossacks. Nicholas calls the plan "degenerate," and claims that, even if he were interested, he could not become involved since his snow shoveller's union does not allow him to hold political office. When Bernstorff chides him for his reticence, Nicholas takes him to the window and shows him the Tobolsk barracks, in which hundreds of thousands of exiles were housed and exterminated. Remorseful, Nicholas refuses to ever hold such unnatural power again. Convinced now that Nicholas will not accept his offer, Bernstorff proposes to make the same plan known to Aliosha. Nicholas agrees to let the boy decide for himself. When Bernstorff details the counter-revolution and promises to return the boy to the Winter Palace, Aliosha screams in fear and demands he be left alone. Defeated, Bernstorff prepares to leave, and Nicholas tells him that, "while empires fall, there will always be snow" that needs shovelling.

Critical Overview — Rice mentions in *Minority Report* (A83) that the play was produced once non-professionally in White Plains, New York. No record of critical response exists.

Help! Help! (unpublished 1919)

Characters — JACK WOODWORTH, CLARICE WOODWORTH: hapless apartment dwellers in post-War New York; PVT. SPENCER DAVIS: their friend, handy with his hands; MONTGOMERY MORGAN: the landlord; MARJORY MORGAN: his daughter.

Plot Summary — ACT I: In the Woodworth's New York apartment in the years following WWI, Clarice sits with her hands bandaged, attended by a surly nurse. Her husband returns and the two lovingly exchange news about their new baby. In series of confrontations, the baby's nurse and Clarice's nurse quit, Morgan raises the rent and hires away Bertha as his cook. Spencer, an old friend of Jack's, arrives having been demobbed. He quickly takes charge and changes the baby's diapers.

ACT II: The Woodworths cannot fend for themselves, and Spencer begins to act as their maid and secretary. Marjory arrives to show the apartment, and is recognized by Spencer as a U.S.O. girl he once kissed. Morgan shows up to evict the Woodworths, and Spencer throws him out not knowing he is Marjory's father. Marjory rebukes him, and Spencer blames Jack before leaving.

ACT III: A real estate agent arrives but cannot satisfy the Woodworths with his few vacancies for them to see. Spencer returns but is still angry. The Woodworth's old maid, Mary, returns and asserts herself with the landlord. She agrees to stay on and take care of the Woodworths.

Critical Overview — The play was not produced.

Wake Up, Jonathan (with Hatcher Hughes, 1921)

Characters — JONATHAN BLAKE: a very successful and wealthy businessman who, after years of living apart from his family, has returned to claim their affection and duty; MARION BLAKE: his wife, who has raised the children to respect compassion and tolerance; HELEN BLAKE: the oldest daughter, courted by both Bernard and Douglas; JUNIOR, CHIPPY, and PEGGY BLAKE: the remaining children; BERNARD RANDALL: a young teacher without worldly ambitions; DOUGLAS BRENT: a young civil engineer bent on a successful career; ADAM WEST: former confidante of Marion, who left when Jonathan proposed to her; JEAN PICARD: a Frenchman traveling with Adam.

Plot Summary — PROLOGUE: At twilight on Christmas Eve on a country road, Adam and Jean appear singing and whistling. Adam, a rural sage, reveals he is on a pilgrimage to a place of great importance for him. They see a houselight in the distance, and Adam decides they will approach it.

ACT I: The Blake home is set for Christmas Eve, and the children are looking up the chimney and discussing Santa. When they ask Bernard if Santa exists, he assures them that he is a reality. Marion enters, and tells the children she is off on a "wild goose chase" to the train station, where she is to meet her husband who left the family some years ago. After she leaves, Adam and Jean arrive at the house, and entertain the children. They are especially fond of Adam, and Chippy tells him that his real name is Adam as well. Behind Adam's back, they wonder if he is actually their father. Douglas enters with Helen, and is immediately on guard against Adam, though he is cordial. Helen suggests that Adam is reminiscent of Bernard in that both are poetic, and Douglas uses this as a means to deride Bernard as a man with no drive or "push." Bernard enters, and he and Douglas exchange insults. After he leaves, Helen quarrels with Douglas, who tells her that he wants her to think seriously about a future with him. Adam enters and Helen, too, asks if he is her father; he says he is not, but that he wishes he were. Adam asks Helen how she feels about Bernard, and encourages her by relating a fable of a young, dreamy man who allowed an ambitious suitor to steal away his love. Helen promises to set Bernard's heart at ease. Marion returns from the station without a husband, so the children surprise her with Adam. It turns out the two do know each other — Adam was the dreamy suitor who lost out to the ambitious man for Marion's love.

ACT II: A moment after their meeting, Adam and Marion reminisce about their shared past. Marion says that she married Jonathan because he "tamed" her with his push and drive, but that these qualities led eventually to an unhappy life with him. As he began to dictate the marriage according to his terms, he spiritually devastated Marion. When children began to arrive, Jonathan called them an encumbrance and began to work away from home. Finally, he moved West to work, and stopped coming home altogether. For some time Marion visited him, but when she felt certain he did not intend to change, she stopped coming. Their only contact had been Jonathan's financial support through the mail, until Marion received the telegram announcing his visit only the day before. Having finished her tale, Marion tells Adam that the children are really his in spirit, and this revives his flagging spirits somewhat. Just then, Jonathan arrives by chauffeured car. He is overbearingly proud of his wealth and power, and hardly recognizes Adam until he recalls besting him for Marion's affections. He describes himself as a twentieth-century

Napoleon who has shaped the world according to his will, and makes no apologies for subordinating his family to his work. He offers to forgive Marion, but does so while also proudly announcing his female conquests around the world. Marion mocks him with a light irony as he tells her to prepare for a second honeymoon and life in New York. He announces he will prepare Junior to take over his vast empire. After Marion goes to fetch the children, Bernard enters and encounters Jonathan. Upon hearing that he is interested in Helen, Jonathan offers Bernard a job writing publicity, an offer that is declined. Jonathan sees this as evidence that Bernard has no push, and brings in Adam to explain how unrewarding it is to build air castles. After Jonathan dismisses him, Bernard goes and speaks quietly to Adam. Alone again, Jonathan meets Helen and tells her Bernard is no suitable lover. When she leaves and Douglas enters, the two businessmen hit it off immediately. Jonathan offers Douglas a job, and grooms him as the proper suitor to Helen. The other children enter, but they do not believe Jonathan is their father. When called upon to attest, Marion amusingly says she is not sure herself if he is the father. The entire family goes off to dinner.

ACT III: After dinner the family sits offstage in a music room. Randall arrives and meets Helen, carrying with him a marriage certificate. He insists they elope this evening, and, after hesitating and suggesting they let Marion know their plans, Helen agrees. After they depart, Jonathan enters with Douglas as he relates the tale of one of his business conquests. He tells Douglas that Marion has raised the children without authority, and promises to become the new boss of the family. Douglas affirms everything Jonathan says, and reveals his desire to help him tame the world. Junior enters, and for a moment appears to be leaning toward his father, as he accepts money from him so that he can crow over those with less in the schoolyard. Marion and Jonathan discuss money, the latter advocating its power and Marion describing it as a necessary but secondary adjunct to life. Jonathan accuses her of instituting "domestic bolshevism" in the house, and insists that it be changed, starting with the eviction of Adam. She tells him to do this himself, and he leaves. When Junior asks Marion if he should continue to follow Jonathan, she suggests he observe him closely then decide for himself. Adam enters after being told to leave, but Marion props up his courage and he decides to stay. Whereas Adam dismisses Jonathan as irretrievably corrupt, Marion insists he may still have "possibilities" for which she will test him. When she goes to Jonathan, she is told she must choose between him and Adam, ambition and dreaminess, to which she responds by asking why both can not be active at the same time. She proposes to allow both Jonathan and Adam to become acquainted with the children, after which they will be free to choose whom to accept as their father. Jonathan agrees, but gets off to a bad start when, cautioning against sentimentality, he goes to remove the Christmas tree to get into a closet. When the children react, he gruffly offers to give them expensive presents in place of the tree. Marion calms down the children by offering to tell them a story. She relates an explicit parable of a giant called "Pater Familias" who is so drunk with power and self-esteem that he has forgotten how to care for his family. In the middle of the story, Bernard and Helen arrive, now wedded. Jonathan is furious, but sees this as a sign that Bernard has some push. He offers him a lucrative job, but again Bernard declines and promises to go his own way. After the newly-weds leave, the children ask for the conclusion to the story, but Marion tells them she does not yet know it. As the children prepare to put up their stockings, Jonathan decries Santa as a myth, and offers five one hundred dollars to anyone who will deny that Santa exists. When no one complies, he takes the stockings from them. Junior, however, has observed Jonathan's behavior, and now rejects him by taking back the stockings. Jonathan admits he is bested for now, but promises to return because his sense of family is bigger than any claim Adam can offer. By showing some remorse for his actions, Marion is now able to end her parable by declaring that the cruel giant eventually realized his past mistakes, and mended his ways. She now tells the children that Jonathan is their father, and there are restrained but loving greetings between them. The play ends with the promise of a slow, but determined reconciliation.

Reviews — R25, R26, R27, R28, R29, R30, R32, R33

Critical Overview — *Wake Up, Jonathan* opened on 19 January 1921 at the Henry Miller Theatre for 105 performances.

The play qualifies as Rice's first uncontested failure. Woollcott (R26) called the play trite and insipid, though he admitted the last act contained some amusements. Reid (R27) thought it "pure hokum" and, like many critics, concentrated on discussing how Mrs. Fiske tried gallantly to save the show. Firkins (R30) took the play to task for avoiding any semblance of probability, while Lewissohn (R31) attacked it for its clutter and sentimentality. Only the *New York Clipper* (R29) saw merit in the play, calling it a tasteful comedy. Palmieri (S141) observes that the plays shows early signs of Rice's preoccupation with the evils of capitalism.

It Is the Law (1922)

Characters — ALBERT WOODRUFF: enemy to Justin Victor; RUTH: Victor's wife; JUSTIN VICTOR: murdered by Wooddruff; "SNIFFER" EVANS: a career criminal.

Plot Summary — Albert Woodruff wishes to pin onto Justin Victor the crime of having killed him. He locates a double for himself in the person of "Sniffer" Evans, a down and out ex-criminal who lends himself for hire to the proceedings, not knowing what the consequences will be for himself. Woodruff brings his double to his rooms, then calls Victor there to discuss a dispute the two men are having regarding Victor's wife. When Victor rings the bell, Woodruff shrieks into the phone that he is being attacked by Victor, then shoots Evans (his double) and escapes down the fire escape. Victor hears the shot, breaks into the apartment, and is found there by the police along with the revolver. Victor is sent to prison for life. Albert, however, returns to gloat over his triumph, and is recognized by Ruth. She fingers him and the situation is resolved

Reviews — R34, R35, R36

Critical Overview — *It Is the Law* opened on 29 November 1922 at the Ritz Theatre for 125 performances.

Critics were impressed by the play's technical achievements, which Theatre Magazine (R36) compared to Rice's innovations in *On Trial*. Corbin (R34) admired the play as a legitimate return to the crime melodrama, and *The New York Clipper* (R35) found it competent as a spine-tingler.

The Adding Machine (1923)

Characters — MR. ZERO: an inarticulate, uxorious, weak everyman figure, characterized as an eternal slave; MRS. ZERO: his shrewish and long-suffering wife; DIANA DAISY DOROTHEA DEVORE: Mr. Zero's co-worker and secret admirer; THE BOSS: Mr. Zero's superior, whom he murders; MR. AND MRS. ONE, TWO THREE, FOUR FIVE, and SIX: friends of the Zeros, who later act as the JURORS in Mr. Zero's murder trial; JUDY O'GRADY: former neighbor of the Zeros, arrested for indecent exposure at Mrs. Zero's complaint; SHRDLU: a tortured soul who murdered his mother and scours the afterlife for retribution; LIEUTENANT CHARLES: a mender of old souls, who cleans them before sending them off to reincarnation; POLICEMAN, JOE, A HEAD.

Plot Summary — SCENE 1: In a cheap room, Mrs. Zero badgers her husband for his lack of initiative and success at his job of twenty-five years. She also discusses the latest movies she has seen, and argues that sentimental love films are superior to westerns.

SCENE 2: Mr. Zero's office at the department store. He argues with Diana Devore as they record receipts in numbingly repetitive order. They sometimes speak as though the other is not listening. Diana ponders suicide, while Mr. Zero ruminates over the arrest of Judy O'Grady for walking in front of her window in only a T-shirt. Both Zero and Diana think about marriage to the other. Zero remembers that the twenty-fifth anniversary of his employment is near, and speculates about a raise. After the whistle sounds, Zero's boss enters, and informs Zero that his position is being replaced by an adding machine, and that he is therefore fired. Cacophonous music and a thunderclap are heard, foreshadowing the violence to come.

SCENE 3: Back at home, Mrs. Zero prepares for a small party, while Mr. Zero remains preoccupied. When the guests arrive and ring the bell, it sounds to Mr. Zero and the audience like the clicking of the keys and levers of an adding machine. The guests arrive (Mr. and Mrs. One through Six), all dressed in similar clothing, and moving with symmetrical and repetitive movements. The party banter is bland and full of cliches, with sudden and violent expressions of vitriolic patriotism and prejudice. A Policeman arrives, seemingly expected by Mr. Zero. As he moves to leave with the officer, Mr. Zero tells his guests that he has that afternoon killed his boss.

SCENE 4: At the Court of Justice, a cramped, windowless room, Zero is dragged before a jury made up of his former guests, who do not acknowledge him. He insists that, though he is guilty of killing his boss, he is not an evil man or a real murderer. He complains that his job, and the "figgers" that haunt him from it, have alienated him to the extent that only his instincts make him feel alive. These include an urge to spy on the scantily-clad Judy, to kill those who stand in his way, and to witness the lynching of a black man. The jurors stoically ignore his story, until Zero says he is just like any of them. At this, they stand and shout "GUILTY!" and move mechanically off the stage.

SCENE 5: In a lower-class graveyard, Judy O'Grady arrives with a man, presumably to engage in sex. She reads a tombstone, and discovers it is Mr. Zero's, whom she remembers as the man responsible for her arrest. She wants to perform sex on his grave, but her trick is too fearful. After they leave, Zero's head pops up from his grave, and he climbs out to stretch his stiff legs. He meets Shrdlu, and the two discuss the manner of their deaths. Shrdlu has killed his mother, a crime he explains as the expression of his "evil nature." He explains to Zero that they can expect to meet terrible retribution for their murders in the form of eternal fire and damnation. As his voice rises, another of the dead chases the two men away to gain some quiet.

SCENE 6: Zero wanders into the Elysian Fields, where he again confronts Shrdlu, who is mortified to discover that he has not been adequately punished for his sin. More gratingly, he has not been able to discover his mother among the pure souls that inhabit this pastoral afterworld. Diana Devore is suddenly heard calling out Zero's name, and the two are reunited. She had committed suicide days after Zero was executed, and has been seeking him since her death. After dismissing Shrdlu, Zero and Diana exchange reminiscences, which lead to declarations of love and regrets that they had not acted on their feelings while still living. They kiss, and suddenly begin to hear the music that the pure are allowed to hear. They dance with great abandon, and dream about staying in this world. Shrdlu returns and, to their surprise, informs them that they may indeed stay here if they wish. However, it turns out that Elysium is filled with various artists, reprobates, and time-wasters (the only ministers available to marry Zero and Diana are Swift and Rabelais), a fact Zero takes as evidence of the low quality of the place. No longer able to hear the divine music, he decides to leave, and Diana recognizes that she will never see him again.

SCENE 7: The sounds of an adding machine are heard as the curtain rises, and we find Zero sitting before it, surrounded by reams of machine tape which he has churned out for twenty-five years. His labors are interrupted by Lieutenant Charles, who tells Zero that his time here is up, and that his soul is about to be used again. Zero resists, saying he did as well in the world as he could the first time, and arguing that he is happy where he is. Charles explains that souls are always reincarnated to "save space" in the afterworld. Zero asks Charles for the history of his own soul, and to his chagrin he finds his is one of the souls which always transmigrates downward to a lower state. Zero asks where he began, and he is told that he was first a monkey before devolving into his present state. Shocked, Zero continues his questioning, only to find that his soul has always been that of a slave — as a primate, a pyramid builder, a galley slave, and finally as an accountant. Zero tries to refuse his reincarnation, but a thunderclap quiets his resolve, and he despairingly asks what his new fate will be. Informed that he will operate a "superb, super-hyper adding machine" with the flick of one toe, Zero is impressed. But Charles explains how this fate simply continues his descent into more and more subservient and alienated lives. Zero bewails his lot, and asks for help; in response Charles says he will provide Zero with a beautiful blonde wife, called Hope. When he calls for Hope, however, no one appears, but the prospect of her arrival is enough to send Zero rushing back into the world toward his new life.

Reviews — R38, R39, R40, R41, R42, R43, R44, R45, R46, R47, R48, R49, R50, R51, R52, R53, R54, R62, R64, R65, R76, R96, R306, R369, R370

Critical Overview — *The Adding Machine* opened at the Garrick Theatre on 19 March and ran for 72 performances.

According to Rice, this was the only play he ever wrote without revision, completing the work in seventeen days. Durham (S114) states that the play's primary theme is "dehumanized man's inability to grasp freedom and love when they are dangled before him." Other critics (Choudhuri [S136]) suggest that the work represents the soundest expression of Rice's understanding of the mechanisms of social life. Largely ignoring thematic issues, contemporary critics attacked or defended *The Adding Machine* around the issue of expressionist technique and the degree of German influence. Hammond (R39) called it "insoluble" and Seidenberg (R46) reviled it as "a concoction of strident modernity." Lewisohn (R43) felt it synthesized expressionist techniques better than did *The Hairy Ape* and Farrar (R49) and Broussard (S89) considered it superior to Lawson's *Roger Bloomer*. Despite claims by critics (Wilson [S120]), Rice himself said he had not read the German expressionists (Cf. Elwood [S108] and Broussard [S89]). Most recent criticism takes the playwright at his word and leans toward analyzing his unique deployment of subjective theatricality (Sievers [S82]; Palmieri [133]; Hogan [S95]).

The play was well received overseas, garnering positive reviews in London (R100), Stockholm (R95) and Paris (R94). Palmieri (S141) argues that Rice's reputation will endure based on the play, and Hogan (S95) says it contains some of the best monologues in American drama.

Black Sheep (1923; published 1938)

Characters — THOMPSON PORTER (alias "TOM HATCH"): the roustabout "black sheep" of the Porter family, a writer; KITTY LLOYD: his older traveling companion, editor, and taskmaster; MRS. PORTER: Tom's mother; MR. PORTER: his father, a well-to-do businessman; ALFRED PORTER: Tom's brother, betrothed to Dorothy; PENELOPE PORTER: Tom's sister, betrothed to Milton; DOROTHY WOODS: Alfred's fiance and a great fan of Tom Hatch's writing; MRS. ABERCROMBIE: a literary bluestocking; MILTON ABERCROMBIE: her son, betrothed to Penelope; ELIZABETH: the Porter maid, with whom Tom has an affair; BERTHA BELKNAP: a society-page journalist.

Plot Summary — ACT I: In the Porter living room, Mrs. Porter prepares to receive the socially superior Abercrombies. Dorothy enters and comforts her by telling her not to worry about receiving such an upper class family. Alfred enters and kisses Dorothy. Just then a telegram arrives, announcing that Tom (called "Buddy") will be arriving later that day. When Mrs. Porter becomes nonplussed, Dorothy asks who Buddy is. Alfred explains that Buddy is Tom, his brother, who has been out of touch with the family for seven years. Mr. Porter enters, and when he hears the news he is angry, calling Tom a loafer and a jailbird and refusing to extend him any hospitality. Penelope enters and reacts similarly, saying that her brother's arrival will ruin the meeting between her family and the Abercrombies. She threatens to break off the engagement with Milton, which occasions Mr. Porter to reverse himself, declare that Tom is still "blood," and as good as anyone from the Abercrombie family. Tom suddenly enters, accompanied by Kitty. He mistakes Dorothy for Penelope, and kisses her brusquely. He also borrows carfare from Mr. Porter, and immediately orders drinks for himself and Kitty. The family watches, shocked, as they toss down their drinks and go up to their room. After they leave, Mr. Porter and Alfred express their dislike of a woman like Kitty, but Mrs. Porter supports her because she is "Buddy's choice." They worry if she is even married to Tom. The Abercrombies now arrive, and Mrs. Porter gets off to a bad start by being too voluble and chatty. Mrs. Abercrombie turns the conversation to her latest book review of her favorite novelist, Tom Hatch, whom she recently met in San Francisco. As they converse, Mr. Porter discovers that Kitty and Tom are not married, and goes upstairs to threaten to throw them out. As the argument gets louder, Mrs. Abercrombie prepares to leave in embarrassment. At that moment Tom comes downstairs, and is greeted by a surprised Mrs. Abercrombie as Tom Hatch. The Porters now beg their son to tay with them.

ACT II: A week later, the same room has been converted into a writing studio for Tom. At the desk, Kitty is reading and copy-editing Tom's manuscripts. Dorothy and Penelope sit nearby, discussing one of his novels. Penelope has no taste for literature, but Dorothy has had her imagination fired by the writing and by Tom's unencumbered and bohemian lifestyle. When Alfred joins them, Dorothy is markedly cooler towards him. Alfred, however, wants to be married immediately, but Dorothy demurs. Milton now enters and, obviously taken by Kitty, compliments her and waits to catch another glimpse of her after she leaves. Penelope and Mrs. Porter join Milton and chat, but his eyes constantly wander to the hall. After the couple leaves, Mrs. Porter confronts Kitty and argues that it is time Tom settled down with a respectable wife. Kitty responds by saying that it is Tom's wildness and rootlessness that makes him a great writer. She tells Mrs. Porter of her meeting with Tom five years ago, and of her own role in pushing Tom towards a writing career. After he had been shanghaied by sailors, Kitty began to drink and drift away from her own husband. When Tom wrote to her from Australia, she left her husband and went to "pull him out by the hair" and fetch him back. Since then, she has been wet-nursing his career and looking out for him. Mrs. Porter is offended that Kitty implies she knows Tom better than his mother, and they argue until Mr. Porter enters. When Tom arrives, Mr. Porter invites him to his golf club, where he can meet prominent men, and Tom says he can "see the business sense" of the proposal. When Mr. Porter follows up by suggesting that Tom settle down at home, Tom admits he is tired of knocking about and feels comfortable at home. Mr. Porter advises him to leave Kitty, but Tom is undecided. At that moment a reporter arrives to do a sentimental story on Tom by interviewing his mother. Tom knows she is a hack, but plays along because he wants to please journalists. After everyone leaves, Tom and Kitty discuss business; she has sold a story he is currently writing, but is convinced he is growing soft and complacent in the family environment. She pushes him to return to his work, and they argue. They are interrupted by a visit from Mrs. Abercrombie. She asks Tom to read one of her stories, and praises his own work. Relishing her attention, Tom encourages her, and she goes on to suggest that, from a "social point of view" Kitty is harming his reputation. She advises him to improve his social position by taking up with a respectable and sophisticated woman — like herself. After she leaves, Kitty returns and encourages Tom to write. He is interrupted by Dorothy, however, who tells him how much she admires his work and his lifestyle. Tom tells her he sometimes wishes for a stable life with a good woman, like Dorothy. He relates a story of one his adventures, and ends by kissing Dorothy passionately. She retreats, and Kitty enters.

ACT III, Scene 1: Four days later, Mr. Porter is reveling in the good publicity Tom has generated by playing golf at his club. When Tom enters, we learn in passing that he has been having an affair with Elizabeth, the maid. Dorothy enters, preparing to leave for home to await her nuptials with Alfred. It soon becomes, apparent, however, that she is actually eloping with Tom. Kitty enters and tells Tom he must finish the story soon. Apparently needing the money to escape with Dorothy, Tom says he is just finishing it and will want the check as soon as he hands the manuscript to the publisher. Kitty ridicules the smarmy newspaper story on Tom, but he defends it as good advertising. After he goes to finish the story, Milton enters and confronts Kitty with his desire for her. She rejects him kindly. After Milton leaves, Mr. Porter enters and tells Kitty that Tom is beginning to fit in down at the club. He blithely tells her that Tom needs a good wife, and that the sort of relationship between Kitty and Tom can never last. He even offers to bribe her to leave Tom. Before she can retort, Dorothy enters to say her goodbyes. Sensing the truth, Kitty tells Dorothy that for Tom, conformity will mean the death of his writing and a good deal of self-abnegation. Alfred then enters to say goodbye to Dorothy, causing her to feel her guilt and nearly to break down in front of him. After he leaves, Dorothy resolves to break it off with Tom, but when she confronts him he convinces her that they are in love. As they part, Kitty and Alfred are seen just beyond the door. After Tom leaves, Kitty enters and confronts Dorothy directly about the elopement. She disillusions Dorothy by revealing Tom's affair with the maid, and advises her to take the train home and to marry Alfred. Dorothy departs, confused, and Tom re-enters with his finished story. Kitty begins to read it, and is shocked at its low quality and sentimental style. After reading a mawkish passage, she tears the manuscript in half. Tom defends himself by saying he is now writing for the wider public. Kitty ridicules his rationalizations, and reveals what has transpired between herself and Dorothy. Tom is enraged at her intervention, and threatens to visit his "ace in the hole," Mrs. Abercrombie. After he leaves, Kitty, now desperate, finds Milton and offers to run off to South America with him. She instructs him on how to buy the tickets, and, though frightened, he departs to make his plans.

ACT III, Scene 2: The next morning, Mr. and Mrs. Porter discuss the surprising news that Alfred and Dorothy have eloped the night before. When Tom enters and hears the news, he dispiritedly announces that he is engaged to Mrs. Abercrombie. Though somewhat discomfited, Mr. Porter congratulates him and again offers to pay off Kitty. Tom rebukes his father as Kitty enters, her bags packed. The Porters leave, and Tom and Kitty argue again about their impending separation. Milton enters, and having heard of his mother's engagement to Tom, waits to speak to Kitty. He asks her if she is running away in reaction to Tom, but she confirms she wants to go with him. She takes the tickets and some money from him, and tells him she will meet him down the block in ten minutes. After he leaves, she calls Tom down and tells him where she is going (though not with whom), tempting him by suggesting that Rio would be the perfect spot for him to write about in his next story. His imagination fired, Tom agrees to go with her, and hurriedly goes upstairs to pack. When Mrs. Abercrombie calls, Kitty tells Elizabeth to tell her that he has left for South America. Tom confronts his mother and tells her where he is going; initially saddened, Mrs. Porter slowly begins to return the room to the old order. Milton arrives, having seen Tom and Kitty leave, and finds a note in which Kitty calls him a "little fool."

Reviews — R129, R130, R131, R132

Critical Overview — The play opened on 13 October 1932 at the Belasco Theatre for 4 performances.

Garland (R130) felt Rice should never have resurrected the play, an opinion with which Atkinson (129) concurred.

Close Harmony; also titled ***The Lady Next Door*** (originally copyrighted as *Soft Music*) (with Dorothy Parker, 1924)

Characters — HARRIET GRAHAM: suburban housewife, fussy and overbearing; ED GRAHAM: her husband, unhappy with the present state of his marriage and his life; ADA TOWNSELEY: Harriet's sibling, equally overbearing and demanding, who visits the Grahams; "SISTER" GRAHAM: the Graham's spoiled and obnoxious daughter; BELLE SHERIDAN: neighbor to the Graham's, a vivacious ex-actress whose spirit is being crushed by her husband and by suburban life; BERTRAM SHERIDAN: Belle's husband, a lazy and unfeeling lout; DR. ROBBINS: physician to Annie.

Plot Summary — ACT I: In Homecrest, a quiet suburb of New York City, Sister practices at the piano while Harriet bustles about the drab house obsessively cleaning. Both of them complain about ailments that are presumably imaginary. Ada arrives, furious that "Daddy" (Ed) was not present to meet her at the station in the city. She advises her sister how she would handle such a man. As they complain about hiring good help, there is a phone call for Harriet's neighbor, Mrs. Belle Sheridan, whose phone is out of order. Before she arrives, Harriet informs her sister of the latest gossip regarding Belle. When Belle arrives, she is pleasant but a bit too "fancy" for Harriet and Ada. The phone call is from Belle's former agent, who is asking her to come back to the stage for the season's follies. She thanks him, but says she is off the stage for good.

Ed enters, apologetic and on the defensive. After berating him for missing Ada at the station, Harriet tells him they will all go see a film that evening. He asks her why the two of them do not go out alone much anymore, and wonders why they do not "enjoy life" more. As they converse, another call for Belle comes through, and Ed suggests that he go to fetch her. Harriet sends the maid instead, and Ed turns his attention to his daughter, who is haughty and distant. Belle arrives, and Ed's spirits improve considerably as he listens to her speak to her husband. Belle hangs up angrily, upset that Bert, her husband, is not coming back from the city again. Ed presents her with a bag of endives she had mentioned wanting a few days earlier, and she thanks him. Belle confides in Ed that she is unhappy and neglected, and admits that she is tempted by the offer to return to the stage. Ed lets slip inadvertently that he is bored and unhappy, too, and this admission makes them both self-conscious. They turn to discussing Sister's music (Belle is her instructor), and Belle invites Ed over to hear his mandolin playing sometime. Harriet re-enters, and Ed suggests to her that Belle stay for dinner. Harriet ungraciously resists, and Belle leaves.

Close Harmony

ACT II: Ten days later at the Sheridans, a more flamboyantly decorated home, Bert is spending Sunday afternoon drinking Scotch. Belle is there, bored and arguing that the two of them should do something together. Bert barely acknowledges her, and treats her requests cynically. They argue about their life together, and she reveals the offer to return to the stage. Bert is unconcerned with what she does, and makes it clear that he is her husband in name only. Ed arrives to ask Belle to help Sister prepare for a recital, and after he leaves Bert mocks his middle-class family lifestyle. Belle defends Ed, and Bert accuses her of having "ideas" about him. He tells her that he is going into town again, and is furious. Sister arrives to practice, and after addressing Belle with disdain she sits down to play, badly, and ignores Belle's instructions. Harriet and Ada arrive to listen, and discuss with Bert how spoiled Ed is. When Ed and Belle leave, they comment rudely on the house and her character. Sister tells her mother that Belle "swore" at her, and Harriet decrees there will be no more lessons here. When Belle and Bert re-enter, there are snide exchanges, and everyone leaves but Belle.

After she is alone, Belle calls Ed and invites him over to play music with her. A garage mechanic arrives at the door, demanding payment for a bad check that Bert had written him. When he threatens to get a summons, Belle pays him with money she had taken from Bert. Ed arrives and Belle serves him a cocktail, a diversion Ed is not often given to. They discuss suburban life and the alienation they find in their lives. When their mood turns somber, Belle suggests they play the "Blue Danube Waltz" on piano and mandolin. After unsuccessfully negotiating the piece, they search for other music, drawing close to each other before self-consciously pulling back. They find some tunes to sing, and eventually begin to dance. Ed, bolstered by the drink, kisses Belle, but she pushes him back lightly. She returns this with a friendly kiss, but will not allow Ed to return it with any passion. They decide to make a snack, and after Ed goes into the kitchen, Bert returns unexpectedly, looking for the money Belle had removed from his trousers. As they argue, he handles her roughly and Ed comes into the room to restrain him. Glowing and self-assured by the drink, Ed is forceful enough to make Bert leave. As he goes, he threatens never to return. Belle is now weeping, and in the heat of the moment they decide to run away together.

ACT III: Back in the Graham's living room, Ed enters and begins packing. The phone rings with news that Sister has suffered some sort of accident at the recital party. Harriet, Ada, and Sister enter noisily, the latter having been kicked in the stomach by a rude boy at the party. As they take her upstairs, they chastise Ed for having forgotten to watch the Sunday roast, now burned. After the doctor arrives and goes to tend Sister, Belle enters and promises Ed she will wait for him outside until he can make his escape. The doctor re-enters, and discusses Sister's condition with Ed. As he listens, his will to run away begins to leave him, and Belle, aware of this change, asks him what he is thinking. When he admits he is becoming apprehensive, she tells him that she understands perfectly, and will not hold him to his vow. She still intends to leave, and to return to the stage in the city. Ed wishes her well, and offers her money, which she graciously accepts. After Belle departs, Harriet comes down and begins harping at Ed again. She is interrupted by the phone, which Ed answers. It is the parents of the boy who kicked Sister, calling to apologize. As Harriet glares at him, Ed cordially forgives the boy's actions. Harriet, now joined by Ada, is furious; after Ada insults him, however, Ed begins to assert himself, asking that she leave his house. After Ada storms upstairs to pack, Harriet, becoming more submissive, and tends to Ed's comforts. He tells her that he has decided that they will begin to enjoy life more

Reviews — R55, R56, R57, R59

Critical Overview — The play opened 1 December 1924 at the Gaiety Theatre for 24 performances.

Reviews were generally positive, with Broun (R55) expressing admiration for the play's humor and pathos and Young (R57) congratulating the authors for their stage instinct. Krutch (R59) thought the social environment bland and felt the play reflected a more general decline in American literature.

The Subway (1924; produced 1929)

Characters — SOPHIE SMITH: an eighteen-year old office worker who dreams of a more fulfilling life; EUGENE LANDRAY: an artist who seduces Sophie and gains inspiration from her; MRS. SMITH, MR. SMITH, ANNIE SMITH, TOM SMITH: Sophie's automaton-like family, whose existence is repetitive and meaningless; GEORGE CLARK: a fellow office worker of Sophie's who had once dated her, but who is preparing to leave for Michigan; JAMES BRADLEY: Sophie's office supervisor; MAXWELL HURST: a rather foppish newspaper writer; ROBERT ANDERSON: a friend of Landray's who wishes to hire him for an overseas job.

Plot Summary — SCENE 1: In a small, oppressive office at the Subway Construction Company, Sophie is discovered filing letters. George enters and presents her with a rose, for which she is grateful. She asks if he would like to see a show, but George says he is busy studying for a correspondence course in auto mechanics. He eventually reveals that he has accepted a job at his brother's auto shop in Detroit, and will soon be leaving. He declaims forensically about his right to "make the best he can" of his life, and expresses little regret at having to leave. Sophie, however, is saddened by the news. After George leaves, Bradley, Hurst, and Eugene arrive in the process of writing a public relations blurb for the company. Bradley explains how the company's filing system has "improved upon nature," and extols the virtues of the office's efficiency. Hurst and Eugene are more interested in Sophie, and convince Bradley that she should be included in a drawing, which Eugene executes. When he finishes, they leave, Eugene casting a long look as he departs.

SCENE 2: On the subway, Sophie is crammed among a crowd of people. The crush of passengers loading and unloading is mimed, and Sophie is left gasping for air. After another train passes by her own, we see in Sophie's car that all the men have now taken the guise of various grotesque animals leering about her. She screams.

SCENE 3: In Sophie's meanly-furnished house (complete with striped wallpaper suggesting bars on a cage), Sophie's family enters and goes through a series of mechanical motions and activities. When Sophie arrives with Eugene, they take no notice of them. After a brief conversation, Eugene leaves, and Sophie relates the story of how she came to feel faint in the dank air of her office, nearly passing out. Eugene had offered to drive her home, rather than making her face the subway ride. Her family does not react to the story, and Sophie moves toward the audience as if to escape. The wallpaper "bars" descend before her, blocking the attempt.

SCENE 4: Sophie prays in her room before going to sleep. She asks for a good sleep not broken by her "awful dreams" of being pursued by some unknown person. As she prays, jazz music filters in the room and lifts her spirits somewhat. She recalls a past date with George, during which she allowed him to kiss her. Thinking of his departure, she cries and fantasizes about suicide. Her mind turns to the awful subway rides she endures each day, and thinks gratefully of Eugene's help that day. She returns to thoughts of death, crying out in her fear that she will die before she has truly lived. Her final prayer is for someone to talk with who will understand her, and she ends by asking Jesus to love her in her solitude.

SCENE 5: Inside a movie theatre, Sophie enters with Eugene. As they watch a newsreel reporting the lives of various celebrities, Sophie expresses her desire to travel on a Cunard luxury liner. Eugene promises to take her to see one, but Sophie says she must work. As the feature begins, Sophie is enraptured by the stars and the simple story that unfolds. In continuous asides, Eugene comments on Sophie's "incredible naivete" while also commenting that "there's something about her" that attracts him. Sophie reads the subtitles of the film, which often comment ironically on her own emotions at the moment. Eventually, Eugene casually touches her hand, first tentatively but then more forcefully. With both of them struggling with their internal voices, they suddenly kiss as the film soundtrack rises to a sensuous blare. Eugene springs up and tells her to come with him, and she yields.

SCENE 6: Eugene reads by lamplight in his studio, and speaks aloud his state of mind. A bodiless voice calls out "Liar!" at intervals. Sophie rings at the door, and upon entering is immediately fearful of being discovered. Eugene says it would not matter, that he loves her. She is wary of the situation and wants them to begin seeing each other more openly. Eugene temporizes by telling her that she is too good for him, that his mercurial temperament would make a steady relationship unbearable for her. He tells her that she has given him a "vision" of an artistic masterpiece he wishes to execute, called "The Subway." He deliriously describes it to her as a work intended to expose humankind's enslavement to the "mechanistic dance" of progress. He envisions the subway as the Beast of a new Apocalypse which presages massive war and the destruction of the modern "skyscraper culture." In the post-apocalyptic world, he imagines the subway tunnels as the burrows into which humanity will descend. Leaping into the far-flung future, he imagines a new civilization stumbling upon the tunnels in an archeological dig. They discover the cheap remnants of the civilization, but also discover a girl who has miraculously survived with her beauty intact. Sophie does not grasp the significance of the vision, and asks only that Eugene love her.

SCENE 7: Sophie arrives at Eugene's studio and decides to wait for him to return. She finds a series of charcoal nudes of herself that Eugene has drawn, and hides them in a portfolio. There is a knock at the door, and Anderson enters, surprised to find her there. He knows her relationship to Eugene, and has even seen the charcoal renderings. He calls Eugene and his work "vacillating and lazy," and tells Sophie she is foolish to love him. He has been asked to publish Eugene's "Subway," but sees it as bad business and a hindrance to Eugene's more important graphic work. He wants to offer Eugene a job as art editor of a new glossy magazine (called *Tripe*), a job which will force him to relocate overseas. Eugene enters, and Anderson makes his offer and tells him to attend a meeting the next morning. Eugene seems unsure how to respond, and Sophie clings to him as he thinks.

SCENE 8: Sophie lies in her bed, feverishly tossing while snickering voices murmur around her. As the voices become clearer, we hear Eugene telling Sophie he loves her and wishes to marry her. Other voices intervene — her sister, Anderson, George, her mother — and accuse her of adultery and blasphemy. When she is able to drop off to sleep, raucous laughter wakens her. Each time a voice accuses her of some sin, Eugene's voice interrupts to comfort her by insisting on his love for her. The other voices reveal she is pregnant and thinking of an abortion, while imaginary fingers point at her mockingly.

SCENE 9: At 3 A.M. in the deserted subway station, Sophie appears wearing a coat over her nightgown. She is frantic and delusional. Hurst happens by at this moment and, recognizing her, begins to seduce her. He offers her a taxi ride, his whisky flask, and finally his rooms for the night. After drinking from the flask, she admits she has had an affair with Eugene and that she has quit her job. As Hurst begins to lead her away, the horn of a subway train is heard in the distance. She breaks away from Hurst, and moves toward the platform. Rhapsodizing about the beauty of the train, she pulls free of Hurst and leaps onto the track.

Reviews — R82, R86, R89

Critical Overview — *The Subway* opened at the Cherry Lane Theatre on 24 January 1929 for 35 performances. It moved to the Masque Theatre and ran for 7 performances.

Begun in 1923 (the same year as *The Adding Machine*), the play languished until Rice allowed an amateur group, the Lennox Hill Players, to stage it. Because of poor productions at both venues and inevitable comparisons to *The Adding Machine* and the currently-running *Street Scene*, critical reactions were negative to varying degrees. Clark (R82) thought it should have remained in Rice's trunk, while the reviewer for *Theatre Magazine* saw moments of real drama in an otherwise rambling piece. Durham (S114) characterizes the play as a significant transitional piece between the expressionist distortions of *The Adding Machine* and the severe naturalism of *Street Scene*. Hogan (S95) praised several scenes and Rice's depiction of Sophie's death as a "rape" by technology. Valgemae (S117) counters that Sophie's language in the final scene represents her willing, even erotic, submission to her death.

The Gay White Way (1925)

Characters — YOUNG MAN; STOUT WOMAN; AGED THESPIAN; EFFEMINATE YOUTH; OVER-RIPE INGENUE; MR. LOVETT; NOVICE; LETTER CARRIER; LATIN LADY.

Plot Summary — In the dingy reception area of Gene Lovett, a theatrical manager, the Young Man reads a copy of *Variety*. The Stout Woman enters and, seeing a "No Casting" sign, wanders over to the magazine rack and takes a Christian Science pamphlet before exiting. A female giggling from the inner office can be heard. The Aged Thespian enters, also sees the sign, and exits. Now the Effeminate Youth enters, sees the sign, and is about to leave when he hears a kissing sound. The Over-Ripe Ingenue exits the inner office, blowing a kiss to the unseen Lovett. The Effeminate Youth tries to enter the office, but the door closes. He turns to leave as the Novice enters. She takes a seat nervously and waits. The Letter Carrier enters and makes a delivery. After he exits the Latin Lady arrives, sees the "No Casting" sign, and leaves. After she exits, Lovett appears. The Novice crosses to leave and is observed by Lovett. He quickly follows her out the door, and returns with her. They enter his office, as the Youth yawns and continues reading.

Critical Overview — *The Gay White Way* is a scene from *Sidewalks of New York*, which was copyrighted in 1925 but never performed. This segment appeared in *The New Yorker* in 1928 and was copyrighted and published separately in 1928. It has never been performed.

The Passing of Chow-Chow (unproduced, published 1925)

Characters — JAMES RUSSELL: a lawyer; CORA WEBB STANDISH: suing to divorce her husband; ROBERT BRETT STANDISH: suing to divorce his wife.

Plot Summary — Cora arrives at Russell's office to discuss her divorce suit. She accuses Standish of hurling her dog, Chow-Chow, down the steps after discovering the dog has destroyed one of his paintings. Russell receives a phone call, and asks Cora to sign some papers while he leaves the room. He goes to meet Standish, who is there to accuse of his wife of infidelity and to seek his own divorce. Upon questioning, Standish reveals it is Chow-Chow upon whom Cora is lavishing her affections. After Russell leaves, the husband and wife confront one another. After they argue, they receive a call telling them that Chow-Chow has passed away. The reconcile and decide to stay together to honor their former pet.

Critical Overview — The play was not produced.

The Sidewalks of New York (written 1925; published 1934, unproduced)

The text is made up of Rice's "Three Plays Without Words."

Landscape With Figures

In front of a drugstore, a young man in a threadbare suit waits amid a crowd. A pretty young woman is in the window demonstrating the effects of mineral salts. A pickpocket works the growing crowd. The sound of an auto accident offstage causes most of the crowd to leave, the young man continuing to wait. An injured man is brought onstage before he and the crowd are led away. The only person left watching the demonstration is a feeble-minded young man. When the demonstration ends, the girl leaves the store, and he follows her. The young man finally gives up his vigil and leaves. A young woman appears, looks for the young man, and leaves in distress.

Rus in Urbe

In the center of Washington Square an ex-soldier sits on a bench near a young boy and his governess. A derelict passes by looking for cigarette butts, while a young man scans a recruiting poster before writing down the address. The little boy sneaks off to chase the sound of a fire truck he hears. A young man enters and sits to read a manuscript he carries. He leaves, inadvertently forgetting his papers. A thirty year-old woman seats herself at the bench, picks up the manuscript and begins to read it. She reacts strongly to what she reads and does not notice the young man return. He watches her reactions intently, and when she finishes reading their eyes meet.

Exterior

Outside a New York brownstone a young couple kisses and parts. An intoxicated man enters the building and is followed by a doctor and a thief. Noises emanate from the building — alarm clocks, music, babies crying, the sound of arguments. An iceman enters as a janitor appears from basement to empty trash. An anxious man hangs a white rosette from the outside door of the building as an organ grinder walks by playing "Sidewalks of New York."

Critical Overview — "Three Plays Without Words" was never produced, though it became the genesis for *Street Scene*.

Cock Robin (with Philip Barry, 1928)

Characters — GEORGE McAULIFFE: the director of a community theatre troupe; HANCOCK ROBINSON: the lead actor in the troupe, an arrogant and wealthy man who intends to ruin Carlotta; CARLOTTA MAXWELL: a young ingenue in the troupe, having an affair with Robinson; RICHARD LANE: an actor in the troupe, known as an expert marksman and a former suitor to Carlotta; JULIAN CLEVELAND: another actor, also Robinson's law partner and brother-in-law; HELEN MAXWELL: Carlotta's mother, who also acts in the troupe; DOCTOR EDGAR GRACE: Carlotta's uncle, who intends to separate her from Robinson; MARIA SCOTT: the shy but observant assistant director of the troupe; HENRY BRIGGS: the stage manager; JOHN JESSUP; ALICE MONTGOMERY; CLARKE TORRENCE: other actors in the troupe.

Plot Summary — ACT I: Within an interior stage, a community theatre group rehearses a performance of a swashbuckling costume drama. After enacting a duel scene, the actors are interrupted by McAuliffe, the director, who is not satisfied with the performance. He summons Maria to critique the scene, and she points out that Robinson could be observed caressing Carlotta while he was supposed to be dead. The somewhat drunken Lane is angry at the flirtation, and stalks offstage. Robinson tells McAuliffe that he will not act that evening if Lane is to play the other duelist, claiming that Lane's jealousy and prowess as a pistol shot might put his life in jeopardy. McAuliffe grudgingly replaces Lane with Torrence, and after explaining the change to the cast, the scene is played again. Although there are problems with the firing of blanks to simulate the pistol shots, McAuliffe explains that with so much noise occurring at once, no one will notice because in the midst of much noise and action, everyone will see something different. He jokingly tells the actors that one is better off killing someone in a crowd, since no one will be able to report the truth. As the troupe disperses, Lane rebukes Carlotta for no longer caring for him, but she dismisses him as jealous of Robinson. Mrs. Maxwell intervenes to tell her daughter that Robinson is manipulating her, and her protests are joined by Dr. Grace's. He accuses Carlotta of planning to elope to Europe with Robinson, but Carlotta says they both just happen to be departing on the same ship that evening. After Carlotta leaves, Dr. Grace tells Mrs. Maxwell that he is tempted to "injure" Robinson during the performance that evening in order to delay his departure to Europe. As the performers depart, McAuliffe first gives them a pep talk, but after they leave he mocks their pretentions as actors.

ACT II: The scene is the same as in Act I, but from reverse-perspective so that we look from backstage out toward the audience. Before the play begins, Mrs. Maxwell addresses the crowd and reports on the troupe's fund-raising efforts. When she departs the curtain goes up on the play. As the dueling scene approaches, Carlotta sees a shadow on the side entrance wall, and is transfixed by it. Just as she screams, the dueling pistols are discharged, and a jug on a wall is shattered. The scene progresses, but it soon becomes apparent that Robinson has truly been shot and killed. The curtain is lowered, the audience dismissed, and the performers decide to try to figure out what happened before calling the police. With Cleveland leading the inquiry, they establish from the angle of the shot that broke the jug that the bullet must have come from Torrence's gun. However, Maria enters and says that from her vantage point in the crowd she saw the side entrance door opening during the scene. Lane admits this was his doing, but that he was only anticipating his cue. Maria also notes that Carlotta screamed before the shot, and under questioning she admits that she saw

Lane in the doorway with two guns. Lane explains that he carried the extra gun in order to help Briggs, the Stage Manager, create the sounds of gunfire offstage. However, once it is pointed out that the shattered jug could not be in Lane's firing path, he is exonerated. Suspicion now returns to Torrence, who argues that even if his gun fired the fatal shot, he was not the one who loaded it with real bullets. After much discussion and several accusations, Dr. Grace admits he put the bullet in the gun. He admits he wanted to injure Robinson with a knife after the show, then decided to use a gun. He was interrupted while loading the gun, however, and forced to leave it with the other props after being assured it would not be used in the duel. Dr. Grace also admits that he later was convinced not to injure Robinson, but he refuses to admit why he changed his mind. Carlotta intervenes and explains why Grace was angry at Robinson, but Cleveland tells her that no elopement was possible because Robinson never intended to get a divorce. Carlotta then tells them that she had gone to Robinson's dressing room that evening, and, Robinson being out, she discovered a letter from Paris. Upon reading it, she discovered that Robinson had taken another woman there and seduced and abandoned her, where she is now dying. This had convinced Carlotta not to elope, and she had told Dr. Grace before the show. Having cleared Grace, suspicion now returns to Torrence, but Maria points out that he is no marksman. Examining the body more closely, Dr. Grace discovers to almost everyone's surprise that the bullet had only wounded Robinson, and that the real cause of death is a stab wound. As the fatal knife clatters to the floor, Mrs. Maxwell shouts, "I did it!"

ACT III: A few minutes later. Now Mrs. Maxwell reveals she confessed only to protect Dr. Grace. McAuliffe now takes charge of the investigation and deduces that one of the five performers surrounding Robinson must be the killer. As he assesses the situation, he mentions in passing that the woman who wrote the letter Carlotta found was Mary Clinton, his former assistant director. The knife is examined for prints, but nothing turns up. Maria suspects it might be Mrs. Maxwell, whose arm she saw raised. Mrs. Maxwell explains this by revealing that she had felt something catch her sleeve; upon investigation, they find a knife slit there. Maria suggests that they walk through the scene to determine who could have done it, and as they begin she notices that a pair of gloves used in the scene have been moved from their usual position. Before she can comment on this, McAuliffe creates a diversion and surreptitiously moves the gloves back, though Maria sees him do it. As Maria directs them through the scene, suspicion falls on Carlotta, who seems to have had the best opportunity to stab Robinson. However, just as the police arrive, Lane suddenly intervenes and points out that McAuliffe might well have done the murder. He concludes that the knife was thrown, and remembers McAuliffe's earlier reminiscences about beginning his performing career as a knife-thrower in a circus. Though he does not admit to the murder, McAuliffe points out that no jury could be convinced of his guilt. Mrs. Maxwell now remembers McAuliffe's earlier slip regarding Mary Clinton, and it becomes clear that McAuliffe killed Robinson in revenge for the latter's seduction and betrayal of the former assistant director, who, McAuliffe now reveals, died three days ago. Lane says he believes McAuliffe had good cause to kill Robinson, and hopes they do not convict him. Maria, whose testimony regarding McAuliffe's manipulation of the gloves he wore during the murder is crucial evidence, pretends she has weak eyes and so will not be able to testify. The police enter while McAuliffe laughs quietly to himself.

Reviews — A07, R66, R67, R68, R69, R70

Critical Overview — The play opened 12 January 1928 at the Fortieth-Eight Street Theatre for 100 performances.

Rice himself admitted in *Minority Report* (A83) that he felt "no great pride of authorship" for the play. Reviews were mixed, with Krutch (R68) and Bellamy (R69) admiring the play's solid illusion of life and its enjoyable resolution. Brown (R70) felt it was stuck between satire and mystery. Hogan (S95) points out that the use of the reverse setting in Act III is similar to that used by e. e. cummings in *Him*.

Street Scene (1929)

Characters — ANNA MAURRANT: an attractive, but lonely and yearning woman; FRANK MAURRANT: her rough and dominating husband; ROSE MAURRANT: their daughter, an attractive and capable woman; WILLIE MAURRANT: the Maurrant's young son; ABRAHAM KAPLAN: an elderly educated Jew with Marxist tendencies; SHIRLEY KAPLAN: his daughter, who has sacrificed everything to put Sam Kaplan through law school; SAM KAPLAN: a radical socialist, in love with Rose; HARRY EASTER: office manager at Rose's place of employment, who wants to put her on the stage and make her his mistress; STEVE SANKEY: a married man having an affair with Mrs. Maurrant; GRETA FIORENTINO: a large German woman living in the tenement; FILIPPO FIORNETINO: her jolly Italian husband, a music teacher; OLGA OLSEN: Scandinavian woman, wife of the tenement janitor; CARL OLSEN: her husband; DANIEL BUCHANAN: husband to woman having her first child; MARY HILDEBRAND: poor resident of the tenement, in the process of being evicted; MAE JONES: a cheap, vulgar woman; DICK MCGANN: her loutish date; VINCENT JONES: cabdriver who flirts with Rose and physically abuses Sam.

Street Scene

Plot Summary — ACT I: Before the exterior of a dilapidated brownstone, of which only the first floor is visible. The neighborhood is run-down and noisy, with buildings nearby being demolished. The residents of the flats are cooling themselves on the stoop, discussing the hot weather. Throughout their conversation are intimations that Mrs. Maurrant, a resident, is having an illicit affair with Mr. Sankey, the milk bill collector. The gossip is sometimes crude and hurtful, until Mrs. Maurrant joins them. As the talk turns to the behavior of young women, there are also hints of racial tension, even though the residents are themselves immigrants from various lands. They go on to discuss the Buchanans, who are expecting a child. Frank Maurrant arrives in a foul mood, compelling his wife to state that "everyone needs a kind word now and then." As Sankey walks in front of the building, there is a palpable tension in the air, indicating that Frank is already suspicious. As the group disperses and re-forms, Mrs. Maurrant again expresses her plea that people should be getting more out of life than hardship and cold words. She then leaves, presumably to speak to Sankey, as the neighbors murmur disapprovingly. Mr. Jones predicts that Frank will kill the two lovers someday. Filippo Fiorentino arrives with ice cream and entertains the group with his antics. A woman from the Charities arrives to tell Mrs. Hildebrand that she is going to be evicted, and Fiorentino gives the family some loose change as Abraham Kaplan chastises the woman about the "kepitalist plot" that makes them all paupers. His comments elicit derisive (and racist) comments from the neighbors, who prefer to believe they live in a free land where such revolutionary talk is not needed. Frank, especially, expresses his strong belief in the status quo, where families are ruled by the will of the fathers. His comments lead to a brief scuffle with Kaplan. Sam Kaplan, a young intellectual, arrives and the discussion turns to music — while the others prefer Verdi, he listens to Beethoven and Tchaikovsky. After Sankey passes by again, Mrs. Maurrant returns and is greeted suspiciously by Frank. Willie Maurrant appears, apparently after fighting with another boy who has insulted his mother. After the Maurrants leave, the gossip begins again until Sam, sobbing, asks them to stop their cruelty. Everyone returns to their respective apartments, as Rose appears with Easter. A married man, Easter forces a kiss on Rose, and tells her he can get her on the stage, while intimating that this includes her becoming his mistress. Their conversation is interrupted as Mrs. Buchanan goes into labor. Rose leaves to help with the preparations. She returns on her way to make a phone call, and is met by Mae and Dick, two drunks, who insult her mother. As she recoils from this, Vincent Jones walks by and grabs her. Sam sees this, and comes to her aid, only to be beaten by Vincent. After he leaves, Sam and Rose sit on the stoop to discuss their mutual unhappiness and despair. Rose tries to cheer up Sam by asking him to recite lines from Whitman's "When Lilacs Last in the Dooryard Bloom'd." As he finishes, Dr. Wilson arrives and Rose prepares to go up. Sam asks to kiss her, and she allows it, though she does not return his ardor.

ACT II: Early morning sounds are heard as the next day begins to break. Mae is just returning from her date, and Dr. Wilson prepares to leave after delivering the baby. Rose, preparing to attend a company funeral, stops to speak with Fiorentino, and they discuss whether it is better to marry for love or money. Mrs. Jones, who had seen Rose and Sam together, tells Rose she is better off not bringing a Jew into the family. As Frank leaves, he argues with Mrs. Maurrant and goes off drinking from a flask. Rose and Abraham converse about the reasons why there is so much suffering in the world. Rose then speaks to her mother, and explains that, though she understands her need for companionship, she is worried that Frank will discover her liaison and do something violent. She gently remonstrates with her mother to be more discrete. After Mrs. Maurrant goes in, Shirley Kaplan comes by and asks Rose to let Sam concentrate on his studies. Rose maintains she is not in love with Sam, and promises not to encourage him. She leaves, and Sam and Rose converse through an open window, discussing spiritual beliefs (Sam is a rationalist) and reasons for choosing life over suicide. Rose believes that she should leave New York, and Sam admits he would like to accompany her, but Rose refuses. Easter arrives to walk with Rose to the funeral, and they depart. Sankey arrives, and Mrs. Maurrant surreptitiously invites him up, after which she closes the window shades. City marshals appear to begin evicting Mrs. Hildebrand. At that moment, Frank returns and notices the closed shades. As Sam tries to stop him, he moves quickly into the building in a rage. Two shots are heard, and then Sankey appears at the window, breaking it with his elbow in an attempt to get out. Frank grabs him and pulls him into the flat as another shot is heard. As a big crowd begins to form, Frank appears at the landing bloody and disheveled, leveling a revolver at the crowd. He escapes into the cellar as the police arrive. As Rose appears on the scene, Sam runs to her and tries to keep her from seeing the sight. An ambulance arrives, and Mrs. Maurrant is taken away in critical condition.

ACT III: By mid-afternoon of the same day, Frank has still not been captured and Mrs. Maurrant has died at the hospital. The tabloids have already produced sensational accounts of the shooting, and curious spectators stop by to gawk at the building. Easter arrives looking for Rose, and asks if he can help her. She declines, and asks Shirley to accompany her into the apartment. Sam arrives and reveals that the police want him to testify against Frank when he is captured. Shots are heard offstage, and everyone rushes out to see the capture take place. Frank is brought in, wounded and filthy, and is allowed a word with Rose. He sees her black attire, and realizes that his wife is dead. He says he was "off his nut" and drunk when he shot the two, and asks Rosie to forgive him. He is taken away and Rose is left with Sam. She tells him she will leave New York with Willie, and again Sam asks if he might go along. Though tempted, Rose believes that people should "belong only to themselves," and, since she is not yet in love with Sam, this is what their relationship would be. She comforts Sam by telling him that someday it may be right for them to marry. He leaves, disconsolate, and Rose departs from the tenement for good. A family of new prospective renters arrives to look at the vacant flat.

Reviews — R72, R73, R74, R75, R76, R77, R78, R79, R80, R81, R82, R83, R84, R85, R86, R87, R88, R92, R94, R95, R97, R98, R99, R100, R101, R107, R111, R114, R123

Critical Overview — *Street Scene* opened at the Playhouse on 10 January 1929 and ran for 601 performances.

Originally entitled *Sidewalks of New York*, the play was a groundbreaking depiction of New York tenement life — Adler (S155) even suggests it is the first important "ghetto drama" in the American canon. Left by necessity to direct the play, its success convinced Rice to begin directing many of his own plays. Atkinson (R72) quickly championed the play and Krutch (R76) argued it represented a significant advance over *The Adding Machine*. Minor qualms were raised by Young (R77) and others regarding the melodramatic plot, but the play was by far the most critically-acclaimed of Rice's career. It easily won the Pulitzer for the season and continues to be produced worldwide and anthologized often. Murphy (S156) considers it among the finest expressions of the type of American realism espoused by Howells and James early in the century.

See Naples and Die (1929)

Characters — CHARLES CARROLL: an American traveller, formerly affianced to Nanette Dodge; NANETTE DODGE KOSOFF: wife of a dispossessed Russian prince, and former fiance of Charles; IVAN IVANOVITCH KOSOFF: Nan's husband, a languid and pathetic aristocrat; KUNEGONDE WANDL: a Viennese traveling with her lover, who plans an affair with Charles; GENERAL JAN SKULANY: Kunie's lover, a Rumanian strongman; MITZI DODGE NORTON: Nan's sister, married to a British citizen, formerly lover to Kosoff; HUGO VON KLAUS: manservant and spy for Kosoff; BASIL ROWLINSON: a moralistic Englishman living in Naples; LUCY EVANS: an elderly American traveling through Naples; ANGELO and HJORIDIS DE'MEDICI: owners of the pensione overlooking the Bay of Naples; LUISA: their sensuous maid; TWO CHESS PLAYERS.

Plot Summary — ACT I: In the de'Medici pensione near Sorrento, several travelers and expatriates come together. Basil is shown executing a horrid still life, which Mrs. Evans compliments. She is excited by the impending arrival of Kosoff, a Russian prince. Von Klaus enters and introduces himself, and is surprised to meet Charles, whom he recognizes but does not acknowledge. After the others leave, Charles sees Kunie on her balcony and beckons to her to join him. They have drinks, and discuss Kunie's relationship to Skulany, whom she wishes to leave before he returns to engineer a coup in Rumania. Charles asks Kunie to run away to Paris with him, though Kunie suspects this is in reaction to the fact that Charles has recently been deserted by his own fiance, Nanette Dodge. Mrs. Evans returns and interrupts the conversation, noting that the Russian prince who is coming is none other than Kosoff, the man who married Nan. Charles reacts angrily, and proposes that Kunie and he leave immediately for Paris. Before they can escape, however, Nan arrives. She wonders at Charles's surprise, maintaining that she had sent a telegram announcing her arrival and her need for his help. Charles affects a glib air, and does not allow Nan to explain her situation. As Charles attempts to leave, Von Klaus returns and intervenes. Nan recognizes him as Kosoff's spy, who has been following her since she left Paris. Von Klaus informs Nan that Kosoff is informed of her whereabouts, and has arrived in Naples in pursuit of her. When Mrs. de'Medici offers to prepare a room, Nan insists she will not be sleeping with her husband. She wants to leave, but is told that the road closes down every afternoon at Mussolini's order, so that an auto race can be held. Nan accosts Charles again, and explains that she is avoiding Kosoff and needs his help, but Charles is hurt and will not listen. After he leaves, Kosoff arrives.

ACT II: When Kosoff confronts Nan they argue in between the loud roars of the racers outside the gates. He is utterly languid and melancholy, but insists that Nan accompany him home. When he tries to kiss Nan, she kicks him. Above the piazza, Skulany is seen dragging Kunie back into their rooms. Charles and Nan have a moment together, and she reveals her reasons for leaving him to marry Kosoff. Her sister, Mitzi, had an ill-advised affair with Kosoff during the war, during which she exchanged erotic letters with him. Now dispossessed by the revolution of his domain, Kosoff has turned petty blackmailer. When Mitzi and Nan are not able to raise a sufficient bribe, they decide that Nan (who is due to inherit money upon marriage) will marry Kosoff, pay him off with the inheritance, and then divorce him. However, Kosoff has reneged and now wishes to keep Nan, and threatens to expose Mitzi with photocopies of the letters which were not destroyed. Nan has recently stolen the copies and destroyed them, so Kosoff is now in pursuit of her, threatening that he will go back and reveal all to Mitzi's husband. Upon hearing this, Charles strikes Kosoff, who does not respond. After he has been helped away by his aides, Nan and Charles lay plans for thwarting Kosoff's scheme. They are interrupted, however, by Kunie's screams. She runs to Charles and reveals that Skulany has struck her and threatened her harm if she leaves him. He tells her that they will still go to Paris together, but that first he must help Nan. They depart, and Kosoff re-enters with Von Klaus; together they plan top abduct Nan. When she enters, Kosoff approaches her and, when she retreats, Von Klaus drags her into a room.

ACT III: After the abduction, Kosoff discusses plans to purchase Skulany's automobile to make his escape from Naples. After flirting with and kissing Luisa, Kosoff goes to barter with Skulany. Mitzi arrives unexpectedly, and runs into Kosoff, who tells her that nan has left with Charles to visit a tourist site. After he leaves, Charles enters and is recognized by Mitzi. At that moment Luisa enters and tells Charles that she has witnessed nan's abduction, and tells him where to find her. He rushes into Von Klaus's room and, after an offstage bustle, emerges with Nan. She sees Mitzi, and the two make plans to escape. Nan ridicules Charles for deciding to stay behind to wait for Kunie, and the two go off arguing. At that moment Skulany and Kosoff appear on the balcony. The two chess players, who have been silently passing time throughout the play, suddenly leap to their feet and produce revolvers. They fire at Skulany, and hit both the general and Kosoff. Mitzi is frozen in terror, but the gunmen motion her to be silent. When the others emerge, she tells them she has seen nothing, and they all go off to investigate. The chess players explain to Mitzi that they are Rumanian freedom-fighters sent to assassinate Skulany. They tell her to remain silent, and take her money and all the luggage that stands in the piazza. When Nan and Charles return, the three decide to remain silent about what Mitzi has witnessed, and to leave Naples after the police finish with them. Kunie arrives and says she will not go to Paris with Charles because she knows he is now free to marry Nan. Charles and Nan kiss, and are led off to be questioned by the police.

Reviews — R90, R91, R92, R96, R126

Critical Overview — The play opened 24 September 1929 at the Vanderbilt Theatre for 62 performances.

Inevitable comparisons were drawn between the play the still-running *Street Scene* (cf. Krutch [R92]). Atkinson (R91) and Young (R90) found it amusing but felt its tone was not appropriate for its themes. Rice's first solo attempt at comedy, the plays was attacked for its non-stop "wise-cracking" (*Theatre Magazine* [R96]).

The Left Bank (1931)

Characters — CLAIRE SHELBY: John's wife and Teddy's mother, living in Paris; JOHN SHELBY: Claire's husband, living in Paris and flirting with Susie Lynde; CLAUDE: the Parisian manservant; WALDO LYNDE: husband to Susie, but pursuing Claire; SUSIE LYNDE: married to Waldo, but interested in John and the modish life of a bohemian; LILLIAN GARFIELD: John's sister, who desires to bring up Teddy.

Plot Summary — ACT I: Claire and John, tenants in Paris, prepare for the arrival of their friends Susie and Waldo Lynde. They discuss their concerns about their son, Teddy, currently undergoing treatment at a psychological clinic for children. They also reveal they are strapped for funds. John refuses to consider returning to America, as he wishes to raise Teddy as a "civilized man" and does not believe this can be accomplished in the spiritual vacuum of America. When Waldo and Susie appear, it becomes apparent that the latter is pursuing John, with some encouragement from him.

ACT II: Celebrating Bastille Day, Claire and Waldo discuss the differences between French and American culture. They also are suspicious of the flirtation between their mates. Lillian arrives and reports that Teddy is turning into a "savage" at the clinic. The three of them turn to the new libertinism of the "moderns," which evolves into a debate concerning the ancients versus the moderns. Alan, an artist pursuing Claire, manages to alienate her with his advances. Waldo asks Claire if she would trust him with her son. As the guests depart, they embrace passionately.

ACT III: John and Susie enter discussing ways to get their mates together, thus leaving them free to pursue their own affair. John rejects the notion, believing Claire needs him and would be devastated at losing him. Susie is tiring of John, and sulks. Lillian arrives and asks John if she may take Teddy from his clinic to care for him herself, but John refuses. When Claire arrives, however, she tells John she wishes to leave him for Waldo and to take Teddy with them. John now acquiesces to Lillian's request, but Claire intervenes and stops him. Susie asks Waldo for a divorce, and Claire insists that John return home with her. She argues that they are aliens in France, and that John hates it because he has not been recognized as a major writer. John ripostes that Claire has given up on her attempt at radical self-reform in order to return to the "old patterns." Claire leaves with Waldo, and Susie re-enters and begins to flirt with John.

Reviews — R102, R103, R104, R105, R106, R108, R111, R112, R116, R117, R118, R120, R143

Critical Overview — *The Left Bank* opened at Little Theatre on 5 October for 242 performances.

Rice's gentle satire of Parisian expatriates and bohemians polarized opinion. Chatfield-Taylor (R104) saw it as a fine example of stark realism and impartiality, and Atkinson (R103) defended it against charges of dullness by complimenting Rice's literate dialogue. Critics like Young (R106) and Beebe (R108), however, attacked the play for its pretentiousness and use of caricatured characters. Palmieri (S141) sees merit in the play's attacks on American puritanism and hypocrisy, while Durham (S114) notes it expresses Rice's typical disapproval for those who turn their backs on America, no matter how politically misguided and culturally sterile it may be.

Counsellor-at-Law (1931)

Characters — GEORGE SIMON: a motivated, well-to-do attorney who has worked himself up from the streets to become New York's most prominent lawyer; CORA SIMON: his wife, who eloped with George while married and the mother of two children; LENA SIMON: George's mother; RICHARD, JR. and DOROTHY DWIGHT: Cora's children by her first marriage; JOHN P. TEDESCO: George's law partner; REGINA GORDON: Simon's private secretary, secretly in love with him: PETER MALONE: a local politician; ROY DARWIN: client of George, pursuing love with Cora; SARAH BECKER; old friend of Simon family; HARRY BECKER: her son, a communist agitator beaten by police, whom George frees from prison; HERBERT WEINBERG: a law clerk who admires Regina; LILLIAN LARUE: actress, and client of George; ZEDORAH CHAPMAN: another of George's clients, whom he has just helped beat a murder charge; JOHANN BREITSTEIN; George's former client, for whom he perjured testimony many years before the events of the play; FRANCIS CLARK BAIRD: an attorney from an old-money family, whose vendetta threatens George with disbarment; CHARLES MCFADDEN: a former criminal, now a process server whom George uses to gather evidence against Baird; BESSIE GREEN: switchboard operator at Simon & Tedesco; ARTHUR SANDLER: clerk at the firm; GOLDIE RINDSKOPF: Tedesco's personal secretary; HENRY SUSSKIND: an office boy.

Plot Summary — ACT I, Scene 1: The curtain rises to reveal the well-appointed and very busy outer office of the Simon and Tedesco law firm in New York City. Bessie is busy at the switchboard as calls come in from clients, business associates, and politicians. We learn that George has just won an important murder case. Zedorah Chapman, the defendant, waits to thank George. Lillian Larue and Sarah Becker also wait for George's arrival.

ACT I, Scene 2: In his inner office, Simon juggles business with prominent politicians, businessmen, and various clients. A careful and calculating man, he makes transcripts of his calls with important clients. Still, he is also revealed as a kind and caring man, as he refuses payment for a pro bono accident case. He conducts business with Lillian Larue and grudgingly sees Mrs. Chapman. She makes overtures to him, but George refuses her attention. When Regina enters, it is clear that she admires and possibly loves George, but she remains silent and dutiful. Mrs. Becker arrives, and George recognizes her from the old days on the streets. She relates how her son, Harry, was arrested and beaten for making pro-communist speeches in public. George immediately offers to take the case, and gives her money. Darwin then arrives, and asks George to compromise himself by refusing a client with whom Darwin has vested interests. George vehemently declines, but still lends Darwin money when he requests it.

ACT I, Scene 3: In the outer office, Darwin runs into Cora Simon as he leaves; the two are very familiar with one another, and arrange to have tea. When Regina greets Cora, however, feelings are noticeably hostile. Lena Simon arrives to visit her son, and while she waits McFadden greets her and tells her how George has saved him from a life of crime. Malone, a city official enters, and recognizes Lena Simon from the old East Side days on the street.

ACT I, Scene 4: Back in the inner office, George meets with Lena and Malone. George speaks movingly of his affections for Cora, but implies that he's been remiss in attending to her. He discusses their planned trip to Europe, a celebration of the fifth anniversary of their elopement. Lena informs George that his brother, David, is in a legal scrape again, and George reacts angrily, though he ends up promising to help. Cora comes in, and leaves with Lena. As they walk out together, they discuss George's work ethic and success. While Lena thinks her son is a dedicated lawyer, Cora prefers that he would rest on his laurels and spend more time with her and his stepchildren. Lena departs, and George joins Cora, who seconds Darwin in asking George to decline representation in a messy contestation of a will. She argues that he is now sufficiently successful to forego such scandalous and ungentlemanly cases, and should pick only the cases appropriate to his station. George, looking to placate her, agrees to drop the case, even though it is transparently winnable. Cora leaves, and George meets with Malone to request that the well-connected councilman get the party to nominate Tedesco, George's partner, for a State Supreme Court judgeship. Malone agrees, but also tells George of Francis Clark Baird's continued attempts to have George disbarred, apparently because the old-money Baird does not appreciate George's working-class roots. George is initially nonplussed, but after Malone leaves he reacts angrily and begins making plans to cover up his past misdeed.

ACT II, Scene 1: Back in the inner office, Bessie is found lying ill, supposedly traumatized because she has seen a man jump to his death from an office window. George enters and prepares to meet Breitstein. He first tries to call Baird, but is rebuffed. When Regina reminds George of various commitments to Becker's free-speech case, George is too busy to pay much attention. Indeed, so caught up is George in planning his defense that he plans to cancel his European tour with Cora. In conversation with Tedesco, George admits to subordination of perjury in the Britstein case, but argues that it was a minor infraction now being blown out of proportion as part of Baird's vendetta.

ACT II, Scene 2: In the outer office, Cora arrives with her children by her previous marriage. They make a point of telling people they have kept their real father's name; yet when Darwin enters, they greet him in a very friendly manner.

ACT II, Scene 3: Darwin meets Cora and makes it clear that he wants Cora to go to Europe alone so that he can follow her. Though Cora does not accept the idea explicitly, she is obviously intrigued. George arrives and confesses his present situation to her. Surprisingly, she responds by saying that she will continue on to Europe alone to avoid the scandal. Simon is hurt, but agrees to the plan. After Cora leaves, George calls in McFadden and tasks him with shadowing Baird to dig up unsavory information. Becker then arrives, and Simon explains that he has copped a plea bargain for the charge of public disorder. Becker refuses to accept the offer, and, out of principle, demands to be sent to jail. He harangues George with accusations laced with crude communist slogans, calling him a bourgeois flunky, a big-business prostitute, and a traitor to his working-class origins. He ends by spitting on George, and storming out.

ACT III, Scene 1: George has returned from Washington, where he had attempted to seek influence with a senator. As he engages in a speech filled with violent recriminations, Regina brings word that Becker has died in prison as a result of his head injuries. George immediately offers to pay for the funeral and to help out Mrs. Becker. Tedesco enters and George admits that his career is all but ended. After Tedesco leaves, McFadden arrives with crucial information on Baird. After tailing Baird to Philadelphia, McFadden has observed him staying at a widow's house. He waited until evening, then broke into the house and retrieved evidence that Baird, a married man, was leading a double life with the widow, by whom he has had a daughter. George immediately cables Cora at the ship and tells her not to leave for Europe.

ACT III, Scene 2: We learn from her conversation that Bessie is likely pregnant. As she finishes her phone conversation, Baird arrives looking anxious. George makes him cool his heels in the outer office before signalling him to come in. George's mother arrives in the outer office, and after a moment George and Baird appear together showing one another constrained politeness. George sees him out, then exuberantly greets his mother. He is very excited about saving his career, but the joy is momentary: Cora calls and tells him she will not postpone her European trip. After hanging up the phone, George divines the truth, and calls Darwin's office. He is told Mr. Darwin has left for Europe — on the same boat as Cora. George is devastated, and even climbs up on the sill to ponder leaping from his office window. At that moment, Regina enters, and the two break out in sobs. As they comfort each other, the phone rings and George discovers he has been handed another prominent case to handle. Putting their momentary dilemmas aside, the two rush out of the office to begin the case.

Reviews — R107, R109, R110, R113, R114, R115, R119, R121, R122, R123, R124, R127, R128, R151, R152, R154, R245, R246, R247, R248, R249, R250, R251, R252, R253, R254, R255, R256, R257, R258, R372

Critical Overview — *Counsellor-at-Law* opened at the Plymouth Theatre on 6 November 1931 for 292 performances. It resumed production on 12 September 1932 for another 104 performances, and again on 15 May 1933 for 16 performances.

One of Rice's perennially popular plays, this story of a good-hearted lawyer at the mercy of past indiscretions has often been praised for its evocation of the rhythms of life in a law office. Most critics (Hutchens [R123], Atkinson [R107]) compare it to *Street Scene* in its capacity for observation and attention to minute atmospheric detail, but Hogan (S95) argues that its craftsmanship exceeds that of the earlier play. Durham (S114) goes further, and argues that the play is architectonically Rice's most complex and skillfully managed drama. Atkinson echoes other critics (*Dramatist* [R119], Wyatt [R124]) and Chatfield-Taylor [R109]) when he complains that the play was talky and too long, yet still deserving of praise. Critics almost unanimously commented extravagantly on Paul Muni's performance in his first Broadway lead. The 1977 revival brought further acclaim from Gussow (R371) and Eder (R372) for the work's continued dramatic vitality.

We, the People (1933)

Characters — HELEN DAVIS: a poor school teacher; WILLIAM DAVIS, FRIEDA DAVIS: her parents; ALLEN DAVIS: her brother, a man with socialist tendencies: FRED WHIPPLE: an arrogant tenant; ALBERT COLLINS: in love with Helen; WILLARD DREW: a banker; WINIFRED DREW: his spoiled daughter; ALBERT, STELLA, SARAH, DONALD and LARRY COLLINS: Bert's rural relatives, facing hard times; STEVE CLINTON: their Black farm hand; MARY KLOBUTSKO; a student radical, in love with Allen; SLOANE and HIRSCHEIN; University faculty taking the side of labor.

Plot Summary — SCENE 1: In a grade school classroom, Helen Davis meets with Louis Volterra, an immigrant laborer, and his son Tony. Louis tells Helen that he is out of work because his shoe shop has been closed by competition with a large manufacturer. Helen listens sympathetically, but then tells Louis that Tony has been speaking out in class against America's business elite. Louis argues that his son is only telling the truth, and provides a litany of burdens his family has suffered because of their class. He goes so far as to say that the school is teaching the children to appreciate war, just as the schools in Italy had done in the past. Helen defends the school and America, and warns him to keep an eye on Tony.

SCENE 2: In the Davis home Mrs. Davis prepares dinner while humming German folk tunes. Allen arrives to announce that he has passed his College Board exams, and will be attending State University. As the rest of the family gathers, everyone congratulates Allen, who announces that he wants to become a chemical engineer. As they sit down to dinner, Helen relates the content of her meeting with the Volterra's. Her father, William Davis, says he hears the same sort of "bellyaching" at his plant, and defends American capitalism. Allen asks why so few should control the means of production, especially when so much of it devoted to military spending. He announces that he supports the laboring classes, and will not fight in a war. William insists that he will, and father and son argue until Allen leaves. Helen and Mr. Davis discuss working conditions at the school and the Applegate plant, where things are bad. Helen has not been paid in five months, and there have been layoffs at the plant. Mr. Davis begins to realize that he will be stretched to pay for his home, especially now that Allen is going to college. He hints that Helen should consider marrying Bert Collins, her beau, but she does not seem hopeful. At that moment Bert arrives, and everyone sits down to dinner.

SCENE 3: That same evening, in a public park, Bert and Helen enter holding hands. As Bert tries to kiss her, Helen self-consciously shies away, afraid to be seen in public. Their conversation reveals that they are already engaged, but too uncertain about future prospects to be married. Both are eager to be together, and Bert suggests that Helen begin visiting him in his rooms. Helen worries that if she is discovered to be either Bert's lover or wife, she will lose her teaching job. Bert, meanwhile, is not hopeful about his prospects about finishing his C. P. A. training. They discuss their bleak prospects, and Bert again attempts to persuade Helen to come to his rooms, but she is fearful of the consequences and so they decide to go to a movie instead.

SCENE 4: In his banking offices, William Drew speaks by phone to a constituent and argues that Labor must begin to share its part of the economic burden of the Depression. Drew leaves and Bert arrives to request a raise from the bank's manager, Cunningham. As Cunningham explains why he cannot authorize a raise, Winifred Drew, the banker's daughter, enters and begins discussing the plans for her upcoming socialite wedding in Westminster Abbey. Drew re-enters, and after speaking with his wife by phone about the purchase of "another Titian" painting for one-half million dollars, he meets with a representative of the Unemployed Charity and agrees to donate $5,000.

SCENE 5: In the dining room of the rural Collins family. Sarah enters and greets Stella, her sister-in-law, and Williamson, the local clergyman. Noting Stella's anxiety, Williamson asks her if she has been attending church lately. When she reports she has not, the pastor notes that many have stopped as times have gotten worse. Mrs. Collins sees this as evidence of dwindling values, but Williamson feels it is due to his own inadequacy. Bert Collins enters on a visit from the city, and talk turns to the failing farm loans that threaten the family. Steve Clinton, a Black farm hand greets Bert and asks him how things are in the city. When Steve hears about the layoffs, he relates corporate exploitation with that of race. After he leaves, the others discuss the deteriorating race relations that have surfaced as Blacks come North and take low-paying jobs from Whites. Stella re-enters and we learn that her husband, Larry, has been out of work and taking to drink. Williamson excuses himself to go speak with her. As Mrs. Collins and Bert continue to compare urban and rural problems, Donald enters and adds that he is about ready to give up on farming. Larry then arrives, drunk and morose, and upsets Stella. It is revealed that Larry is a WWI veteran who was gassed and suffers from shell shock, and who now subsists without any government aid. Alone with Stella, he lashes out at her to defend his eroded sense of manhood. When the others come to dinner, she covers up for Larry. After Williamson says grace, she breaks into tears and leaves the table, as the others silently prepare to eat.

SCENE 6: Back in the city, Helen and Bert lie across the bed in Bert's rooms, half-clothed. They are talking about the spectacular Drew wedding and comparing their state to that of the rich. Helen still fears discovery of her relationship with Bert, and he is upset at his family's situation in the country. They cannot figure out a solution to their dilemmas, and Helen leaves.

SCENE 7: In the Davis home there is cause for momentary celebration, as Helen comes home with three months of back pay from the school. They have also received a letter from Allen, which reports that he is passing his college courses with honors while becoming a leader in student government. When Mrs. Davis suggests that Helen not remain out so late, Helen reveals that she and Bert have been going to his rooms. Davis enters and reports that he has received another 10% cut in pay at the plant. Becoming more bitter toward the corporate bosses, he now considers telling Allen that he cannot afford to remain in college. Another option he suggests is to rent Allens's old room to Bert. Without deciding upon a plan, the family decides to tighten their belts and to persevere.

SCENE 8: In the country, Bert is visiting his family home again. Williamson and Steve Clinton are present, and the latter reports that he is reading H. G. Wells's *Modern Utopia*. Bert is told that Stella has left Larry and run off to California with another man. Mrs. Collins is shocked, while Bert seems unsurprised and Williamson ready to forgive her action. It is also reported that, after hearing of Stella's departure, Larry went into a rage and beat his son Donald, who has also run away. Larry now enters looking for drinking companions. After he leaves, Donald sneaks back in to report that he is leaving to join the Marines in the hopes of going to "lush, tropical Haiti." Steve tells him that if he goes to serve there he will be oppressing the indigenous Blacks who are fomenting revolt. Mrs. Collins reprimands Steve for his radical notions, and Donald leaves with her comment that the Collins's have always provided America with soldiers.

SCENE 9: In the Davis house, Allen's old room has now been rented to Whipple, an obnoxious man who likes to make lewd remarks to Helen about her relationship with Bert. Helen and Davis enter, talking about the arrest of Louis Volterra and his imminent deportation. Whipple butts in and makes a bigoted, jingoistic speech about foreigners before he departs. Mr. Davis tells Helen he wants to throw Whipple out, but cannot afford to. She reports that their bank has closed, swallowing up their entire savings.

SCENE 10: At State University, the student government is in session discussing the issue of compulsory military training. While many of the students want to table the discussion, Allen and others fight to have it resolved. Mary Klobutsko strongly opposes the plan, arguing that no one would ever attack the United States. A faculty advisor with liberal sympathies, Sloane, urges them to take a stand against mandatory military training, and the motion is carried. Sloane speaks to Mary and Allen, telling them he admires their brains and their hearts. After Sloane leaves, Allen asks Mary to the freshman dance, and she accepts.

SCENE 11: Helen is at home with Whipple, who is bragging about a date and threatening to expose Helen's relationship with Bert. Davis enters and it is apparent he has been fired from the Applegate plant and has not been able to find other work. Allen is also home, working as a coal hauler. He speaks out against the rich, and argues with his father about whether or not things will ever improve under the current form of economic organization. Bert arrives, and Helen tells him that Whipple knows about their trysts. They discuss ending the meetings, and sit down to pass the time playing checkers, since they can no longer afford to go to the movies.

SCENE 12: In Drew's opulent library, six wealthy industrialists, educators, politicians, and capitalists (including Applegate, the owner of the plant) discuss what to do with "agitators" who have been protesting the economic downturn. Senator Gregg disagrees with Applegate, suggesting that the unrest is spreading even to "decent" working men. Applegate espouses an isolationist stand, and Drew remarks that the people must be made to understand that the interests of big business are the interests of the country. Drew's new son-in-law, Meadows, has been named Ambassador to Haiti, primarily to protect American banking interests there. Drew announces to Professor Purdy, president of State College, that everyone in attendance has agreed that they want to draft him for the presidency. Those in attendance envision him as the right man to end government interference with big business, and promise him that they have the political machinery, money, and media connections to get him elected. All rise to toast the prospect.

SCENE 13: The Davises are preparing to move from their home. Three men from the plant arrive to tell Davis that, after a meeting the night before, the men fired by Applegate have planned to march on the plant, and want Davis to lead them. Allen tells them they are wasting their time. As Davis ponders the offer, a marshall arrives with a warrant to arrest Allen for stealing coal. Davis accuses his son of being a crook, but agrees to march with the workers.

SCENE 14: At the Applegate plant, the an employee and a security guard witness the approach of the marchers. They call in Moulton, the manager, who wants to call out the National Guard. When the marchers arrive, accompanied by women, they demand to speak to Applegate. Moulton refuses, and a woman marcher spits on him. He orders the guards to evict the marchers, and a scuffle breaks out. Soon the sound of shots being fired is heard, and the march turns into a melee.

SCENE 15: In the President's office at State University, Purdy receives telegrams of congratulations on his candidacy. He then calls in two faculty members for reprimand. He rebukes the first, Hirschein, for attending a meeting of the Liberal Club, which had gathered to protest the killings at the Applegate protest. When Purdy refuses to support his attendance at the event, Hirschein calls him Applegate's apologist. The President accuses Hirschein of violating the University's disciplinary code by his attendance at the meeting, but Hirschein argues it is a free speech issue. Purdy then dismisses Hirschein from his post, though the teacher protests that Applegate and Drew were on the board that rendered the decision. He parts with bitter accusations of anti-Semitism. Sloane enters next, believing he will be dismissed as well. However, Purdy says they have decided only to reprimand him; Sloane, however, resigns in protest over the favored treatment, which is the result of his connections to a prominent old-money family. Purdy tries to convince him to stay, but Sloane notes that one of the men seriously wounded at the Applegate protest was Davis, the father of his prize pupil Allen. As soon as Sloane leaves, Applegate is on the phone to Purdy plotting strategy.

SCENE 16: In the Washington office of Senator Gregg, Applegate discusses the growing unrest at his factories. War veterans are picketing outside the Senate offices, which Applegate sees as a sign of communist agitation. He is anxious about the government investigation into the massacre at his plant, and reasons that if the government were better prepared to rid the country of outside agitators, the protest would never have taken place. Before departing, Applegate tells the Senator that he feels a war would be good for the economy. After he leaves, a pacifist group which includes Pastor Williamson and Hirschein enters to lobby for the League of World Peace. While the talk is bland, Gregg appears sympathetic; but when Hirschein asks him about his connections to the Drew bank, Gregg sends the delegation away. Williamson lags behind to ask Gregg to look into getting Allen Davis out of jail and to help out veterans (Donald Collins, we learn, has been killed in Haiti). Williamson leaves convinced that Gregg will help.

SCENE 17: Mary Klubotsko is working on a speech when Allen arrives at her rooms. He has been freed from jail, and wants to renew their acquaintanceship. Mary has left the University in protest of the faculty firings, and is now speaking regularly at labor meetings and doing manual labor. Alen tells her that he fears he will be sent back to prison, and so has bought a revolver. He thinks he is not welcome, but as he turns to leave, Mary invites him to live with her, and they embrace passionately.

SCENE 18: In a public square dominated by a monument to those who fought in WWI, a speaker relates the depredations suffered by the veterans. Allen speaks next as "the son of one of the victims at the Applegate Harvester Plant." He tells the crowd that they must not take their pain like sheep. A policeman interrupts to silence him, and a scuffle ensues. When the crowd scatters, a civilian and a police officer lie dead on the ground.

SCENE 19: In a packed courtroom, Allen is being tried for the murder of the police officer. Though the murder weapon was owned by him, he maintains he had left it in Mary's apartment the day of the riot. The prosecutor inflames the jury by calling Allen an ex-con who "raped" Mary and who has shown a consistent disregard for the law. The judge, Cleveland Thomas (one of those in attendance at the Drew dinner) refuses to set aside the verdict. In sentencing Allen, the judge makes clearly racist comments about how Allen, who comes from solid White American stock, was unable to take advantage of the manifold opportunities which America offers its citizens. He rebukes him for his weakness, and sentences him to hang.

SCENE 20: At a mass meeting in a public auditorium (in which the theatre audience is placed in the position of the public audience), a parade of speakers — Sloane, Hirschein, Mary, Williamson, Helen, and others — gathers to protest Allen's execution. The case has by now attracted a great deal of national and international attention. The speakers plead that Allen was framed, that he was a victim of class, and so on. Mary reveals that she is pregnant with Allen's child. Sloane is the last speaker, and he reads from the Constitution and condemns those who would contravene its message. He refers to Mary, Allen, Hirschein, and others as "the youth upon which a new, strong, and free people" could be built, but who instead are abused and slaughtered by their country. He ends by claiming that the country is "our house: this America. Let us cleanse it and put it in order, and make it a decent place for decent people to live in!"

Reviews — R245, R246, R247, R248, R249, R250, R251, R252, R253, R254, R255, R256, R257, R258, R372

Critical Overview — *We, the People* opened on 21 January for 49 performances.

This sprawling pageant drama depicting America during the Depression brought Rice a great deal of notoriety as a social critic. As might be imagined this polemical play divided critics along political lines. Conservatives like Brown (R134) and DeCasseres (R148) were offended by the play's proletarian themes, Garland (R135) going so far as to accuse Rice of biting the hand of the economic system which had made him wealthy. Moderate to liberal critics such as Young (R143) and Atkinson

(R133,138) praised Rice's ability to stir indignation in the audience, while McKenna (R155) lauded the structure of the work. Some liberal critics, Krutch (R139) among them, found it disappointing as a sociological drama because it did not draw the audience into it. Hogan (S95) compares the work favorably to Odets's *Waiting for Lefty* as a work of agit-prop, while Durham (S114) calls the play a "protest vote" against certain policies, rather than a true "revolutionary" drama. Behringer (S143) points to inherent contradictions in Rice's political thoughts which would lead him eventually to move away from explicitly political theatre.

Judgment Day (1934)

Characters — DR. MICHAEL VLORA: a principled member of the High Court of Justice; DR. PANAYOT TSANKOV: a Nationalist Party tool, also a Justice; COLONEL JOHN STURDZA: another member of the Judiciary; PROFESSOR PAUL MURUSI: a jurist and High Court Judge, easily swayed to Party principles; COUNT LEONID SLATARSKI: an aristocratic Court Judge, but a believer in democratic principles; ALEXANDER KUMAN: an imprisoned revolutionary; LYDIA KUMAN: his wife, a defendant accused of plotting to kill Minister-President Vesnic; GEORGE KHITOV: a co-defendant and eloquent spokesperson for democratic freedom; KURT SCHNEIDER: a half-mad erotomaniac, accused of co-conspiracy but unknown to Lydia and Khitov; DR. WOLFGANG BATHORY: the xenophobic State prosecutor; DR. STAMBULOV: defense attorney representing Lydia; DR. MENSCH: representing Schneider; CONRAD NOLI: Lydia's American brother, who assists Stambulov in her defense; DR. CONSTANTIN PARVAN: Secretary to Minister-President Vesnic; VASSILI BASSARABA: a waiter and witness for the prosecution; MARTHE TEODOROVA: wife of a government clerk and witness for the prosecution; SONIA KUMAN: daughter of Alexander and Sonia, and a witness for the defense; GENERAL MICHAEL RAKOVSKI: Minister of Culture and Enlightenment, a cover for the State's internal police; GIULIA CREVELLI: an Italian opera singer, linked to Rakovski and Schneider; GRIGORI VESNIC: Minister-President of the State, reportedly recovering from an assassination attempt; MAREK, SRAZHIMIR, GHEREA, GLUCA, PEKMESI, VIDIN, JORGA, ZOGU: guards, many of whom are secretly sympathetic to Alexander Kuman.

Plot Summary — ACT I: In a Court of Justice in a vaguely Balkan/Slavic state, a trial is underway. Five judges sit, but there is no jury. The scene opens on a loud altercation between Khitov, who is demanding to make a statement and who accuses Judge Tsankov of bias, and the judges and State prosecutor, Bathory. Khitov is eventually forcibly removed. Noli presents his petition to represent his sister, even though he is an American. Despite sneers directed toward American non-totalitarian political and judicial principles, the judges allow him to sit. Charges are read, accusing the three defendants of belonging to the opposition People's Party and of attempting to assassinate the Minister-President.

The trial begins with Parvan taking the stand (he swears his oath on the Greek crucifix) for the prosecution. He claims Lydia and Schneider arrived together in order to plead with Vesnic for clemency in the case of Alexander Kuman, an opposition leader who was captured and sentenced to death. Lydia and Khitov remonstrate during the testimony, but are silenced. Next, the obeisant Bassaraba, the waiter at the Café Danube, takes the stand. With Bathory obviously leading his answers, he testifies that Schneider, Lydia, and Khitov often met at the café, and that at the last meeting — on the day before Vesnic was shot — he witnessed Khitov passing a revolver to Schneider. Bathory calls Schneider next, and the German is apparently not altogether in his right mind (also, since he is Protestant, he is not allowed to take the oath). He admits to shooting Vesnic for reasons of liberation, but his answers are mechanical and unconvincing. Khitov again intervenes with shouts for freedom, and is again forcibly removed.

Lydia now takes the stand, and attempts to refute all the previous testimony. She claims she has never known Schneider, though she noticed him staring at her in the Minister-President's antechamber before she entered to see Vesnic alone. After Vesnic brutally refused her plea for Alexander, she left, only to hear the sound of a shot behind her and to see Vesnic fall. Bathory then produces what he claims is Alexander's confession, which implicates Lydia. Claiming it is a forgery, Lydia demands that Alexander be brought in to testify. Bathory then informs her that Alexander has hanged himself in his cell. Lydia grabs the revolver held in evidence and points it at her own breast, before being subdued by Noli.

ACT II, Scene 1: Several days later in the same courtroom, Lydia is seen sitting dispiritedly, listening to Mme. Teodorova's testimony, which is contradictory and muddled on several points. Noli leaves and returns with Sonia Kuman, whose testimony he proposes to use for the defense. Despite Lydia's pleas, Sonia takes the stand. Bathory insinuates that, because she is not a member of the Party Youth, she is not a patriot. Sonia answers that she is "not in sympathy with the politics of the National Party." She also supports her mother's contention that the two of them had met only with Khitov at the café, and that no gun was present. As Bathory continues to badger her, Alexander's name comes up, and Judge Tsankov brutally informs her that her father is dead. After Sonia is led away in tears, Khitov takes the stand, and speaks eloquently in his own defense. He charges that

General Rakovski has masterminded the entire prosecution. As he speaks, a guard, Vidin, is seen passing a note to Lydia. Tsankov notices this, and demands that Vidin be arrested and questioned. Lydia swallows the note, and refuses to divulge its contents. At that moment, the sound of crashing glass is heard in the Court antechamber, followed by a tremendous explosion as the curtain falls.

ACT II, Scene 2: Two days later, court is again in session, though the damage from the bomb attack is evident. Lydia is testifying, though she is weak from two day's deprivation of sleep and water. The judges question her about the contents of the note, but she refuses and is led away. Vidin is called, but Bathory informs the Court that the guard has fallen into a coma. Khitov is called next, and again accuses Rakovski of a Nationalist Party plot to concoct the assassination attempt in order to steer sympathy towards Vesnic and to indict the opposition. He maintains that Vesnic was never really shot, and asks that objective parties examine the Minister-President. Rakovski enters at that moment, and peremptorily demands to be placed on the stand. He brusquely asks Schneider if the two have ever met, and Schneider corroborates his claim. Noli and Khitov attempt to question Rakovski further, but he is haughty and unwilling to answer. Khitov is again dragged out of the Court.

Noli's next witness is Mme. Crevelli, a self-absorbed Italian prima donna who is often seen in public with Rakovski, though she says she detests his attentions. She has had a dispute with the Opera, and is returning to Italy. After some questioning, she reveals that Rakovski used to meet with Schneider at in her rooms, and that the two were present on the day before the assassination attempt — exactly the time when Schneider was supposedly meeting Khitov and Lydia to receive the gun at the café. Raskovski again interrupts the proceedings, claiming Crevelli is lying in a jealous rage. She galls Raskovski by admitting that Schneider had indeed spent the entire night with her after the general had left.

ACT III, Scene 1: Later the same day, the five judges meet in executive chambers. Vlora and Slatarski are beginning to waver in their judgments. Accusations of intrigue and dishonor are exchanged between Slatarski and Tsanov. Eventually, the judges decide to treat the defendant's cases separately, over Tsankov's objections. They all agree on the death penalty for Schneider. When they come to Lydia, there is disagreement: Tsankov and Sturdza (who is drinking) demand death, while Murusi ponders the "moral point" of his judgment, which he construes as identical to the "welfare of the State." As he wavers, Tsankov reveals that, in just a short time, the State will make membership in the People's Party a capital crime. Thus, he argues, Lydia and Khitov are guilty by virtue of association. An argument ensues over whether this information should affect their deliberations. Murusi, pressured by Tsanov, relents and agrees that Lydia is "constructively guilty" and should be put to death. Slatarski intervenes, speaking as the eldest tribunal and a man with an honorable family history. He argues that Lydia and Khitov are innocent, and that a death penalty will be tantamount to murder. As he concludes, Rakovski, against all precedent, interrupts the executive session. He informs the judges that a unanimous guilty judgment is necessary and expected: citizens have begun to agitate in the streets, and the police have refused orders to fire on the crowds. The three guilty votes fall into line, but Slatarski adamantly refuses to join them. Since four out of five votes constitutes a unanimous judgment, the burden falls on Vlora to break the deadlock. As he vacillates, Raskovski springs another surprise: the information in the note passed to Lydia was that Alexander Kuman is not dead, and in fact has escaped from prison. Though it is pointed out that this means Raskovski perjured himself by his testimony, he responds by declaring that the Party has put aside all "decadent philosophies" of liberalism and Christian ethics for the greater good of the State. In order to convince Vlora that Lydia and Khitov have, indeed, committed a crime, Raskovski offers to bring Vesnic in to testify. All the judges except Slatarski leave together.

ACT III, Scene 2: An hour later, guards prepare the courtroom for an evening session. They discuss their support for the opposition, and plot some kind of maneuver to take place during the session. A "Father Sebastian" arrives, and is hidden in the curtains. As the trial continues, Noli speaks first, asking the Court to consider "world opinion" in passing their sentence. Khitov follows, and reasserts his accusation that Vesnic has not really been shot. As he reaches the height of his peroration, Vesnic is dramatically wheeled into the courtroom to testify. He is haughty and petulant, angry that he has been forced to testify. He begins by denouncing Alexander, but before he can finish a long whistle is heard. Father Sebastian — actually Alexander Kuman in disguise — steps out from the curtains, and denounces Vesnic. Parman raises a revolver at Alexander, but is restrained by a guard. Tsankov also draws a gun, which Slatarski wrestles from him. Vesnic attempts to intervene, and in the struggle is shot dead by Slatarski. The aristocrat then cries out "Long live the people!" before turning the gun on himself.

Reviews — R156, R157, R158, R159, R160, R161, R162, R163, R164, R165, R166, R167, R168, R169, R170, R172, R175, R188, R189, R190, R192

Critical Overview — *Judgment Day* opened at the Belasco Theatre 12 September 1934 for 93 performances.

Based on the recent trial surrounding the Reichstag fire, this incendiary melodrama of political intrigue in a Balkan country sharply divided critical opinion. Brown (R157) and Garland (R159), predictably, censored

Rice for indulging in political polemic, Brown suggesting the play was as old-fashioned as *The Drunkard* and therefore unintentionally funny for audiences. Atkinson's (R156, 164) measured response took account of the exciting early scenes while noting that the play eventually devolves into predictable melodrama. Marxist critics like Garlin (R162) felt Rice had not gone far enough in implicating capitalism. Less ideologically-committed critics (Lockridge [R161], Hammond [R160]) admitted that audiences were aroused by the performance.

More recent accounts (Hogan [S95], Durham [S114], Smiley [S116], Palmieri [S141]) point to the play's simple characterizations and neat plot resolution as signs of weakness. The London production fared much better (Fleming [R189]).

Between Two Worlds (1934)

Characters — MARGARET BOWEN: a transatlantic traveler; FREDERICK DODD: a university wit; N. N. KOVOLEV: a prominent Soviet filmmaker, returning from Hollywood, who pursues Margaret; EDWARD MAYNARD: a liberal intellectual, in love with Margaret; GIUSEPPE MORETTI; JAMES ROBERTS; RITA DODD; VIVIENNE SINCLAIR; ROSE HENNEFORD; RICHARD NEILSON; MATILDA MASON; HILDA BOWEN; ELENA MIKHAILOVNA GOLITZIN; LOUBERTA ALLENBY; LLOYD ARTHUR; ELEANOR MASSEY; CHRISTINE MASSEY; HENRY FERGUSON; HELEN EDDINGTON; EDGAR HOWELL; CLARA ROBERTS; DR. DAVID MacKNIGHT; DAISY COOPER; CHESTER COOPER; HAROLD POWERS; EUNICE STAFFORD; HENRI DESCHAMPS; BILLY EDDINGTON: travelers of various nationalities and social backgrounds.

Plot Summary — SCENE I: Late on an afternoon aboard the S.S. Farragut, bound for Europe, a potpourri of characters representing various classes, nationalities, and lifestyles are gradually introduced. Lloyd's father has committed suicide after the Wall Street crash, and he is trying to establish himself as a poet as he begins a career in government. A vapid Hollywood screen starlet, Vivienne Sinclair, is aboard, as well as Eva, Princess Golitzin, a displaced young Russian aristocrat. A collection of wits and sports, including Louberta, Moretti, and Edward, enliven the dialogue.

SCENE II: The next morning. As more passengers board, conversations are heard regarding the approaching war. Lloyd and Edward engage in debate over the relative merits of Hollywood and Soviet film-making. Lloyd is envious of Edward's brash self-confidence, but Elena comforts him by saying she admires his soul. Vivienne is revealed as a casual bigot as she mistreats her handmaiden Rose.

SCENE III: The next afternoon. The older women on board discuss current morality, while Vivienne studies for her upcoming role in a film version of Lucretia Borgia. Elena recognizes Kovolev as a Bolshevik, and avoids his gaze. Later Elena's companion Margaret, after spurning brash advances by Edward, is confronted by Kovolev, who details his opinions on post-revolutionary art and religion.

SCENE IV: The next day, after lunch. Matilda and Howell swap travel stories, and the former sings a folk song. Kovolev encounters Rose after she has been treated curtly by Vivienne. Rose reveals she is educated, and married to a doctor. Kovolev asks her about race relations in the U. S., and calls her "comrade" as they part. Margaret, who has overheard their conversation, remarks that Kovolev was kind to speak to Rose. Kovolev responds with a speech outlining the division of labor in the world and the interesting experiments in ideology-control being conducted in Russia. Margaret warms somewhat to him, and reveals her upbringing, which is characterized by a proclivity to choose the paths of least resistance. They leave, and Elena and Lloyd appear to provide a juxtaposition to Kovolev's descriptions of Russia. Elena describes the revolution and remembers seeing her family dragged out to be executed. Lloyd suggests that there is more to life than the "material plane," and Elena agrees that spiritual values are important (she quotes Francis Thompson).

SCENE V: The next evening, at a cocktail party. A large group including Margaret, Edward, Lloyd, and the Dodds are sharing drinks and playing a game in which each admits to something they have never done before. Edward says he has never proposed to anyone, while the Purser has proposed but never been accepted. The talk then turns to social revolutions, and Edward declares that one is immanent which will wipe them all away, for which he is grateful. Lloyd counters Edward by stating that there are other aspects of life that are interesting. Edward argues that it will not matter, that the revolution will eliminate the parasitical middle class to which he and the others belong. He proclaims himself a "first-class whore" for expending his considerable energies in advertising. Lloyd suggests it is his dissatisfaction with his career which makes him so eager for change. Edward then ridicules Lloyd and his poetry-writing, asking if he thinks his poems matter to the working class. The guests, embarrassed, depart for dinner. Margaret returns and chastises Edward for his tactlessness, for which he apologizes. He then proposes to Margaret, pointing out that both are in a rut and wasting their lives "playing lost generation." Margaret says she will consider the proposal.

SCENE VI: Later the same evening. A promenade-scene, with individuals and couples entering and exiting throughout. There is a full moon, and various manifestations of romance are expressed. Rita and the Captain engage in friendly flirtation, Christine and Richard kiss and avoid her mother, and Cooper tries to steal kisses from different women. Lloyd explains to Elena his earlier embarrassment at the hands of Edward, and admits that he, a former nature lover, is now out of touch with his wellspring of being, quoting Wordsworth as evidence. Elena responds by expressing her devotion to Lloyd, and by asking him to commit to her. Lloyd reveals that this prospect makes him happy, but admits to her that his marriage had failed because he was not able to physically satisfy his wife. Kovolev appears with Margaret and makes advances, noting that jazz dancing excites the sexual emotions. Margaret at first spurns him, but when he accuses her of cowardice in the face of the biological urge, she half-heartedly succumbs, and is lead, zombie-like, into his quarters while Edward searches for her above deck.

SCENE VII: At a costume party the next evening, amid much celebrating, Kovolev and Edward meet. Edward is worried about Margaret, whom he has not seen all day. Kovolev divulges nothing of his liaison with her, and tries to steer the conversation in other directions. After Edward leaves, Kovolev seeks out Elena in order to gloat over the reversal of their respective fortunes. The Kovolev family had been serfs on a Golitsin estate, where Kovolev's grandfather had been crippled by beatings, and his father driven into exile. As Elena tries to depart, Kovolev reveals that it was he who gave the order to execute the Golitsin family. Elna tears at him in a rage, and he slaps her.

SCENE VIII: Early the next morning, several passengers are preparing to board a tender which will take them to England. Margaret is finishing a long letter to Kovolev, but he appears and she tears it up. Margaret chastises Kovolev for mistreating Elena, but he is not remorseful. Margaret accuses him of being heartless and indecent toward herself, but Kovolev maintains a darwinian and materialist view of love and sex, and argues that he does not have patience for sentimentality. Margaret delivers an impassioned speech declaring that American democracy, for all its romantic notions, is superior to any other political system because it recognizes the individual and insists upon mutual respect among its citizens. Their conversation is interrupted by Elena's departure.

SCENE IX: Later that evening, the ship approaches Cherbourg. Margaret and Edward are seated together, but not speaking much. When Edward tries to discover what has fallen between them, Margaret coolly changes the topic. As they prepare to disembark, Edward leaves and Kovolev approaches Margaret. He apologizes for his earlier rudeness, explaining that as a soldier still fighting an uncompleted revolution, he often is cruel without intending to be. Margaret accepts his apology, and admits that Kovolev has made her see things in her life differently. She confides that she is breaking off her engagement, possibly to accept Edward. Kovolev invites her to Russia, then kisses her fiercely before she leaves. Rose appears on deck, and also thanks Kovolev for being kind to her.

Reviews — R171, R173, R174, R176, R177, R178, R179, R180, R181

Critical Overview — *Between Two Worlds* opened at the Belasco Theatre 25 October 1934 for 32 performances.

The least successful of Rice's three Depression-era plays was also responsible for sending the playwright into a well-publicized four-year retirement from the theatre. Krutch (R174) admired the pithy social discussion that takes place in the play, but considered it too static and undramatic to be of interest. Rudolph Schildkraut's acting was universally applauded, but the writing was characterized as directionless (Van Rensselaer [R181]).

Not for Children (1935; Revised and reproduced 1951)

Characters — ELIJAH SIVLERHAMMER: a "Universal Broadcasting Company" broadcaster; TIMOTHY HARRIS: a Broadway producer; AMBROSE ATWATER: a former Professor of Applied Psychology, and one of the play's interpreters; THEODORA EFFINGTON: Ambrose's foil, a Lecturer; CLARENCE ORTH: a critic, married to Irma and father of Eva; IRMA ORTH: an aspiring playwright, married to Clarence and mother of Eva; PRUDENCE DEARBORN: the Orth's maid, a former cabaret singer; HITCH IMBORG: the stage-manager who "plays" a stage-manager; PENSACOLA CRAWFORD: offstage factotum to Harris.

Plot Summary — ACT I: In a forestage set, two chairs face one another from each side of the proscenium. Further back are drawn tableau curtains. Silverhammer enters and announces the play in an overtly presentational manner, showering accolades on Rice, the author, but mistakenly ascribing to him a Nobel, rather than Pulitzer, Prize. After shilling for Perspiro deodorant, Silverhammer gives way to Harris, the producer of the play. Harris represents the typical cog in the Broadway machine; his recollections of his dealings with Rice for accepting the play allow for a debate regarding the definition of good drama (as well for some jabs at journalistic critics). Rice has, however, convinced Harris to accept the "novelty" of using a pair of compéres to comment on the play's proceedings: as Harris says, "Why make you try to figure it out for yourself, when I can hire somebody to do it for you?" This brings on the raissoneurs, Theodora and Ambrose, the names apparently intended to evoke those of earlier famous exegetes. Ambrose, a former professor of Applied Psychology, will present the masculine view, while Theodora, a "well-known lecturer on literature and the drama," will provide the feminine response. He is rather melancholic, with a "masculine" tendency for explaining everything. Theodora, on the other hand, is suitably vivacious, a sort of post-Shavian woman without the same degree of irony. The two discuss various topics, personal and theatrical, including the nature of theatrical illusion (with an overt nod toward Pirandello), which Ambrose loathes as hollow and deceitful, while Theodora exalts its preferability to the harsh realities of life. After this exchange, the tableau curtain rises to reveal Clarence and Irma Orth; before their scene can begin, however, the two interlocutors analyze the set and the expectations it creates. When the scene begins, Clarence and Irma are in the process of negotiating their impending divorce. When Prudence, a maid (and former cabaret singer) enters, her dialogue with Clarence reveals him to be a theatre critic, while Irma mentions that a play she has written has interested a possible producer, who turns out to be Harris. Eva arrives with Digby, and as they part the tableau curtain falls. Theodora and Ambrose continue their earlier discussion, using the scene as reference: Ambrose again feels the scene cannot capture the complexity of human personality, while Theodora admires the way the scene captures the totality of a character. When Ambrose attacks the use of multiple actors for a role and the use of masks and interior monologue (possibly with O'Neill in mind), Prudence sings a song, "Multiple Personalities." Theodora and Ambrose then go on to consider the audience members and their "performances" in the stalls. The tableau curtain opens again, and Clarence appears looking for Mrs. Effington, that is, Theodora. She rises from the forestage chair and enters the action of the tableau stage. As Clarence's former mistress, Theodora comforts him about his divorce, and ends up accepting his overtures for lovemaking. As the tableau curtains close, Theodora returns to her forestage chair, where she discusses the scene with Ambrose. Other metatheatrical incidents follow: Harris interrupts the two critics at several points, as when Ambrose declares that the play is "propaganda," which elicits dramatic scenic effects and the staged departure of an audience member. Several other plot lines are also introduced: Hugh and Prudence are revealed as lovers who enjoy rather violent foreplay, Digby is proposing to Eva, (who rejects him because he wants her too much), and Ambrose unveils that he has earlier proposed to Theodora. The first Act ends with Silverhammer taking the stage and again pitching deodorant.

ACT II: The second Act begins in the tableau stage, where Eva is seen backstage, now appearing as the actress-playing-Eva. Harris visits her and tries clumsily to proposition her, but is interrupted by the actor-playing-Digby. As she and Digny prepare to rehearse their next scene, the tableau curtain falls, and Harris crosses the forestage The tableau curtain rises again to reveal the actor-playing-Clarence, who is visited by Hugh, his agent. They discuss the failure of the first act, but when Harris arrives they hypocritically rave over the show. The tableau curtains close, then reopen to show Theodora and Ambrose in their dressing room. We discover they are actually man and wife, though they snipe at one another's performance. Pensacola (who, we discover, is Harris's not-too-secret-mistress) visits them and praises their work, and is joined by Harris. Ambrose and Theodora reassume their forestage chairs, and the topic turns to censorship. A list is produced of censored groups (excepting only "Shintoists, the passport photographers, and the window cleaners," as well as the Manx). After further discussion, Harris appears in the tableau stage and enacts a scene with Digby, who has brought him a highbrow play to read. Digby cannot lower himself to accede to Harris's practical revisions, and leaves. Irma Orth then appears with Hugh to discuss her own script. Harris accepts it, with the proviso that Irma work on it with a play doctor (Rice is mentioned as one choice, but rejected). Afterwards, Harris comes downstage to ask Ambrose for help in understanding the play within the play complications, which leads to a further discussion of the reality-illusion debate of Act One. We switch to the tableau stage, where Irma is visited by Digby, who, after being rejected by Eva, now propositions her mother ("The incest motif," comments Ambrose drily). After more debate between the interlocutors, the upstage curtain is drawn to reveal a bed, toward which Theodora and Ambrose direct an analysis of its many possible symbolisms. Prudence puts their thoughts into a song, "Ev'ry time I hit the pillow," after which we return to the tableau stage to find Eva, dressed in mountain climbing gear and speaking from the top of a mountain. She delivers a long speech relating her discovery of God, at the end of which both curtains fall.

ACT III: Silverhammer introduces the critic, Clarence, who lectures the audience on the merit of the play of which he is a part. A scene between Ambrose and Irma is meant to follow, but it has been reduced to a telephone conversation, which goes somewhat awry. In the same botched mode, a murder scene (actually the enactment of Irma's playscript) follows in which all manner of stage trickery and plot manipulation is exposed — presumable to justify Ambrose's contention that "the more nearly a play is good theatre, the less likely it is to be a reflection of reality. . . . theatre and life are antithetical." Ambrose critiques the play as the exposure of Rice's unconscious desires. Clarence interrupts and proposes to explain his paper on the decline of tragedy, and is in turn interrupted by Digby, who contests Clarence's thesis. Eva suddenly reappears, and in the best deus ex machina tradition reunites her parents and accepts the "new" Digby as a worthy husband. Theodora and Ambrose, and Harris and Pensacola, are likewise united. The play ends with Silverhammer announcing that, in response to thousands of telegrams, this will be the last performance of *Not for Children* (though not the final appearance of Perspiro deodorant).

Reviews — R182, R183, R184, R185, R186, R187, R307, R308, R309, R310, R311, R313, R314, R315, R316, R317, R318

Critical Overview — The play opened in London at the Fortune Theatre on 28 November 1935. It opened in Los Angeles at the Pasadena Playhouse but was not brought to New York. It was revised by Rice and produced in New York on 13 February 1951 at the Coronet Theatre for 7 performances.

The London premiere gained lukewarm praise, Verschoyle (R183) crediting Rice with dissecting the fundamentals of dramatic illusion though suggesting the play was too long. Morgan (R184) called it a "devil of dullness," while he later (R185) blamed a lack of awareness on the part of the audience for the play's failure. The revised 1951 script fared much worse, with Guernsey (R310), McClain (R312) and Chapman (R308) condemning Rice for playing boring theatre games and waxing too abstruse.

American Landscape (1938)

Characters — CAPTAIN FRANK DALE: Spanish-American War veteran and owner of the Dale homestead and factory, tiring and on the verge of selling his holdings; CARLOTTA DALE: his daughter, a widow; FRANCES DALE SPINNER: Carlotta's eldest child, now living in California; GERALD SPINNER: her husband, a writer who has sold his services to a Hollywood combine; CONSTANCE DALE: Carlotta's youngest daughter; JOE KUTNO: foreman at the Dale Shoe factory; BETTY KUTNO: his sister, the maid in the Dale house; WILLIAM FISKE: the Dale's lawyer, who intends to marry Constance; KLAUS STILLGEBAUER: a prospective buyer of the Dale home, who wants to turn it into an Aryan exercise camp; PAUL KUTNO, ABBY KUTNO: parents of Joe and Betty, longtime retainers of the Dale's; PATRICK O'BRIEN, ABRAHAM COHEN, NILS KARENSON, HENRI DUPONT, REVEREND JASPER WASHINGTON; spokesmen from the Dale factory and the community who try to convince Frank not to sell; CAPTAIN TONY DALE; the ghost of Frank and Carlotta's eldest son, blinded and killed in WWI; CAPTAIN SAMUEL DALE: Frank's deceased relative, a veteran of the revolutionary War; CAPTAIN HEINRICH KLEINSCHMIDT: Carlotta Dale's deceased grandfather, a veteran of the Army of the Republic in the Civil War; MOLL FLANDERS: the ghost of Defoe's literary creation, a distant relative of the Dales; HARRIET BEECHER STOWE: ghost of the American writer, a longtime friend of the Dale family.

Plot Summary — ACT I: In the solid but rambling Dale country house in Connecticut, a blind war veteran stumbles into the living room. Betty enters and receives him, but he is looking for the Dales. After he leaves, Carlotta, Fran, Jerry, and Bill return from playing tennis. When Betty reports the visit, Carlotta is troubled. Fran and Jerry are visiting from California, and there is a noticeable strain in their marriage. Connie enters and is met by Bill, who wants to plan their marriage. However, she seems to have changed her mind and now desires to be a local teacher. After they leave, Carlotta asks Fran what is troubling her, and Fran responds with a bitter denunciation of the empty life she leads with Jerry in California. She suspects him of an affair, and reveals that she is considering a divorce. As they speak, the soldier re-enters, and Carlotta recognizes him as her dead husband Tony. He has appeared because some unstated threat to the house has compelled him to return. He promises that other relatives will appear as well. Joe recognizes Tony as they pass in the garden, though he is startled by the appearance. Frank has asked Joe to come to the house to tell him that he has decided to sell the Dale factory to an Eastern firm. As they speak, another spirit appears, this time Captain Samuel Dale, the founder of the family business. He advises Frank not to sell. The others return, and after greetings are exchanged, they leave. Joe speaks to Connie, and tells her that Frank's decision to sell is based on the outcome of a recent union meeting, in which the workers voted to accept representation by the union. He tells Connie that selling the plant will result in its closing, and criticizes the Dales for not having real loyalty to the town and company they founded. Connie tells Joe that she, for one, intends to stay, and that she has decided not to marry Bill.

Stillgebauer enters, and reports seeing a woman dressed in eccentric clothing in the yard. This turns out to be Moll Flanders, Frank's relative by many removes. Stillgebauer has arrived to discuss purchasing the house, but before he can negotiate another ghost arrives, this time Carlotta's grandfather Heinrich, who is accompanied by Harriet Beecher Stowe, an old friend of the family. After they are introduced, Frank reveals that he is selling the house in addition to the firm. Everyone moves to the terrace, expressing dismay and concern, while Moll and Harriet lag behind and express their wish that something terrible did not have to happen to someone in the family.

ACT II: Several hours later, Connie and her father are discovered speaking about her future. Tony tells her she should marry Joe, and leaves her to speak to him. Together they plan strategies for saving the firm, and along the way express their regard for one another. They leave, and soon Jerry enters with Moll, his favorite literary heroine. She reprimands him for his Hollywood affair and lifestyle, but they are interrupted by a phone call for Jerry, with the news that he must return to Los Angeles immediately. After he leaves, Fran speaks to Moll, who counsels patience and forgiveness. Fran then goes to speak to Stillgebauer, and discovers his plans to turn the house into a retreat for an Aryan group. The spirits intervene, and give the history of the house and its traditions of freedom, castigating Stillgebauer for his racist intentions. Jerry enters and tells Fran he is leaving, and she tells him she wants him to quit his L.A. job and help her buy the Dale house. Jerry is interested, but will not commit to the plan. Fran threatens divorce, and Jerry leaves bewildered. After they leave, Moll and Harriet return and again discuss the tragedy due to strike the Dale family. When Frank enters, they finally acknowledge to him that it is his time to die. Before he can respond, Abby and Joe Kutno enter with Fran, and make their argument against selling the house. They are followed by the delegation from the factory and community, who support the Kutnos' argument. Frank responds with a moving speech regarding the circumstances that have conspired against him and convinced him to sell: the bad mortgages he has picked up to help others, the Wall Street speculators who are driving private businessmen to ruin, the government's intrusive regulations into farming, and above all, the new unions. Connie blurts out that what Frank wants is "feudalism," to which Frank responds by promising to extend the workers' severance pay. Joe retorts that this is charity, not a true recognition of the rights of workers. Frank defends himself by saying that this is a "new America" that he does not understand, and he wonders if he can be expected to function in a world that is so different from his own. As angers rise, Stillgebauer interrupts and presents the bill of sale to be signed, at which point O'Brien intrudes to protest the "legacy" Frank is leaving them by selling to preachers of racial and religious intolerance. The ghosts join in the argument, and just as Frank prepares to respond a bugle is heard, and Frank collapses in a seizure, shouting "Not yet!"

ACT III: Ten days later, Connie and Fran are seen responding to sympathy cards commemorating Frank's death. Jerry returns from L.A., and after expressing condolences, asks Fran why she has not written. He tells her that by rushing back for the funeral he has been dismissed from his job. Bill enters to read the will, and makes peace with Connie regarding their canceled marriage plans. The ghosts enter, and everyone prepares to hear the will. The house is given to Fran, and the business is divided among Connie and a trust made up of her, Joe, and Bill for the benefit of all the employees. Frank's stated hope is that the idealism of youth will find solutions for problems that had become too burdensome for old age. Bill, after finishing the reading, advises them in his capacity as family lawyer that they should sell both house and factory. As the ghosts leave, Tony lingers and makes a plea for the living to oppose being put into uniforms, "whether of the body or the mind." As the captains prepare to leave, Frank's ghost appears among them, and he notes sadly that he was the last "pure" Dale. Recovering himself, he tells Fran and Connie to fuse their blood with the new stock, for "that is the chemistry of America." After they depart, the remainder toast "the next day and the day after."

Critical Overview — *American Landscape* opened at the Cort Theatre on 3 December 1938 for 43 performances.

Marking Rice's return to the stage, this critical view of America's past was greeted warmly if not effusively by the critics but shunned by audiences. Coleman (R196) expressed the most common sentiment, noting that although the play's theme was worthy, the dramatic execution was lacking. Similar feelings were expressed by Mantle (R198) and Atkinson (R194, 201). Only Whipple (R200) was explicitly condemnatory, though Young (R204) thought both the writing and Rice's direction were flat. Critics, including Palmieri (S141), Collins (S73) and Hogan (S95) unanimously criticize the overly-oratorical speeches that dominate the play.

Two on an Island (1940)

Characters — MARY WARD: a young and vivacious woman from New Hampshire,, arriving in New York to pursue a vocation as an actress; JOHN THOMPSON: a friendly Iowan who comes to New York pursuing a career as a writer; LAWRENCE ORMANT: a harried and somewhat cynical Manhattan director/producer; RUTH ORMANT: his unhappy wife; RUTH ORMANT: their daughter; WILLIAM FLYNN and SAMUEL BRODSKY: Manhattan cabbies, the former a "cultured" man and the latter his antithesis; A SIGHTSEEING GUIDE: who takes Mary and others on a revealing tour of Manhattan; MRS. DORA LEVY: a widow now residing in New York, who briefly befriends Mary; FREDERIC WINTHROP: very cerebral and academic, from a rich family, but given to supporting "the working classes"; KATHERINE WINTHROP HOLMES: his sister, an elite snob; GRACIE MULLEN: down and out friend to Mary and John; CLIFTON ROSS: well to do artist, though physically handicapped; DOROTHY CLARK: wealthy dilettante who enjoys experiencing a variety of lifestyles; MARTIN BLAKE, HEINZ KALTBART, MARTHA JOHNSON, SONIA TARANOVA, DIXIE BUSHBY: occasional acquaintances of Mary and John.

Plot Summary — ACT I, Scene 1: At a busy Manhattan intersection, two cabs wait for fares. In one, Brodsky, a self-styled bookworm listens to an informative documentary, while in the opposite cab Flynn, a blue-collar type, listens to dance music. Mary enters Brodsky's cab, revealing her naivete when she does not tip correctly. She asks to go to the nearest YWCA. John enters Flynn's cab and heads to a YMCA. He reveals he is from

Iowa. After John and Mary disembark from their respective cabs, the two drivers collide and begin to argue the cause of the accident.

ACT I, Scene 2: On a Manhattan sightseeing bus an ethnically-diverse group prepares for a trip. May meets Mrs. Levy, and confides her desire to become an actress. John arrives, but does not notice Mary. The tour begins, and collapses an entire circuit of Manhattan into a short period. The bus travels not only through Times Square, but also Greenwich Village. the Bowery, Shantytown, and Harlem. The guide mixes cliched travel dialogue with ironically penetrating social commentary (e.g. "having the highest disease rate, the highest crime rate, the highest death rate... the Negro never loses his native gaiety and happiness").

ACT I, Scene 3: In Ormant's cluttered Broadway office, the producer prepares to audition actors for *Long Island Honeymoon*. He treats the performers curtly but with great panache. John enters and asks Ormant to read the manuscript of *Red Cloud*, a play about dust bowl farmers. Ormant is humorously impossible to please, and dismisses John by admitting that *Long Island Honeymoon* is up and running only because Dorothy Clark, a spoiled rich girl, is putting up the money so that she can play the lead. John responds good-naturedly, and leaves. Alone, Ormant excoriates himself and the sleazy business he is in. Dorothy arrives, and Ormant does an about-face, convincing her that the play is marvelous and destined for success. After she leaves, Mary enters and tries to tell Ormant about her dream of becoming an actress for the pure love of the profession. Ormant anticipates her at every turn, and tries to discourage Mary by telling her that "Broadway is paved with the little white psyches of renegade schoolteachers." He does, however, invite Mary back to read for a small part in the play.

ACT I, Scene 4: Two months later, another miscellany of characters, some of whom were along for the sightseeing tour, move in and out of a BMT subway car. Katherine and Frederic Winthrop debate class issues, before Ormant and Ross appear to discuss business. Apparently *Long Island Honeymoon* has flopped, though Ormant himself managed a profit. John then enters as they leave, and meets Martin Blake, an All-American football player from Iowa. Blake now successfully sells insurance in Manhattan. John unburdens himself to Blake, noting that Ormant has had his play now for two months, and that work is getting harder to find. He exits as Mary enters. She runs into Mrs. Levy again, and, like John, confides to her that she is becoming lonely and alienated in Manhattan, even though she did land a small part in *Long Island Honeymoon*.

ACT II, Scene 5: In Ross's apartment, Mary is posing in a swimsuit for an advertising commission. Ross is cynical about his "popular" work, yet he recognizes that his commercialism does not necessarily preclude him from doing real art. He calls himself and his work an "in-betweener." There is a telephone call from Dorothy, who wants Ross to do her portrait, but he declines. Mary confides to Ross that she was in one of Ormant's plays, and that he had tried to seduce her during the run. Ross, too, is attracted to Mary, and kisses her. At that moment John arrives, selling prints for an arts publishing company. Ross nastily rebukes him, and John answers him pointedly before leaving. Mary composes herself, and leaves despite Ross's pleas that she stay.

ACT II, Scene 6: The by-now familiar faces of several characters are gathered at the Coffee Pot Café, where John is now working. Ormant enters with his wife, but does not recognize John. John addresses him, and reminds Ormant that a year ago he had left him a manuscript. Ormant remembers, and says he hated *Red Cloud*. John accepts this, and says he is now writing comedies, one of which has been sent to Ormant. He apologizes for intruding, and retreats. Helen criticizes Ormant for not giving John any encouragement, and for becoming overly hardened and cynical since coming to New York from St. Louis. Ormant responds with a self-pitying apology about his recent failures. Helen tries to convince him to return to St. Louis, but Ormant resists. Mary enters and sits with Gracie and her date, who want her to join them for dancing. Too tired from working at a five and dime, Mary declines. Winthrop, seated with Sonia, has been agitating at the store for the workers to form a union, but was physically removed from the premises. As he notices Mary, Ross and Dorothy arrive to taste the decadent pleasures of the café, an attitude that causes Sonia to curse their snobbery. She and Winthrop argue over the matter. After dining, Ross and Dorothy leave, as does Sonia. Winthrop then sits with Mary, and gives her literature on forming a store union.

ACT II, Scene 7: A docent leads several older women through a slide show and vapid commentary on modern art at the Metropolitan Museum. Mary enters in the company of Winthrop and recognizes Mrs. Levy among the listeners. They speak and plan to meet later. Off to the side John enters, wearing Dorothy's livery. As Winthrop and Mary look at a Degas, they argue its merits and begin to quarrel about Mary's decision to take a part in a play that is sure to flop. There is a sudden disturbance offstage, and Mary goes to investigate. Meanwhile, Ormant enters with his daughter, Ruth, who asks him why her parents are separating. They are followed by Ross, who, upon hearing from John that Dorothy has stood him up, angrily dismisses his affair with her. John admits he also has just quit her employment, and the two exit to drink together. Mary returns with the news that Mrs. Levy has suffered a fatal heart attack in the next gallery.

ACT III, Scene 8: At the Silver Bar in the West Forties, John is seen panhandling while Dorothy promenades with a Hindu spiritualist. Ormant enters and runs into Mary, for whom he says he has a part in a new play. He begs her to join him inside for a drink. John runs into Gracie, now a prostitute. The two discuss financial hardships, which leads John to suggest that they pool their resources and live together, with no attachments. Ormant and Mary come out of the bar, and are interrupted by Ross. John recognizes Mary, and moves toward her as if to speak. At that moment Gracie returns and tells John she has agreed to accept his offer. As they leave, Ormant presses Mary to take him to her apartment, and they leave together.

ACT III, Scene 9: Inside the viewing deck of the Statue of Liberty we find John and several tourists. Mary arrives, and John finally speaks to her. They discover their mutual link with the theatre and with Ormant, but this freezes Mary into silence. John reveals he has sold two stories to a penny press for $75, a third of which he has given to Gracie as a goodbye gesture. He tells Mary he is giving up on Manhattan, and plans to return to Iowa to take a share in a Chevrolet dealership with his brother. Both admit that New York has been hard on them, and they confide to one another their failures and loneliness. John thinks he is close to becoming a Bowery bum who cannot leave New York, while Mary admits that Ormant has made it clear that her getting the part in a good play depends on her sleeping with him. After listening to John, she decides she will not accept the offer. John asks Mary to accompany him on a last blow-out dinner before he leaves New York. She refuses, saying she believes a man like John should stay and pursue his dreams, no matter the cost. They agree to share a drink, and leave.

ACT III, Scene 10: In a Chelsea apartment, Mary is setting a table for two. Her landlord comes to collect the late rent, and Mary cheerfully apologizes and makes a partial payment. Ormant enters, and demands to know why Mary had turned down his offer to act in the play, which has since become a blockbuster hit. She responds that she simply was not interested. Ormant asks her if she regrets the missed opportunity, to which she answers no. He offers her another part, but is still pursuing his seduction. When she demurs, he even offers to marry her. When she refuses, he notes for the first time the dual settings at the table, and recognizes that she is living in "a love nest." John enters, and there are amazed recognitions all around. He tells Mary he has found a job — as a manuscript reader, in fact, for Ormant, who did not know John was living with Mary. Ormant is amazed at the couple's tenacity and toughness: he invites himself to dinner, then leaves momentarily. John and Mary happily acknowledge their good fortune, and John asks Mary to be his wife. As she accepts, Ormant returns with champagne.

ACT III, Scene 11: The same two cabs and drivers from the first scene appear. Mary and John enter one, and prepare to leave for Niagara Falls. In the other, Winthrop and Dorothy (who now shares Winthrop's marxist zeal), also recently married, head to the same location. As John and Mary disembark from the cab, she tells John she is pregnant with "a native New Yorker." After they leave, their cabs are taken by another man and woman fresh from rural areas who are coming to try their luck in Manhattan.

Reviews — R210, R211, R212, R213, R214, R215, R216, R217, R218, R219, R220, R221, R222, R223, R224

Critical Overview — *Two on an Island* opened at the Broadhurst Theatre on 22 1940 for 96 performances.

As was often the case with Rice, this comedy follows a series of plays on serious social themes. Perhaps because of the contrast, most reviewers viewed the play as an idyllic departure from earlier work. Brown (R212), Whipple (R216) and Mantle (R214) were entertained by the witty dialogue and unpretentiousness of the play, and Krutch (R218) felt it revealed Rice's skill for capturing the accent of contemporary urban life. Only Atkinson (R217) and Nathan (R221) admonished Rice to forsake comedy for his more significant social drama.

Flight to the West (1940)

Characters — HOWARD INGRAHAM: an American political writer in the midst of a crisis of conscience; CHARLES NATHAN: an American newlywed escaping from Europe; HOPE TALCOTT NATHAN: his wife, who desires to settle down in isolated America; DR. HERMANN WALTHER: German consul worker travelling to his country's embassy in Washington, D. C.; COUNT PAUL VASILICH VRONOFF: a Russian emigré with a history of intrigue; MARIE DICKENSEN: a Belgian refugee, escaping from the destruction of Louvain; EDMUND DICKENSEN: her husband, a scholar who has been left blind after the bombardment of Louvain; LISETTE DICKENSEN: their daughter, whose arm was crushed in the bombardment; LOUISE FRAYN: a Texas-based American journalist, virulently anti-fascist; COLONEL ARCHIBALD GAGE: an army reservist, now in business, who wants Americans to accommodate Hitler; CLARA ROSENTHAL: a Jewess fleeing from Europe; CAPTAIN GEORGE McNAB: American pilot of the Pan-Am air clipper; RICHARD BANNING, THOMAS HICKEY, AUGUST HIMMELREICH: officers aboard the flight; CAPTAIN ARTHUR HAWKES: a British immigration officer, stationed in Bermuda.

Flight to the West

Plot Summary — ACT I, Scene 1: Aboard a Pan-Am clipper in July of 1940, several passengers wait to embark on a flight from Lisbon to New York. The first is Edmund Dickensen and his family, who are fleeing from the destruction of Louvain by the German army. Edmund, made blind in the battle, is followed by his anguished wife, Marie, and their daughter, Lisette, whose arm was mutilated in the attack. Eventually, they are joined by Charles and Hope Nathan, George Ingraham, Colonel Gage, Louise Frayn, Clara Rosenthal, Hermann Walther, and Paul Vronoff. After the ship takes off, Hope reveals in conversation to Ingraham that she is pregnant, but afraid to tell her husband until they are safely in America. In passing, she also mentions that Vronoff looks familiar, though she is unable to place him. When she leaves, Charles speaks with Ingraham, who had written a book, *The Betrayal of Democracy*, which in its critical view of America's role in attenuating the League of Nations had greatly influenced the Nathans' socialist political beliefs. Charles is disturbed, however, by the destruction he has seen in Europe, and feels his pacifist leanings are no longer relevant. Ingraham's response is that events have caused him to reconsider his beliefs as well. He has seen his writings against war picked up and turned into propaganda by both rabid American isolationists and by the fascists in Europe. A "confused liberal," Ingraham has not yet decided his position on the European situation. Charles admits that he may begin training as a pilot, should America enter the war. Ingraham, knowing Hope is pregnant, advises caution. Hope returns and confides her desire to settle in America and put the madness and war in Europe behind her. She wants Charles to settle down with her in peaceful, isolationist bliss, partly because, as we discover, she has led a transient life, having been born in China and lived in the Levant and Europe. Marie interrupts the conversation and relates the story of the destruction of Louvain and its library. She is anxious about her family's future in America, and blames the Germans for the destruction of her way of life. As she leaves in tears, she passes the German embassy official Walther, and grimaces in anger.

ACT I, Scene 2: Mid-afternoon over the Atlantic. Walther is discussing his hobbies, entomology and butterfly-collecting, with Charles. Hope stops by, and discusses her fear that they are bringing Europe's troubles to America. Vronoff joins the conversation, and expresses his happiness at leaving decadent Europe behind him: a scholar and seemingly a fatalist, he says he is not concerned with politics. As he leaves, Hope finally remembers him, though under a different name, as a teacher she knew in Jerusalem who found himself in some sort of trouble with the British authorities. Louise overhears this and, smelling a story, asks if she may radiogram Hope's father for more information. While this conversation ensues, Walther and Vronoff are seen secretly exchanging information. As soon as other passengers arrive, they break apart. A general discussion concerning the war ensues among the passengers, with Walther speaking of the necessary "pacification of Europe" and Louise and Ingraham disputing his version of events. Gage suggests that Americans will learn how to do business with Hitler, to which Ingraham responds that America will remain unconquered only if she creates a true democracy that will serve as a viable alternative to fascism. Gage retorts with a jingoism laced with anti-Semitic overtones, and the group breaks up when Mrs. Rosenthal rushes from the room. Charles then asks Walther how Germany could bomb Louvain, but the German refuses to discuss the question with Charles, who is a Jew. Ingraham asks the same question, and Walther stuns him by replying that the answer is found in *Betrayal of Democracy*, which argues for the autonomy of sovereign nations. As he describes the pain he felt at "having" to shell Louvain, Walther is attacked by Marie, who calls him a murderer. With the cabin in chaos, the plane lands for fuel in the Azores.

ACT II, Scene 1: Having left the Azores, Ingraham is speaking to Hope, advising her to tell Charles about the baby. Walther and Vronoff again speak furtively, but are interrupted. Walther goes to Lisette and shows her his butterfly book, while telling her stories about the toy factories in Nuremburg. When Himmelreich passes by, Walther asks him, in German, if he knows Nuremburg. The attendant responds that he is now an American, but that he remembers touring the torture chambers in Nuremburg's castles. Marie enters and, seeing Lisette with Walther, slaps her daughter and tells her to stay away from the *bosch*. Louise enters with her response to the radiogram, which reports that Vronoff is actually an alias for a man who was suspected of espionage in Jerusalem some years back. Louise wants to stop Vronoff, who is traveling under a British passport, from entering the U. S., and goes to enlist Captain McNab's assistance. Meanwhile, Walther and Vronoff secretly discuss plans to use Vronoff's new position at Berkeley to spy on American aviation and shipping. Walther advises Vronoff to sound off as a foe of Communism in order to make himself popular among his American colleagues and students. When he is ready to report information, Vronoff is instructed to use a code devised by Walther, indexed to his book of butterflies.

ACT II, Scene 2: Later that evening, the passengers are engaged in socializing. Louise reports to McNab that she has received confirmation from British authorities that they would like to detain Vronoff in Bermuda. Meanwhile, Vronoff and Charles play chess, while Mrs. Rosenthal and Hope discuss family issues and the tensions between race and nationality. Mrs. Rosenthal ends by telling Hope never to have children, as it is a bad time for Jewish children to be born, even in America. When Charles joins his wife, he tells her about the news of Vronoff's past, and uses that as a pretext for confiding to her that he will begin training as a pilot to fight such men. Hope is chagrined, having lived a vagabond existence and now hoping to settle into comfortable domesticity. She reveals that she is pregnant and accuses Charles of simply wanting to play hero. They quarrel. After she leaves, McNab enters and informs Louise and his crew that they will make an unannounced landing in Bermuda, presumably for fuel but for the intention of having Vronoff questioned.

ACT III, Scene 1: The next morning, Charles and Hope renew their discussion about their future, but nothing is reconciled and Hope even threatens an abortion. Banning enters and tells the passengers about landing for fuel in Bermuda, asking at the same time for their passports. Marie enters the cabin in a daze just as Vronoff takes a revolver from his pocket and hides it under his seat. Worried over her husband's illness, she seemingly does not notice this. After the plane lands, Captain Hawkes comes aboard to inspect passports. He thanks Louise for her information, and proceeds to pass through the passengers. When he comes to Vronoff, Hawkes has him searched for weapons and accuses him of carrying a forged passport. Vronoff is taken off the plane, and Walther enters. He too is searched, and his valise is taken from him under protest. As he is led off the plane as well, Marie enters the cabin and secretly removes Vronoff's hidden revolver.

ACT III, Scene 2: Several hours later, the plane is in the air again. Walther is again on board, but Vronoff has been arrested. As the other passengers play bridge, they discuss the incident and Walther's possible complicity. The conversation turns toward the issue of confronting Germans like Walther, or seeking appeasement with them. Marie enters and stalks Walther, hiding the pistol in her lap. Walther collars McNab, and insists the captain corroborate a document describing the diplomatic abuses he suffered in Bermuda. When McNab balks, Walther delivers a shrill lecture on American meddling, and threatens that Germany will soon deliver a message, first to Britain and then to America. McNab, furious, nevertheless agrees to contact his superiors and report Walther's complaint. At that moment, Marie stands and levels the revolver at Walther; Charles, seated closest, leaps up to stop her and is inadvertently shot.

ACT III, Scene 3: Two hours later, Charles is seen unconscious across the cabin seats as Hope and Ingraham tend to him. Walther is quietly reading while the other passengers express muted sympathy for Hope. McNab enters and tells Walther that Department of Justice officials are waiting in New York to question him; Vronoff has just talked to British officials in Bermuda and has implicated Walther in the espionage scheme. Ingraham leaves Charles to speak to Walther, asking him what his reaction is to the irony of having a Jew save his life. Walther responds by rejecting the "human equation" and sentimentality he perceives in Ingraham, and by speaking as a "scientist" and "realist." He claims that, since human races are interested only in survival and domination, Charles' actions could only be ascribed as atavistic and illogical, and are therefore not to be admired but repudiated. He also says he hopes Ingraham will not be capable of learning this moral, as this will make the conquest of a "weak-minded" and liberal America that much easier. Ingraham returns to Hope, who tells him she will have the baby because Charles' act has convinced her emotionally that to fight is necessary. This reifies Ingraham's intellectual response, that in comparison to Walther's supposedly rationalist and Darwinian worldview, an "insane" act such as Charles', which proceeds from men "thinking with their feelings," is more in tune with the organic flux of life than Walther's rigid fascist dogmas. As Ingraham leaves to prepare for landing, Charles wakes and indicates that he will be alright. Hope tells him she is proud of him, and reveals that she intends to have the baby.

Reviews — R225, R226, R227, R228, R229, R230, R231, R232, R234, R235, R236, R237, R238, R239, R240, R242, R243, R244

Critical Overview — *Flight to the West* opened at the Guild Theatre on 30 December 1940 for 136 performances.

The last of Rice's explicitly anti-fascist dramas, the play enjoyed moderate success even though critics were almost unanimous in their distaste for it. Brown (R227) repeated his earlier criticism regarding Rice's unwillingness to dramatize when he could discuss, and other reviewers (Freedley [R232], Lockridge [R228] and O'Hara [R237]) echoed the complaint. Young (R241) focused on the play as an example of the continuing difficulty of American playwrights to universalize the theme of war while keeping their characters believable. Other reviewers like Wyatt (R243) and Atkinson (R226, 239) congratulated Rice for facing difficult topical realities and attempting to bring them into the American consciousness. Palmieri (S141) points to the fine touches of humor as a saving grace in the piece.

A New Life (1943)

Characters — EDITH CHARLES CLEGHORNE: an independent-minded radio singer about to give birth to her firstborn, believing that her husband has been killed in the war; CAPTAIN ROBERT CLEGHORNE: her husband, son of a wealthy industrialist, who returns from heroic action in the Pacific; SAMUEL CLEGHORNE: his father, a willful businessman who has temporized with Hitler, only to reap rewards from war contracts; ISABELLE CLEGHORNE: his sickly wife; OLIVE RAPALLO: Edith's

A New Life

friend from the stage; GUSTAVE JENSEN: Edith's former fiance, who has fought in Spain and since joined the merchant marine; MILLICENT PRINCE: former girlfriend of Robert, now working as an aide in the hospital; GROVER CHARLES: Edith's father, a blue-collar worker; DOCTOR LYMAN ACTON: Edith's doctor; THEODORE EMERY, RUTH EMERY: parents who lose their child; HOSPITAL NURSES, PATIENTS.

Plot Summary — SCENE 1: In New York's East River Hospital, Edith arrives with her friends Olive and Gus at the maternity ward. The hospital personnel express some embarrassment when they realize she is not accompanied by her husband. It is soon explained that Robert is missing in action and presumed dead in the Pacific. After Edith is conducted to her room, Olive and Gus argue about how best to be helpful. Their conversation reveals that Edith and Robert had been married only two weeks before he left for the war. Sam and Isabelle Cleghorne arrive from Arizona, wanting to see the daughter-in-law they have never met. They tell Olive that they had invited Edith to Arizona during her pregnancy, but that Edith did not want to give up her promising contract to sing on the radio. After Gus leaves, Millicent enters and is recognized by the Cleghornes as Robert's longtime girlfriend. They speak to her while Edith calls in Olive.

SCENE 2: In Edith's maternity room, Dr. Acton and Miss Kingsley, the birth nurse, are checking the patient's rate of contractions. Olive enters, and after the staff leave, Edith asks her to look after the baby if anything goes wrong. They also discuss the arrival of the Cleghornes, which worries Edith. Isabelle enters, and though she treats Edith rather condescendingly, they part under good terms.

SCENE 3: Back in the hospital foyer after midnight, Gus and Edith's father, Grover, are asleep. Olive enters, having come straight from a show without taking off her makeup or changing out of her costume. She wakes Gus and tells him she believes that the Cleghornes intend to "move in" on Edith and claim the baby for themselves. Gus mocks Samuel, telling Olive that he had been an early appeaser of Hitler before cleaning up on war contracts when the winds shifted. Olive suggests that Gus marry Edith, as he had been her fiance before she met Robert and ended a whirlwind romance by marrying him. Cleghorne returns and interrupts, looking down his nose at Olive in her stage costume. Grover awakes, and is introduced to Cleghorne. When Grover predicts that Edith will be able to raise the child herself, Cleghorne mentions that he will "relieve her" of many responsibilities. Gus confronts him on the point, and insinuates that Cleghorne is more interested in profits, power, and an heir than he is in Edith's rights as a mother. They exchange insults, and Gus leaves. Isabelle enters, and Cleghorne rages to her about how "Reds" like Gus are trying to resist their attempts to bring the baby back to Arizona with them. He departs to take a phone call, and when he returns he reveals that he has news that Robert is alive and on his way to New York.

SCENE 4: In the famous birth scene (the first on the American stage), Edith's face is visible in a beam of light, while the hands of doctors and nurses cross over her. She deliriously speaks of the horrible effects of the war, and wonders aloud if it is worth bringing more people into the world. As she cries out that she will not give birth, the baby son is delivered.

SCENE 5: Robert arrives at the hospital foyer, where he is greeted by his parents. He tells them of his mission, and of his heroic deeds while leading his men to safety on a Japanese island. Bewildered, he reveals that he did not know of Edith's pregnancy when he shipped out, and is therefore not prepared for the news of becoming a father. Dr. Acton arrives with the baby, and is followed by Edith. She is told of Robert's return, and greets him woozily but happily before being carted off.

SCENE 6: In Edith's room, everyone is congratulating her on the fine son she has produced. As Dr. Acton leaves, we discover that another baby, belonging to the Emerys, has died the night before. The Cleghornes enter, and again treat Edith condescendingly as they tell her that Robert has news that he must return to service. They press her to make plans for the baby's future, and offer the use of their private railway car to transport her and the baby to Arizona. Cleghorne is already planning additions to his house. When Edith balks, Isabelle tells her that, now she is Robert's wife, she will have to make sacrifices for the good of the Cleghorne line. After they leave, Olive arrives and discusses the Cleghorne threat. Olive suggests that the decision will ultimately be Robert's to make, and assures Edith that everything will turn out fine. Robert then arrives, and Olive leaves. After warmly greeting one another, they comment on how much the other has seemed to change since Robert went to war. He tells her he must go to Washington in order to receive the Congressional Medal of Honor from the President (a New Dealer with whom Samuel Cleghorne does not get along). He also asks her what she thinks of the plan to settle in Arizona, and she responds that she feels the baby won't grow up independent in such a protected, elite atmosphere of privilege. They come to no conclusions, and Robert leaves.

SCENE 7: A few days later, in the foyer, Isabelle enters agitated and runs to make a phone call. The Emerys are checking out, and they balefully look into the nursery to see all the healthy babies. Robert returns bearing his medal, and Isabelle remarks that it was too bad he had to receive it from such a man. Robert defends Roosevelt, and says he believes in what he stands for. Isabelle tells him she is concerned about Edith, who is resisting their wishes to go to Arizona. Millicent enters, and Robert begs

A New Life

a moment of her time. Robert apologizes to her for the manner in which he left her, explaining that he was beginning to notice that they were "drifting" in their relationship. He says that Edith represents a more stable love, and Millicent accepts the explanation and shakes his hand as she parts. Edith is wheeled into the room, and tells Robert that she's made plans for them to spend some time together at her apartment. Isabelle interrupts and accuses Edith of causing everyone a great deal of trouble. Edith responds warmly, and Robert does not intervene on her behalf. When he kisses her to go, she responds passively. After Edith leaves, Isabelle tells Robert she does not want him making the decision about the baby, because it is apparent he has allowed himself to be seduced by Edith. They leave arguing about how to proceed.

SCENE 8: In Edith's room, Miss Woolley, a dry nurse, arrives to tell Edith that Cleghorne has engaged her to look after the baby on the trip to Arizona. Edith dismisses her angrily, and she leaves just as Gus arrives. He has come to tell Edith that he is shipping out soon. She apologizes to him for having left him for Robert, but he defends his choice to go fight with the Spanish resistance. He is beginning to question the deeper meaning of the war, however, wondering if, once it is over, everything will simply return to normal, or if it will motivate more widespread social change in America. He sees Edith's baby as the next generation for which this war is being fought, and tells her he would prefer that the child not be brought up with Cleghorne's corporate "trademark" affixed to him. Robert enters, and treats Gus coldly. After Gus leaves, Robert angrily confronts Edith about Miss Woolley's dismissal, accusing his wife of not considering his mother's feelings. They argue, Robert insisting that Edith "live in the present" and recognize that during a war certain sacrifices have to be made for the good of all. She retorts that her baby is the future, and so must be brought up ready to face the postwar world. He tells her he is glad to be returning to the Pacific, and ends the argument by insisting that he has moral and legal rights to the baby.

SCENE 9: In the foyer, Cleghorne is searching for Robert, who has been missing since the previous night. Robert enters, haggard after a night of drinking. His parents tell him Edith is packing to go home, and they insist he stop her. He tells them Edith wants to divorce him, to which Isabelle responds with threats of lawyers. Robert tells his parents firmly that if they interfere in the dispute, he will never speak to them again. After he leaves to make a phone call, Cleghorne tells Isabelle that it is in their best interest that the case should go to court, where he can pull strings to win custody of the child for Robert. Edith enters, ready to leave the hospital, and is met with Isabelle's accusations that she has no right to divorce her son. Robert enters with the news that he must report back to his unit the following day. He tells his parents to leave him alone with Edith, and sits to speak with her. He explains that he was out drinking when he ran into Gus at a bar. The two men stayed together all night discussing the war and America's future. Robert admits to Edith that Gus opened his eyes, forcing him to acknowledge the guilt he had always felt at being wealthy and privileged. He tells her he went to war in the first place to break away from his father's influence and business mentality. While on the Japanese island, he had the chance to ponder his family situation, and came to the conclusion that he wanted to work for change in the postwar world. Hearing this, Edith tells him she'll be honored to wait for a man "not afraid to look life in the face." As they prepare to leave and begin their new life together, another expectant couple enters.

Reviews — R259, R260, R261, R262, R263, R264, R265, R266, R267, R268, R269, R270, R271, R272, R273, R278

Critical Overview — *A New Life* opened at the Royale Theatre on 15 September 1943 for 70 performances.

Produced just after the birth of Rice's first child with Betty Field, this optimistic look to a future beyond the war was almost uniformly rejected by audiences and reviewers. Collins (S73) rates it "just short of a being a poor play," and a number of critics (Kronenberger [R262], Waldorf [R266] and Gilder [R272]) felt the birth scene was gratuitous and in bad taste. For the most part, the play was faulted for tedious writing (Garland [R261]), intellectual pretention (Rascoe [R265]), and, in perhaps the most developed critique, for Rice's inability to invest his work with the values of life and art (Young [R269]).

Dream Girl (1945)

Characters — GEORGINA ALLERTON: a young, vivacious woman, part owner of a bookstore and given to intense daydreaming; LUCY ALLERTON: her mother, a sharp-witted pragmatist; GEORGE ALLERTON: her father, a civil liberties lawyer; MIRIAM ALLERTON LUCAS: Georgina's older sister, married to and then divorced from Jim Lucas; JIM LUCAS: Miriam's idealist husband, a book reviewer, with whom Georgina thinks she is in love; CLAIRE BLAKELY: Georgina's partner in the Mermaid Bookstore; CLARK REDFIELD: a sarcastic newspaper reporter who believes in facing reality; GEORGE HAND: a book jobber who wants Georgina to travel with him as his mistress; VARIOUS "DREAM" CHARACTERS, MANY PLAYED BY THE PRINCIPAL ACTORS.

Plot Summary — ACT 1: In Jo Mielzner's presentational set a bed slides into view, carrying the just-awakened Georgina. As she lolls about, she muses upon the lack of direction in her life, and seeks understanding through analysis of her dreams. It becomes obvious that she is enamored of Jim Lucas, her brother-in-law. As she ponders seeking psychiatric help, the first of a series of Walter Mittyish daydream sequences unfolds. Georgina fantasizes herself as a patient on "Dr. Percival's Radio Counseling" show, where she admits to her love for her in-law and also reveals that a businessman has been trying to date her. The sequence ends when Mrs. Allerton interrupts. As Georgina dresses, she reveals that she has written a novel currently under review (by virtue of Jim Lucas's recommendation) by a city press. As she goes to breakfast, she ponders George Hand's proposal to escalate their intimacy. While dining, she receives a letter informing her that her book has been rejected. Discussion turns to Jim Lucas's bleak career prospects — it is obvious that Mrs. Allerton does not think much of his idealism and lack of professional drive. Mr. Allerton is preparing to fight an idealistic, pro bono court battle against the prosecution of a polygamist group. After he leaves for Washington, Miriam enters and announces to Georgina that she is pregnant again. As she departs to tell her mother the news, Georgina's mind again wanders to an imaginary birthing-scene, in which she plays the part of the brave mother bearing Jim's twins. In the dream, Miriam demands custody of the children, but is content to take only one. Jim avows his undying love for Georgina, before the fantasy is interrupted by the news that Jim has just been fired from his job as a book reviewer for being too much the dreamer and idealist.

The scene changes to the interior of the Mermaid Bookstore, where everyone is looking for a racy romance, *Always Opal*. Georgina and her partner, Claire, are not faring well at this location, and are on the verge of bankruptcy. They have been offered the chance to buy a better store, but have no recourse to the money needed for the purchase. Georgina's mind takes flight, this time imagining that her mother has died, thus freeing up her inheritance from her grandfather's estate. Her reverie is interrupted by Clark Redfield, a crude and somewhat cynical newspaperman who is also in the process of reviewing Georgina's novel. In the process of their conversation, Clark reveals that he has little regard for his job (his aim is to become a sports writer), sometimes reviewing books he has not read. Georgina is shocked, and asks if her own novel has received the same treatment. Clark admits he has read it, but says the book "stinks." They argue, and Clark leaves. Georgina, smarting from the review, imagines a courtroom scene where she is exonerated (through the defense of her counsel, Jim Lucas) for killing Clark on the grounds that he brutalized her book.

Georgina prepares to meet George Hand for a lunch date. Before she can leave, Jim arrives to announce that he and Miriam have agreed to a divorce, though he wants to remain great friends with Georgina. After he leaves, Georgina departs to meet Hand, who comes across as a cavalier sexist who believes all women are like those found in *Always Opal*. He entices Georgina with offers of a trip to Mexico, which sends Georgina's imagination into a Hispanic daydream of life as a comfortable gringo mistress. As Hand presses his suit, Georgina begs for more time to decide.

ACT II: Back at the bookshop, Georgina discusses Hand's proposal with Claire, arguing that she can, like a man, approach the problem logically and determinedly. Her next daydream, however, projects her as a prostitute who is confronted by Hand, who pities her before being rebuked by Georgina. Clark then appears and recognizes her, for which he earns a slap in the face. After Clark runs for a policeman, Georgina takes poison. As she slips toward death, Jim appears and thanks Georgina for getting him back with Miriam. Georgina expires quoting Dickens. The daydream is interrupted by a phone call from Clark, who asks Georgina to accompany him to the opening of *The Merchant of Venice*. After they are cut off, Hand also calls and asks her out. She turns down the latter offer, and grudgingly accepts the date with Clark. After she hangs up, Jim enters and confesses that he has always loved Georgina. She admits her own feelings to him, and he invites her to come to Reno with him as he prepares for his divorce. She demurs, but accepts his offer to see him off at the airport at midnight.

Later that evening, at an Italian restaurant, Georgina and Clark discuss their lives. Georgina admits she once aspired to the theatre, after having played Portia in a school production. Clark reveals he is about to be promoted to sportswriter, which will unencumber him from writing book reviews. Georgina's novel again comes up, and Clark accuses her of not putting any "real life" into it. He chastises her for plagiarizing the sensibilities of other female writers, and points out that the idealist hero and heroine of her book sound much like herself and Jim Lucas.

At the theatre, Georgina and Clark continue arguing, stopping only when Hand appears with another woman as his date. After introductions are made, the play begins. Georgina immediately fantasizes that the female lead falls sick, and that the manager asks her to perform the role of Portia. Her rendering of the "Quality of mercy" speech leaves Clark in tears, begging her to forgive all his mistaken notions regarding her character. The daydream ends when the first act lights come up.

After the show Georgina and Clark enter a jazz club and order food and drinks. Clark accuses Georgina of daydreaming at the theatre, and uses the charge to explain that this is characteristic of Georgina's whole life — that it is a refusal of reality in favor of an idealized dream world. Georgina argues that this is the function of art, but Clark disagrees, offering that art is created to reveal reality, not to screen people from it: "dreaming is easy,

Street Scene

but life is hard," he concludes. Clark then shrewdly guesses Georgina's true feelings about Jim Lucas, but senses that she is wavering. He convinces her not to leave for the airport to see him off, and instead they dance. As Clark lists his faults to Georgina, she inverts them into the virtues of a man willing to face reality. In her last daydream, Georgina imagines marrying Clark (where neither of them like the "obey" clause of the vows), but the wedding is interrupted by the arrival of Jim, dressed as a western cowboy. He offers to fight Clark for Georgina's hand, but Georgina dismisses him. She "awakes" to tell herself that she is tired of dreaming, and wants to act instead. Though she says she will go to meet Jim, she accepts Clark's invitation to ride through Central Park. As we fade in to Mr. and Mrs. Fullerton's bedroom, the phone rings: Georgina is calling to say she has just married Clark in Greenwich Village.

Reviews — R275, R276, R277, R279, R280, R281, R282, R283, R284, R285, R286, R287, R288, R289, R290, R291, R319, R320, R321, R322, R323, R324, R325, R326, R327

Critical Overview — *Dream Girl* opened at the Coronet Theatre on 14 December 1945 for 349 performances.

Rice's best-known comedy, in which the use of interior monologue to depict the character of Georgina Allerton (a vehicle for Betty Field) made the play popular with both audiences and critics. Many commented on the fine acting and imaginative sets (Nichols [R278], Chapman [R275]) and several commented favorably on Rice's dexterity in mingling fantasy and realism (Morehouse [R277], Garland [R276]). Recognizing the play as a departure from Rice's usual social criticism, Rascoe (R279) and Young (R286) point to it as evidence of Rice's more gentle nature.

Hogan (S95) criticized the lack of wit and absurdity in the dialogue, but Durham (S114) credits the play as a vehicle for a jocular look at one of Rice's serious interests, psychoanalysis. The title role may have been too closely matched to its star, as Judy Holliday's revival in 1951 garnered almost exclusively negative reviews (Coleman [R321], Kerr [326]). A 1993 revival at the Milwaukee Repertory Theatre elicited comparisons between Rice and Eric Overmeyer (Jaques [R373]).

Street Scene (1947; musical; book by Rice, lyrics by Langston Hughes, music by Kurt Weill)

Reviews — R292, R294, R295, R296, R297, R298, R299, R300, R301, R302, R303, R304, R366

Critical Overview — The musical opened on 9 January 1947 at the Adelphi Theatre for 148 performances.

The musical, coming almost twenty years after the play, polarized critical opinion. Several critics, including Barnes (R293), Morehouse (R297) and Kronenberger (R299) described the work as a folk opera in the mold of *Porgy and Bess*. Others (Chapman [R294], Hawkins [R296], and Lardner [R300]) classified it as opera. Atkinson (R292, 301) championed both Weill's modern score and Rice's perceptive book, but others found it lacking in unity (Garland [R295]), bereft of energy (Lardner), and floating between stage realism and opera (Brown [R304]).

The Grand Tour (1951)

Characters — NELL VALENTINE: a middle-aged Yankee schoolteacher on her first tour; RAYMOND BRINTON: a banker on the run from a failed marriage and a shady past; HARVEY RICHMAN: lawyer for Raymond's bank; ADELE BRINTON: Raymond's former wife.

Plot Summary — ACT I, Scene 1: In a New York city travel agency, Nell Valentine, a schoolteacher, arrives to purchase passage to Europe. She reveals to the agent that she has never allowed herself much pleasure before, and so wishes to make an extensive tour of the Continent. She has planned her own itinerary, which includes Paris, Rome, Geneva, and other cities. After haggling a bit over prices and accommodations, she takes her leave.

ACT I, Scene 2: Onboard a steamer to Europe, Raymond Brinton is seen composing a letter that appears to give him difficulty. Nell interrupts his labor, and the two begin to exchange pleasantries. Upon hearing that he was formerly a banker, she confides to him that she has come into $50,000 in life insurance recently, and asks that he manage the money for her. He responds brusquely, advising her not to be so open about money with strangers. He leaves abruptly, and Nell is left in tears.

ACT I, Scene 3: Several nights later, Ray is seen carrying an attache on deck, into which he places a letter. He then climbs the ship's railing, but is interrupted by Nell, who is being pursued by Professor Coogan, an amorous ornithologist with a gift for puns and for quoting poetry about birds. As Nell tries to disengage herself from Coogan, Ray intervenes casually to rescue her. Left alone, the two apologize for their earlier behavior. Ray reveals to Nell that he is being divorced from his wife, from whom he had become estranged as they climbed the social ladder in Minneapolis. After rebuking him for his fear of being emotional in front of her, Nell takes him to the bar for a drink.

ACT I, Scene 4: In Paris, Ray and Nell enjoy a frenzied tour of the city, presented as a series of presentational tableaux of the Louvre, the Bastille, and other sites. Nell pretends to be caught up in the whirlwind tour, but several asides reveal that she is thinking more about Ray than Paris. She entertains him with various literary references to Paris, but beneath her social veneer she is feeling inadequate in making him really happy. They eat and drink until the early morning, but in the end go their separate ways.

ACT II, Scene 1: Having travelled to Chartres to see the cathedral, Nell and Ray become more intimate. She asks him to tell her about himself, and he obliges by revealing his real aspiration to be a forest ranger. When Nell asks him about going back to the bank, his face clouds over and he dismisses the question. Impulsively, he suggests that they spend the night together in the local hotel, but, though tempted, Nell is hesitant. She forces him to admit that he had spent a similar night there with his wife, and rebukes him for trying to relive his past through her. She departs angrily.

ACT II, Scene 2: Now in Monteux, Nell is travelling alone. She is interrupted by the arrival of Ray, who admits he has followed her because he wants to apologize. She declares that "French Nell" was not really her, and that she is back to normal in the less heady environs of Switzerland. Still, she agrees to talk, and Ray grasps the opportunity to explain that he would like to marry her, but cannot: he is in fact an embezzler on the run from the law. Explaining that he became entrenched in debt by living beyond his means and by playing the commodities market, Ray also reveals that he had intended to commit suicide the night he was interrupted on deck by Nell and Professor Coogan. He also admits that his outburst of anger onboard the ship was caused by the great temptation he felt to accept her offer to manage her money, which he might then have used to make good his debts. After he finishes, Nell surprises him by proposing, arguing that the crime does not deter her from loving him.

ACT II, Scene 3: At a hotel in Rome, Nell and Ray await the arrival of the divorce decree from America, and make plans for their own wedding. She has been offering to bail him out of debt with her inheritance, but he adamantly refuses. The phone rings, and Ray announces that a lawyer from the Minneapolis bank has arrived to speak to him. Nell is flustered at being seen with him, and leaves the room. Harvey Richman then arrives, and confronts Ray with the irregularities that have been discovered at the bank. Ray freely admits his guilt, and his willingness to pay for the crime by making restitution over a period of time. Richman is sympathetic, but says the directors have insisted that the money be forthcoming immediately, or they will force prosecution. After Ray departs, Nell accosts Richman and explains that Ray did not embezzle the money to lavish on her. She offers to pay his debts, but Richman says it can only be done with Ray's consent. In addition, Richman reveals that Adele Brinton is arriving to see Ray the next day. Nell tells him to set up a meeting between herself and Adele.

ACT II, Scene 4: The following day, Adele arrives unexpectedly without having seen Richman first. Nell explains who she is, and gives Adele the news that Ray and she are to be married. Adele is shocked at the news of her husband's crime, and logically assumes he embezzled the money to spend on Nell. Nell pleads her innocence, and explains why Adele must convince Ray to accept her money. Adele is by degrees persuaded to exert her influence, though she requests that it be done after she has rested. After she leaves, Nell surprises Richman by preparing to leave for Naples without Ray. Declaring that she is a solid, straight-thinking Yankee, she tells Richman that her plan is to leave the money with him, and allow Adele and Ray to be reunited. She leaves, telling Ray that she is merely going shopping.

CODA: Back in Bridgeport, Nell addresses her schoolchildren with a slide show of her trip to Europe. As she recalls Paris and Rome, she begins to cry quietly.

Reviews — R328, R329, R330, R331, R332, R333, R334, R335, R336, R337, R338

Critical Overview — The play premiered on 10 December 1951 at the Martin Beck Theatre for 8 performances.

A tepid performance seems to have affected the play's reviews, which were kind but not ardent. Atkinson (R328) praised the first half for its originality, but felt it declined thereafter. Hawkins (R331) voiced a common complaint when he noted that the plot complications dragged down the generally witty dialogue, and Kerr (R332) took Rice to task for "merely chatting" with his audiences instead of discussing ideas with them. Hogan (S95) castigated earlier critics for not recognizing the true theme of the play, "the relationship of morality to money." Rice notes in *Minority Report* (A83) that the play saw numerous foreign productions and more radio and television productions than any play he had written.

Love Among the Ruins (1951; produced 1963)

Characters — ARTHUR DEWING: an aging archeologist overseeing a dig at Baalbeck; SUZANNE DEWING: his attractive and younger wife; CARL HANNAY: Dewing's student apprentice, enamored of Suzanne; NEIL DAVIS: Suzanne's former husband who left her long ago, and has returned to reclaim her; BISHOP PAUL BICKNELL: a middle-aged cleric unsure of his faith; ALMA BICKNELL: his wife; FLORENCE BICKNELL: their hard, cynical daughter; LAURA HARDWICK: a widower traveling alone; CLINTON GRUE: a rich American traveler with an ugly

Love Among the Ruins 89

disposition toward foreigners; ZAKHARATOS: the group's Greek tour guide.

Plot Summary — ACT I, Scene 1: Amid a section of ruins at Baalbeck, Carl listens to Arabic radio while trying to learn the language. Suzanne enters, and though she is friendly to Carl it is apparent that she does not welcome his clumsy attempts to flatter her. After Carl leaves, Dewing arrives and discusses Carl with his wife, concluding that he will have to fire him. Suzanne convinces him to keep him on, and their conversation turns to their own lives. Dewing fears Suzanne is bored with him, and asks if she has considered adopting a child. Before Suzanne can answer, Zakharos arrives with a tour group, which includes Neil Davis, Suzanne's former husband. Suzanne recognizes but does not acknowledge him. After viewing the ruins, the tour group returns and greets Dewing. They leave to look at other sites, leaving Neil and Suzanne alone. He tells her that he has left the woman who broke up their marriage, and that he has come to speak to her about starting over. She initially rejects him, and he stalks off. The tourists return, and are confronted with a Bedouin traveling with his daughter, who wants to sell them an eagle he has shot. Grue, a jingoistic American, insults the natives and tensions arise. After the Bedouins leave, news comes that the tires on the tour bus have been slashed; plans are made for the tourists to spend the night at the camp. As they prepare for their guests, Dewing asks Suzanne if Neil is her former husband, a truth he ascertains through his "long experience in digging up the past."

ACT I, Scene 2: Late the same afternoon Dewing entertains his guests by serving arrack and discussing Middle Eastern civilization. Bicknell tells of his faith in the narrative of Paul's conversion on the road to Damascus, while Carl and Greu are skeptical. Most of the group leaves to see nearby sites, and Neil finds Suzanne alone again. She rebukes him for slashing the tires on the bus. When the group suddenly returns, they are discussing the uses of archeological knowledge, which Grue dismisses as frivolous (unless it includes knowledge of oil deposits). Bicknell argues that the past teaches spiritual knowledge, while Dewing suggests that studying fallen civilizations reminds us of humanity's ability to self-destruct. Neil intervenes to argue that humanity must now turn to understanding the life force which sustains civilization — which occasions Grue to accuse him of being a communist. As tensions rise, the group breaks for dinner, while Neil finds a moment to tell Suzanne that he wants her to return to him.

ACT II, Scene 1: Several hours later, an intoxicated Grue is obnoxiously asking Carl to set him up with the Bedouin girl they met earlier. Carl angrily dismisses Grue, and both leave. Neil and Suzanne enter, and we hear the story of their marriage. Neil had left her for Jeanette, a heroic nurse with whom he served in France while in the army. He pleads an indulgent upbringing, and argues he has both a "creative" and "destructive" side (as did the gods who were worshipped at Baalbeck). They argue some more, but end by kissing passionately. They are interrupted by Laura and Mrs. Bicknell, who wait until they leave separately before beginning to gossip about them. This occasions Laura to confide to Mrs. Bicknell her own earlier choice to cut short an affair with a soldier during WWI, and to express her lifetime's sense of regret for doing so. The bishop enters, and Laura leaves; he speaks to his wife about his own regrets and failures as a priest, and they leave. Carl and Florence arrive, slightly drunk, and flirt with one another. She admits to being three times married, and to having troubled siblings. She teases Carl about his infatuation with Suzanne, but they kiss and go off to be alone. Suzanne and Dewing enter, and discuss their situation. Suzanne admits to being in love with Neil, but insists she still loves Dewing as well. He is magnanimous and philosophical, but admits that losing her would leave him desolate. Before they can arrive at any conclusions, Grue and others return and, after some commotion, are led off to bed.

ACT II, Scene 2: The next morning, Neil is waiting for Suzanne. Other tourists come and go, until Dewing enters to speak with Neil. They openly discuss their positions, and Neil is impressed with Dewing's lack of self-interest and his eloquent defense of individual choice. Suzanne arrives, and Dewing hurriedly excuses himself. After some discussion, Suzanne reveals that, although she is still in love with Neil, she has decided to seek stability and tranquility by staying with Dewing. Neil acknowledges the justice of her decision, and says he will return to the "stream of life" and accomplish something worthwhile in her eyes. As the guest prepare to leave, it is noticed that Grue is missing. He enters in a rush, carrying the eagle's carcass he had tried to trade for earlier. Dewing arrives, and admonishes him to leave quickly. The Bedouin pursues Grue with a rifle, but Dewing wrestles it out of his grasp. As he falls and is about to be stabbed by the Arab, Suzanne and Neil interpose themselves and save Dewing. Neil says he believes Dewing's was "a life worth saving," and acknowledges that Suzanne's decision has been made. They part with good wishes toward one another.

Review — R368

Critical Overview — The play was produced non-professionally at the University of Rochester, New York, on 3 May 1963.

While no critical reviews of the play are extant, Hogan (S98), who directed the play, noted that the production caused Rice to take a dimmer view of university dramatics than he had expressed in his article "Drama on Campus" (A74).

The Winner (1954)

Characters — EVA HAROLD: a young and vivacious, but somewhat hardened woman of small means; MARTIN CAREW: a well-bred lawyer, cynical and world weary, but capable of sincerity and compassion; DAVID BROWNING: Eva's fiance and lawyer, though still married; ARNOLD MAHLER: a rich older man, enamored of Eva; IRMA MAHLER: his wife, who fights for his estate; HILDE KRANZBECK: chief accountant for Mahler's import business; JUDGE SAMUEL ADDISON: presiding over probate hearing of Mahler's contested will.

Plot Summary — SCENE I: In her sparsely-furnished apartment, Eva entertains Carew, with whom she has just had dinner. She is worldly, and a little supercilious, about the dating game and the intentions of most men, though she admires Carew for not acting out the stereotype. Eva reveals she had once married an idealist for love, but that he had left her for another woman. Martin, on the other hand, has been an indolent socialite, not taking his life or career very seriously. Eva is now "half engaged" to David, who is still married, but still dates various gentlemen because she is bored with her life. After exchanging these confidences, Martin leaves when David arrives. David, who warns Eva that Carew is a dangerous philanderer, has come to tell her that his wife's father is ill, necessitating his departure for the south. As the two discuss their relationship, they are interrupted by a call from Mahler, an older man Eva has dated occasionally. He asks to come up, but Eva refuses. David then leaves as Eva prepares for bed. Mahler startles her by knocking loudly at the door, and shouting that he is ill and must come in. She allows him to enter and gives him a drink. He raves to her that his doctor has told him that a heart condition will give him only two or three more years to live. He wants to liquidate his business, desert his wife, and run away to Cuba with Eva. Hoping to convince her of his sincerity, he produces a hastily-scribbled will which leaves his entire estate to her. Eva balks, which causes Mahler to accuse her of loving David rather than him. As he grows more agitated, his heart gives way and he collapses in Eva's bed. She phones a nearby doctor, but when she opens the door she is greeted by Irma Mahler and a private detective, who snap a picture of Mahler lying in Eva's bed with her standing over him dressed only in a nightgown. The doctor then arrives.

SCENE II: Three days later, Eva sits in her apartment fending off telephone requests for interviews with tabloids and fretting about all the adverse publicity she has received. David calls, and promises to visit soon. Carew arrives, and reveals that he represents the estate of the deceased Mahler. They have found a copy of Mahler's latest will, and are looking for the original. Eva accuses Carew of dating her only to bring Irma and the detective to her door. Carew denies this, but presses Eva to accept Irma's offer of $20,000 if she will not contest an earlier will. Before she can respond, David arrives and Martin leaves. After producing the copy of the later will, she discusses the offer with David, questioning whether it would be ethical to accept Irma's offer and thereby benefit from Mahler's death. On the other hand, she wants a chance to clear her name and reputation, though this would mean creating a scandal. David generally supports her desire to take the money; however, after speaking to her mother (who believes she is innocent), Eva does an about-face and vows to refuse the money and to fight Irma in court.

SCENE III: Several weeks later, in the Probate Court chambers of Judge Samuel Addison, Eva arrives on the day she is testify on her own behalf. Carew takes her aside and sincerely presses her to accept Irma's offer, now up to $75,000. As he grasps Eva's hand, Irma enters. After Eva leaves, Irma claims Carew is smitten with Eva, but Carew says he is only working to resolve the claim. The hearing begins with Irma finishing her testimony that Mahler had shown increasing signs of erratic behavior after he met Eva. Carew presents several erotic letters written by Mahler to Eva, though never sent to her. David then cross-examines Irma, seeking to prove that Mahler had indulged in affairs before he met Eva, and that Irma herself had taken several lovers. Carew objects to the line of questioning, and is sustained by Addison. After she steps down, Irma appears agitated when Hilde Kranzbeck is called to the stand. Hilde corroborates Irma's claim that Mahler had acted irrationally after meeting Eva. When David cross-examines, he gets her to admit that she is bitter at Mahler for leaving her only a small sum in his earlier will. She also admits, under intense questioning, that she had been Mahler's lover until he met Eva. Having discredited Hilde's testimony, David then calls Eva to the stand. She recalls her first meeting with Mahler, their occasional dates, and his continued (but unsuccessful) attempts to seduce her. During the testimony, Eva lets slip that Carew had dated her the night of Mahler's visit. The Judge is suspicious, and Carew is asked to explain his presence there. He admits only to having used the date as a pretext to find out more about Eva. Carew then cross-examines Eva, and manages to compromise her testimony by forcing her to admit that she dated men without the intention of having serious relationships with them, and that she is currently engaged to David, a married man. The judge calls for a recess, but first pleads with the parties to come to an amicable agreement among themselves, citing Christian doctrines of forgiveness. Eva responds by saying that her own sense of honor, and not the money involved, makes it necessary for her to continue the fight for her honor.

The Winner

SCENE IV: Some weeks later, Eva is back in her apartment, feeling exuberant at the news that she has won her case against Irma. She invites David over, and he brings champagne, though he appears a bit tense. They read part of Addison's decision, in which, though deploring Eva's "dubious" lifestyle, he recognizes her basic honesty and integrity. The decision concludes that Eva likely did not exert undue testamentary influence on Mahler, thus invalidating Irma's claim and recognizing the viability of Mahler's last desire to leave everything to Eva. However, as Eva fantasizes about how she'll spend the money, David soberly informs her that an appeal is likely, which will tie up the money in probate for a long time. When Carew calls to say he will be stopping by, Eva assumes he is going to announce his design to appeal. However, David tells her it is Irma herself who will make the case, in hopes of getting Eva to pay her off for dropping the suit. Carew enters, to David's discomfort, and announces that he is now out of the case. To David's increasing chagrin, Carew reveals that Irma had revealed to him certain of Mahler's tax manipulations, and that her late husband's real reason for going to Cuba was to avoid arrest by the IRS. Hilde, who knew of the accounting fraud, was prepared to turn in Mahler before he could leave. After Mahler's death, and in light of Eva's case, Irma convinced Hilde to keep silent, promising to take care of her with money from the estate. Now, Irma and Hilde want at least half of the estate, or else they will turn federal witnesses and reveal Mahler's tax fraud. Since the penalties are now greater than the value of the estate, Eva is in a bind. Carew leaves, and Eva accuses David of dishonesty and of "chaperoning" her as if she were a child. She debates her options, wondering if agreeing to Irma's terms will implicate her morally in deception and fraud. Though David tells her it is her decision, he seems more eager to lay hands on the money than he was before. Eva cannot decide, so David leaves to stall Irma for a day. After he goes, Martin returns, having watched David leave. He has come back to tell Eva how much he grew to admire her during the hearing, and how sad it would be to see her relinquish her morals in light of Irma's threat. He invites her to dinner, and Eva is poised to accept when the phone rings. It is Eva's mother calling, and Carew takes the phone to explain what is going on with her daughter.

Reviews — R339, R340, R341, R342, R343, R344, R345, R346, R347, R348, R349, R350, R367.

Critical Overview — The play opened on 17 February 1957 at the Playhouse for 30 performances.

Originally written as a vehicle for Betty Field (who was unwilling to do it), the production suffered from poor casting and a weak script. While praising the courtroom scene, most critics found the majority of the play loquacious and tedious (Hawkins [R342], Chapman [R340]). Many appreciated that the play marked Rice's fortieth year in the theatre, but the consensus was that this effort did his reputation no credit (Atkinson [R339], *Newsweek* [R347]).

Cue for Passion (1958)

Characters — GRACE NICHOLSON: mother to Tony and a widow recently married to Carl; CARL NICHOLSON: former business partner to Mr. Nicholson, now married to Grace; TONY BURGESS: Grace's acerbic son, returned from adventures in the Far East; LLOYD HILTON: Tony's friend, now a criminologist at Alcatraz prison; LUCY GESSLER: a young neighbor the Nicholson's, attracted to Tony; HUGH GESSLER: Lucy's father, a physician; MATTIE HAYNES: the Nicholson's housekeeper.

Plot Summary — ACT I, Scene 1: Grace receives a telegram from Tony announcing he will return that day from a long trip to Asia. Apprehensive about his return, she asks Lucy if Tony had tried to sleep with her before he left. Lucy admits he tried, but she had refused, a decision she now regrets. Carl arrives, and also seems tense about Tony's return. Tony arrives wearing a mourning band for his deceased father. They discuss how Tony received the news of his father's death during an earthquake. Tony is surprised to hear that his mother has remarried Carl so soon.

ACT II, Scene 2: Next morning Grace announces that Lloyd will visit Tony. Carl explains the details of the fatal accident, describing how a bust of Tony (which Carl had carved) fell on his father's head during a seismic quake. Lloyd arrives, followed by Lucy and her father. Tony is sarcastic to her, and she leaves crying. Mattie tells Lloyd that, as a young man, Tony had expressed a wish that his father would die.

ACT II, Scene 3: While Tony plays a distracted game of chess with Lloyd, the others discuss various forms of mental illness. Tony becomes violently angry when he loses the chess game, causing Lloyd to leave the room. Alone, Tony and Mattie test the hypothesis that the bust could have fallen on his father's head during a quake. After Mattie leaves, Tony becomes progressively drunker, until he hallucinates a conversation with his father's ghost.

ACT I, Scene 4: Next evening Lloyd questions Hattie further about Tony. The others arrive and begin to plan strategy for helping Tony relieve his depression. Carl and Dr. Gessler suggest institutionalizing him. Tony enters and speaks alone with Lucy, telling her to forget him and showing her a revolver he has bought. She leaves as Grace arrives. Tony hints to her that he left abruptly because he suspected Carl was his father. He also nearly accuses Carl of murdering his father. Grace replies angrily that

Tony is in the grips of an oedipal dilemma. He kisses his mother passionately, then sees a shadow. He fires his gun, wounding Dr. Gessler.

ACT I, Scene 4: Lucy and Grace discuss the previous night's commotion, revealing that Dr. Gessler received only a flesh wound. Tony arrives and tells Lucy he is sorry, explaining that he had planned to use the gun to kill himself. Lloyd analyzes his psychological state, suggesting that Tony did not kill Carl because it would symbolize his own extinction. Grace enters and says she now believes Carl did kill her husband, but that she had nothing to do with it. She tells him it would be best to go away, and he agrees. He bids farewell to Lucy and departs. Carl and Grace receive each other coolly as the curtain falls.

Reviews — R352, R353, R354, R355, R356, R357, R358, R359, R360, R361, R362, R363, R364, R365

Critical Overview — *Cue for Passion* opened at the Henry Miller Theatre on 25 November 1958 for 39 performances.

Rice's last professionally-produced play revises *Hamlet* along Freudian lines — or perhaps, given the happy ending Rice imposes, along the lines by which Freud was read by Ernest Jones and others. Reviewers were divided on the question of the facility of the adaptation, Atkinson (R353, 361), Chapman (R354), and Tynan (R360) all complaining that Rice's version was reductionist and tepid. Kronenberger (S99) went so far as to call Tony an "Oedipus uncomplex Hamlet." Watts (R359) and Kerr (R357), on the other hand, were willing to acknowledge the play as compelling and a modified success. Rice complained that a newspaper strike made advertising the play adequately an impossibility.

Court of Last Resort (copyright 1965; published 1984)

Characters — JUDGE LAWRENCE SWAIN: a distinguished jurist, nominated for the Circuit Court; LAURA SWAIN: his wife; EDWARD SWAIN: his brother, formerly a promising lawyer but disbarred, now acting as his brother's secretary; PHYLLIS SWAIN: Edward's wife; CONGRESSMAN SAMUEL HOLMAN: a powerful friend of the Judge; GEORGE INGERSOLL: a prosecutor; JAMES ROGERS: a State's defense counsel; KATHERINE NICHOLS: formerly a maid, now on trial for kidnapping; SETH CLIFFORD: a reporter from a law school; GOVERNOR LEWIS WILLOUGHBY: a political foe of Judge Swain's.

Plot Summary — ACT I: In the office of Judge Swain, Edward Swain arrives in time to overhear a phone call from the President conveying the news that the Judge has been nominated for the Circuit Court of Appeals. Amidst the celebration, Congressman Holman arrives. He congratulates the Judge and intimates that he pushed the nomination forward. He also suggests that it might be a first step toward nomination to the Supreme Court. The Congressman leaves when Judge Swain is called to pass sentence on a convicted kidnapper, Katherine Nichols. Preparing for the task, Judge Swain reveals he does not favor sending people to jail, in part because his brother Edward was confined to one in the past. The prisoner enters with Ingersoll, the prosecutor, and Rogers, her defense counsel. After Ingersoll presents his argument for a stiff sentence, Rogers pleads that his client was acting out of desperation and loneliness when she kidnapped a neglected baby. Judge Swain considers the arguments, and passes a relatively light sentence of five years. Edward disagrees with the decision, and tells his brother so after the defendant has left. Laura Swain calls and hears the news of her husband's nomination.

ACT I, Scene 2: Judge Swain sits alone in his study. He picks up the phone and calls the jail to make an appointment to speak to Katherine before she is sent to prison. Laura enters and tells him she will be traveling to London for the birth of their grandchild. He says he needs her to stay in America during his transition to life in New York City. She then reveals she intends to stay in London with their son, whom she feels has been cast adrift by her husband. When Swain asks her if she's going to London to be near a suspected paramour, she admits she is leaving him for good.

ACT I, Scene 3: Judge Swain is in his chambers with Seth Clifford, who is interviewing him for a law journal. Swain tells him that he owes his success and stature to the American dream. They discuss the current generation of young people, and Swain advises them to seek self-knowledge and integrity. Clifford admits he idolizes Swain, and the two part on friendly terms. After Clifford departs, Katherine arrives for her interview. He reveals that he knows she is actually Kate Flanagan, a woman with whom he had a brief affair and a child. He recounts how he paid her off to have an abortion, and she responds by detailing her history after they split up. She married a man who left her, began feeling a compulsion to mother babies she saw left unattended, and spent some time in jail for her crimes. Swain relates that Edward, too, has spent time in jail for manslaughter, and repeats his claim that he does not enjoy sending people to prison. He ends by telling her he will seek a way to ease her sentence, and asks for her forgiveness.

ACT I, Scene 4: Back in chambers, Judge Swain phones Congressman Holman and hears that there may be problems with his nomination. Edward enters and hears the news of Laura's departure for London. He commiserates with his brother, but also asks if he plans to find room for him on his New York staff. Swain appears uncomfortable with the idea, but promises to find Edward something. Edward leaves and the Judge calls in Rogers to discuss possible appeals or a pardon for Katherine. He ends by promising to make a personal appeal to the governor, a political enemy. Congressman Holman now enters, and Swain tells him about Laura. He also admits that he had always loved Phyllis, Edward's wife, but that marriage to Laura promised a better career. Holman asks him if the impending divorce can be delayed until after his confirmation. Swain hesitates, then pours out his story regarding Katherine, telling Holman how he had met her while on holiday when he was young and she was working as a maid. After their affair ended and she became pregnant, he gave her $5000 for an abortion. Swain wants to repent, but Holman counsels a pragmatic course, pointing out that his nomination is finished if he confesses. Swain argues that he still has moral obligations to Katherine. The Congressman ends by saying that it is Swain's choice to make, but that he will surely lose the nomination if he comes clean.

ACT I, Scene 5: At Governor Lewis Willoughby's office. Judge Swain requests a pardon for Katherine, arguing that her intent was never to harm the child she kidnapped. It is revealed that the Governor, too, attended parties at the resort where Swain met Katherine, but he has no recollection of her. He turns down the Judge's request for a pardon.

ACT I, Scene 6: At the prison where Katherine is being held Swain arrives for a visit. He recounts his failure to secure a pardon, but promises her he will continue to work on her behalf. She insists she does not hold him responsible for her condition. At that moment the Judge receives a phone call telling him that Edward has been hit by a bus.

ACT I, Scene 7: Edward Swain's funeral.

ACT I, Scene 8: At Phyllis Swain's house, the Judge arrives to comfort his sister-in-law. She accuses him of forsaking his brother and driving him to what she considers a suicide. She refers to him as cold and calculating, a "careerist": he does not respond, and leaves broken and anguished.

ACT I, Scene 9: Congressman Holman enters Judge Swain's chambers, visibly upset that Swain has visited Katherine. Swain argues that he should admit his guilt and avoid hypocrisy, thus maintaining his integrity. He says that his life has been a series of hypocritical evasions, from his wife, his son, and Katherine. He feels he must rehabilitate himself in his own eyes. He then proceeds to dictate a letter to the President, claiming "deficiencies of character and in the conduct of [his] life" as reasons for withdrawing his nomination. Holman is saddened by the decision, but blesses Swain for his integrity.

ACT I, Scene 10: At the prison, Swain arrives and tells Katherine that he, too, has been a prisoner from human warmth. He says he wants to begin anew, and to make amends for the past. He asks Katherine to marry him, promising that they will adopt as many children as she desires.

Critical Overview — The play has never been produced.

Primary Bibliography

This section is divided into three sections, locating Rice's original writings by: I. Non-Dramatic Works, II. Dramatic Publications, and III. Unpublished, Collected Materials.

I. NON-DRAMATIC PRIMARY WORKS
The following is an alphabetically ordered primary bibliography of Rice's significant nonfictional and fictional published material, designated by the prefix "A."

A01   Rice, Elmer. "Out of the Movies [story]." *Argosy* 32 (May 1913): 440-44.
        An early short story dealing with fantasy.

A02   _____. "Some Lame and Impotent Reflections." *New York Times* 11 April 1915: 6.
        Argues that naive playwrights extricate themselves from blind alleys without regard for verisimilitude. Most modern playwrights are too indolent to write a good last act.

A03   _____. *On Trial* (novelization of play). New York: Grosset and Dunlap, 1915.
        Rice steadfastly maintained that he wrote a novelization of his famous play, but no record of publication exists to substantiate the view. Hogan (S95) and Durham (S114) discount the story and insist that Rice merely corrected this manuscript prepared by D. Torbett.

A04   _____. "A Letter About *The Adding Machine*." *New York Times* 1 April 1923, VII, 2.

Rice defines expressionism as a willingness to interpret rather than describe, and claims that his play was not influenced much by German models.

A05 _____. "Writing Directly for the Screen." *The Author's League Bulletin* 9 (June 1923): 16.

Argues that the motion picture industry in its present state is not comparable to the major arts. It has produced no masterpieces, owing to the limitations imposed on it by technical necessity. While in the other arts the creator addresses himself directly to the audience, in film (as, to a lesser degree, in drama) the creator's impulses are mediated by other collaborators and technical mechanisms.

A06 _____. "Zero et Shrdlu." *Masques, Cahiers d'Art Dramatique* Sixieme cahier, ed. Hanry-Jannet (Paris: 1927). [Rice's character notes to Dudly Digges and Edward G. Robinson for the first production of *The Adding Machine*. Translated, unpublished in English.]

A07 _____. "The Barry-Rice Letters." *New York Times* 15 January 1928, VIII, 2.

A humorous account of his collaboration with Philip Barry on *Cock Robin*.

A08 _____. "Conscience [story]." *Collier's* 81 (11 February 1928): 11. Reprinted in *Ellery Queen's Mystery Magazine* April 1946.

A crime story dealing with remorse.

A09 _____. "New York Childhood." *New Yorker* 4 (14 September 1928).

Nostalgia piece recalling his youth in the ethnic enclaves of New York, the adventure of trips to Central Park and the Bowery, youthful race tensions with the Irish, and learning about women.

A10 _____. "Preface" to *One-Act Plays for Stage and Study, Fifth Series*. (New York: Samuel French, 1929).

Rice discusses the mechanics of playwriting, especially in regard to his one-acter *A Diadem of Snow*.

A11 _____. "Mr. Rice Throws a Bouquet [letter]." *New York Times* 3 February 1929, VIII, 4.

Praises Brady for having the courage to produce *Street Scene*.

A12 _____. "A Short History of Street Scene." *New York Times* 24 February 1929, IX, 4.

Non-Dramatic Works 101

Recounts the happy experience of directing the play, noting its genesis in *Sidewalks of New York*. Describes his search for a model of the tenement used in the play.

A13 _____. "New York: Raw Material for the Drama. *Theatre Magazine* March 1929.

Recollection of how the city molded and colored his sensibilities. Rice explains how the rhythm of the city has changed in the last thirty years, due mainly to increased immigration. Argues that New York provides all the material needed for great drama, so long as the playwright lets the environment speak for itself rather than using it as a catalyst for his own ideas.

A14 _____. "The Playwright as Director." *Theatre Arts Monthly* 13.5 (May 1929): 355-60.

Discusses the function of the tenement in *Street Scene* and argues that plays need the creative input of a director, especially one skilled in visualization. However, too many directors live in a self-contained world and their work projects the world as a bag of theatre tricks, rather than reality.

A15 _____. "Mr. Rice Would Say ---." *New York Times* 6 October 1929, IX, 2.

Describes how *See Naples and Die* came about during his travels after an illness.

A16 _____. "Great Disappearance Movement, 1934-1937 [story]." *New Yorker* 7 (25 October 1930): 23-25.

Beginning with General Griff, people begin to disappear from their lives with large amounts of cash. The practice quickly becomes a trend, and soon New York City is again a peaceful village operating on a barter economy. However, General Griff returns, initiating a trend of reappearances, and soon things are back to normal and peace is just a memory.

A17 _____. "The Theatre Again faces the Censorship Problem." *New York Times* 14 December 1930, IX, 1-2.

Speaking for dramatists, Rice defines theatre as a public institution protected by civil law, and argues that no theatrical productions fit the legal description of obscenity. Pleads that ideas be allowed to be discussed in free and open forums.

A18 _____. *A Voyage to Purilia*. New York: J. J. Little and Ives Co., 1930.

Rice's first novel is, unexpectedly, a wild fantasy tale describing a plane trip to the planet Purilia, where everyone seems to have materialized from a Hollywood soundstage. The atmosphere is rosy and the people all stereotypes who heed the directives of an impersonal voice, called simply The Presence. This satire of Rice's experiences in Hollywood was reviewed by F. T. Marsh (*Nation* 130:426, April 1930) as an admirable satire and worthy of film treatment. John Carter (*New York Times* 23 March 1930. p. 2) thought it nimble-witted and a satire of high order, but the *Saturday Review* (150:318 13 September) considered it tendentious and too long to support its sober irony.

A19 _____. "A Chat With the Bishop [story]." *New Yorker* 6 (10 January 1931): 15-16.

A reporter named Merrick interviews a Bishop whose ideas are surprisingly liberal and tolerant. He advocates better race relations, acknowledges a need to explore open marriages, and reports he opens his church doors to the destitute. In the middle of the interview, Merrick suddenly awakes and realizes he is dreaming.

A20 _____. "Towards an Adult Theatre." *The Drama Magazine* 21 (February 1931): 5, 18.

Argues that mature people cannot take theatre seriously because it remains in an "imbecile and puerile state." Theatre creates a mob-mindedness, and playwrights have been content to appeal to that lowest denominator. In the last decade, however, more playwrights reveal a willingness to confront and represent life honestly. They are scorned and threatened with censorship, but if America resists religious demagoguery, the adult theatre can survive.

A21 _____. "Program Notes [story]." *New Yorker* 7 (28 March 1931): 20-22.

Comic description of an opera, "Le Bruiser," which combines music with a plot from the Saturday night bouts.

A22 _____. "Questionnaires [story]." *New Yorker* 7 (6 June 1931): 18-21.

Expresses distaste for all the questionnaires he receives, especially those from the "who's whoers" and non-professional writers and academics seeking the "secret" of successful drama and criticism.

A23 _____. "Organized Charity Turns Censor." *Nation* 132 (10 June 1931): 628-30.

Reports examples of censorship in various media, then details experience of combatting the Welfare Council of New York City, which took offense at the portrayal of Miss Simpson, the social worker in *Street Scene*.

A24 _____. "The Joys of Pessimism." *Forum* 86 (July 1931): 33-35.

Non-Dramatic Works 103

A tongue-in-cheek defense of himself as a "congenital pessimist." Proposes that in America pessimism always signifies a negative state of mind, whereas actually the opposite is true. Optimists are the ones always anxiously awaiting some reward for their efforts. The pessimist, on the other hand, always responds freshly and directly to good fortune just because it is so unexpected. Joy, says Rice, is an abnormal state enjoyable for just that reason. Also, the optimist always flees reality into illusion (and is thus susceptible to any manipulation), while the pessimist confronts reality with a skeptical defense.

A25 _____. "Sex in the Modern Theatre." *Harper's* 164 (May 1932): 665-73.

Rice links the sensual appeal of theatre and sex and proposes the two institutions are rivals. He analyzes sexual exhibitionism, the performance of sexual acts, the use of taboo language, sexual themes and the representation of love and sex in the theatre. His conclusion is that, though there is greater frankness now than before, modern drama's treatment of sex is timid, squeamish and superficial—a sign of theatre's continued conservatism.

A26 _____. "Things I Have Never Done [story]." *New Yorker* 8 (15 August 1932): 24, 26.

A record of reminiscences by an older man.

A27 _____. "The American Minimum Basic Agreement." *The Author, Playwright and Composer* 42 (October 1931): 20.

Responding to letters by Shaw and St. Ervine regarding American payments for film rights, Rice argues that the existing collective bargaining agreement (or "Minimum Basic Agreement") worked out by the Dramatist's Guild has been a boon for writers.

A28 _____. "A Playwright Sees Russia." *New York Times* 4 September 1932, IX, 1-2.

Descriptions of Russian theatre later used in *The Living Theatre*.

A29 _____. "Mr. Rice on a Repertory Theatre [letter]." *New York Times* 6 November 1932), IX, 3.

Commenting on Atkinson's essay calling for a Repertory Theatre, Rice argues that there is a distinctly American drama that should be produced through a repertory company. Discusses benefits of actor training in such an arrangement.

A30 _____. "Mr. Rice States His Case." *New York Times* 12 February 1933, X, 3.

Responding to box office failure of *We, the People,* Rice briefly describes his career in the theatre and claims this play is the culmination of his desire to write meaningful rather than popular plays.

A31 _____. "Project for a New Theatre." *New York Times* 8 October 1933, X, 1-2.

Call to organize a People's Art Theatre in which poetry and drama work to replace religion as the source of meaning in the modern world. Suggests low admission, production of exclusively American plays, and no government subsidy.

A32 _____. "Method of Treatment." Unpublished manuscript, Elmer Rice Papers, University of Texas-Austin.

This description of *Street Scene* was submitted with his film scenario in 1933. Here, Rice argues that the milieu of the play is accumulated as a painter gathers unimportant details into a "totality of effect." The play attempts to show that life is "complex and diversified" and made up of countless incongruities and contingencies.

A33 _____. "And on the Other: The Author of Judgment Day States His Case for Vigor and Also of His Play." *New York Times* 23 September 1934, X, 1-2.

Responding to Atkinson's companion review which attacks the stridency of his play, Rice argues that intemperateness is allowed if a play's subject matter calls for it. Theatre, as exemplified by *Judgment Day,* is an arena for the clash of cultural wills.

A34 _____. "Elmer Rice Says Farewell to Broadway." *New York Times* 11 November 1934, IX, 1, 3.

Relates substance of his remarks at Columbia University, defending himself and attacking the commercial theatre. Ends by rejecting Broadway and theatre in general, promising to find another outlet for his vision.

A35 _____. "Theatre Alliance." *New York Times* 12 May 1935, 1-2.

Description of the Theatre Alliance, focusing on logistics and finances.

A36 _____. "Theatre Alliance: A Cooperative Repertory Project." *Theatre Arts Monthly* 19 (June 1935): 427-30.

A reprint, slightly revised, from the 12 May article in the *New York Times.*

Non-Dramatic Works   105

A37 _____. "Introduction" to *Rice: Two Plays*. New York: Coward-McCann, 1935): v-xvii.

Rice argues here that art always seeks to communicate, as opposed to being a mode of self-expression. This imposes on the writer a need for craftsmanship and technique in order to organize his material into communicable form. Dramatic writers, especially, have to always keep in mind the "imposing and fearsome machinery of the stage" as part of the medium of their art. Rice provides an overview of this machinery in the form of a critique of current theatre's economic, psychological, and physical demands on the playwright. Along the way, he castigates a conformity-seeking autocracy of investors who determine the production of plays, the prestige-seeking directors and actors who place status above all else, and the pleasure-seeking sensibilities of American audiences, who seem content with a uniformity of perception, a low collective mentality, and the appeal of theatre glamour.

A38 _____. "The Federal Theatre Hereabouts." *New York Times* 5 January 1936, IX, 1, 3.

Explains aims of the WPA and Federal Theatre Project, with brief descriptions of the latter's agenda, including the Living Newspaper, a Popular Price Theatre, and Allied Arts units.

A39 _____. "The Russian Stage." *New York Times* 4 October 1936, IX, 1, 3.

Material on Russian theatre included in *The Living Theatre*.

A40 _____. "The Theatre in Moscow." *New York Times* 11 October 1936, X, 1, 3.

Material for *The Living Theatre*.

A41 _____. "The Stage of Far China." *New York Times* 18 October 1936, X, 3.

Material on Chinese theatre gleaned from his travels, focusing on symbolic and stylized mode of presentation.

A42 _____. "The Drama of Japan." *New York Times* 25 October 1936, X, 3.

Material on Japanese theatre incorporated into *The Living Theatre*.

A43 _____. "On the Modern Theatre of Japan." *New York Times* 1 November 1936, X, 1, 3.

Material for *The Living Theatre*.

A44 _____. *Imperial City*. New York: Coward-McCann, Inc., 1937.

Rice's most ambitious and well-received novel concerns the interrelated stories of Fanny, a dissipated ex-actress, and her three sons: Christopher, a heartless corporate magnate; Greg, a public nuisance and man about town; and Gay, a liberal professor at Columbia. All the sons meet a bad end as the result of their association with a woman, and the novel ends ambivalently by not reporting the consequences of their failures. The novel was acclaimed for its extraordinary range and precise rendering of numerous strata of American life (cf. L. Kronenberger, *Nation* 145:565, 1937), recalling the praise lavished on *Street Scene* almost a decade earlier. There are suggestions that the relative lack of success of Rice's pageant-style plays of the thirties, especially *We, the People*, may have induced him to attempt a similar scope in novel form.

A45 _____. "Art at the Fair [letter]," *New York Times* 6 February 1938, X, 9.

States agreement with a *New York Times* editorial condemning the World's Fair for failing to fairly represent American artists in the exhibits.

A46 _____. "Five Playwrights, Plus Brotherly Love." *New York Times* 28 August 1938, IX, 1-2.

Provides the story behind the formation of the Playwrights' Company and announces upcoming productions of *Abe Lincoln in Illinois* and *Knickerbocker Holiday*. Argues the need for more efficient and integrated production practices. States the "idealistic notions" which gave rise to formation of the Company, and concludes by stating that he has never been more interested in the theatre until this time.

A47 _____. "Apologia Pro Vita Sua, Per Elmer Rice." *New York Times* 25 December 1938, IX, 3, 5.

Marking his twenty-fifth anniversary as a playwright, Rice admits that despite his experience he sees no principle or system which governs the critical and popular reception of his plays. He states that he writes out of "sheer exuberance" and is unable to judge the soundness of his own plays. Despite having no love for the theatre as such, he nevertheless has a passion for formulating ideas. His primary focus has always been, no matter the dramatic form used, the idea that freedom is the preeminent principle in life, "and that nothing is more important in life as the freedom of body and mind." Advocates a drama which seeks to liberate human potentiality for freedom, and adduces several of his plays as examples. Ends by arguing that *American Landscape*, which had recently been panned by critics, is the most important and emotional play he has written to date.

Non-Dramatic Works 107

A48 _____. "Tickets Going Down." *New York Times* 24 September 1939, IX, 1, 2.

Argues that the next step after the Federal Theatre Project and the Playwrights' Company is the lowering of theatre ticket prices in order to build an audience for the future. Offers overview of current theatre economics and relates how the Playwrights' Company intends to use *Abe Lincoln in Illinois* as a test case for a lower-priced admissions policy.

A49 _____. "Two Dollar Top Results." *New York Times* 3 December 1939, IX, 5.

Afterview of experiment with lower ticket prices. As a business venture the idea failed, losing $15,000; however, as an experiment it was a success, since now the Playwrights' Company has a better grasp of the economic factors involved and will take them into account in their next effort.

A50 _____. "Theatre Takes Stock." *Theatre Arts Monthly* 24.5 (May 1940), 353-55.

Rice pitches both lower ticket prices and union contracts based on continuous employment as solutions to the current economic plight of Broadway.

A51 _____. "Of Lower Ticket Prices." *New York Times* 16 March 1941, X, 1, 3.

Flight to the West has been chosen as the next experiment in lowering ticket prices, moving from the Guild Theatre to the Royale. Uses the announcement to review current theatre economics and to propose long-range planning with fair labor policies, reductions in production costs, and so on. Argues that the theatre cannot be left to the well-to-do, especially when plays are concerned with promoting social and economic equality.

A52 _____. "Victim of an Air Raid." *New York Times* 23 November 1941, X, 3.

Reports the death in a Nazi bombing raid of the Russian playwright Alexander Afinegenoff, whom he had met in Berlin and Moscow before the war. Laments the loss, calling Afinegenoff a "spiritual symbol" of the horrors of Hitlerism.

A53 _____. "Elmer Rice, Why He Selected *The Adding Machine* [letter]." *This Is My Best*, ed. Whit Burnett (New York: The Dial Press, 1942).

Records the process of writing the play with no revision, and points out he had no specific agenda in writing the play.

A54 _____. "Two Views of Eisentstein's *The Film Sense.*" *Soviet Russia Today* X (September 1942), 27-8.

  Along with James Gow, Rice reviews Eisenstein's classic text. Rice sees the book as a philosophical essay on aesthetics, and argues that film will never develop out of its infancy because it is too dependent on technology.

A55 _____. "A Letter." *New York Times* 10 January 1943, VIII, 2.

  Supports Paul Green's call for a decentralized theatre, but speaking as the President of the Drama Guild he objects to Green's accusations that the Guild is responsible for hampering efforts to produce plays regionally.

A56 _____. "Tom Paine, Prophet of Liberty." *New York Times Book Review* (25 April 1043), 1, 18.

  A review of Howard Fast's fictionalized autobiography *Citizen Tom Paine*, which Rice characterizes as a "vivid portrait" of a neglected and misunderstood hero. The essay celebrates Paine's forthrightness and passionate idealism, claiming that historical neglect was caused by Paine's continued criticism of privilege and economic injustice of the burghers who profited most after the Revolution.

A57 _____. "The Pitchfork With Prongs at Both Ends." *Saturday Review* 27 (25 March 1944), 4-5, 20-21.

  A review of Ben Hecht's book on anti-Semitism, *A Guide for the Bedevilled*. Rice was disappointed in the book because he claims Hecht only fitfully analyzed the psychological and socioeconomic aspects of race hatred. Accuses Hecht of recuperating race hatred in his treatment of Germans, whom he claims are all bigots and murderers. Rice believes race hatred can only be expunged through education and enlightenment, along with economic equality. He questions why Hecht did not provide a "social prophylaxis by which race prejudice can be localized and kept under control."

A58 _____. "Elmer Rice Answers Daryl Zanuck [letter]." *Saturday Review* 27 (22 April 1944), 18.

  Zanuck had written to chastise Rice for attacking Hollywood in his review of Hecht's *Guide to the Bedevilled*, imputing that Rice was claiming that no liberal minds existed in the movie industry. Rice responds by acknowledging that many creative and liberal people work in Hollywood, but that they are not the ones who control the means of production there. The industry is dominated by greedy plutocrats who want to sustain the eco-

Non-Dramatic Works

nomic status quo by giving lurid and distorted pictures of American life.

A59 _____. "Who Speaks for Russia?" *Saturday Review* 27 (27 May 1944), 12-13.

An answer to another reviewer who had claimed that Russia was merely trying to emulate the "industrial materialism" of America. Rice recalls his trips to Russian in 1932 and 1936, where he saw a country transformed by a new collective spirit intent on forging a better future (which he contrasts to Depression-era America). He also claims that the productivity of the Russian people made the defeat of Hitler possible, and ends by suggesting that Americans should praise the Russian revolution instead of parodying it.

A60 _____. "The U. S. O. and *The Races of Mankind*." *Saturday Review* 27 (15 July 1944), 13.

Attacks the U. S. O.'s suppression of an anthropological study refuting the fallacies of racial characteristics and differences. Rice supports the pamphlet's view that intellectual and moral differences between people are determined largely by environmental, rather than racial factors. He accuses the U. S. O. administrator responsible for the pamphlet's suppression of aiding the cause of white supremacy.

A61 _____. "An Open Letter." *Saturday Review* 29 (12 January 1946), 20.

Addressed to the Bar Association of Boston, who had supported a legal ban of the novel *Strange Fruits*. As President of the Author's League, Director of the ACLU and of the National Council on Freedom from Censorship, Rice is appalled at the flimsy legal language the lawyers used to support the ban. Likens the ban of the novel to the ban in Boston of O'Neill's *Strange Interlude* many years earlier.

A62 _____. "Arthur Hopkins Reaps Rebuttals [letter]." *New York Times* 10 August 1947, II, 1.

Expresses disagreement with Hopkins for writing that American theatre should not strive for social significance.

A63 _____. "The Supreme Freedom: Three Hundred Years After Milton [essay]." (New York: Graphics Group, 1949). Reprinted in *Great Expressions of Human Rights* (New York: Harper & Bros., 1950).

An explication of *Areopagitica* and its applications to contemporary America. Describes censorship practices in America and links it to accelerated processes of industrialization and monopolization in the country. Lashes out against the Hays Office and church-related pressure groups.

A64 _____. "The First Decade." *Theatre Arts Monthly* 33.1 (January 1949): 53-56.

An overview of the Playwrights' Company. Rice explains the company name by deriving it from the medieval guilds who regulated their own working conditions to further common interests. He points to the members' dissatisfaction with the "anarchic" Broadway theatre to provide any continuity to the theatre profession. Rice assesses the Company's reputation for excellent productions and its ability to attract the best performers. Rather than stay pat, however, he feels the Company should move ahead by including younger writers and by continuing to fund the Sidney Howard Award for new playwrights. Includes three pages of production photos.

A65 _____. *The Show Must Go On.* New York: Viking, 1949.

Rice's last novel, an exposé of Broadway as seen through the eyes of Eric, a laborer from Connecticut and an ex-GI, and his immoral mentor. Every possible tribulation of a playwright's life is rendered, and the novel ends ambivalently with Eric's play closing before its premiere. C. J. Rolo (*Atlantic* 184:99 November 1949) called it good entertainment but weighted with too much reportage, while A. C. Spectorsky (*New York Times* 9 October 1949, p. 4) calls it well-intentioned if not flawlessly styled. Rice admitted in *Minority Report* (A83) that the novel contains memories of his own affair with a woman he calls "Laura."

A66 _____. "A Letter." *New York Times* 12 February 1950, II, 2.

Defends the Dramatist's Guild proposal to cut royalties during the tryout period of new plays.

A67 _____. "Tribute to the Late Arthur Hopkins." *New York Times* 26 March 1950, II, 2.

Recognizes Hopkins' integrity, tenacity and resourcefulness, citing the producer's discovery of the jacknife stage on which *On Trial* was mounted.

A68 _____. "Free Expression in the U. S. A. [letter]" *Saturday Review* 33 (1 April 1950), 24.

Congratulates a recent article's exposé of censorship in Russia, but argues that Americans should not complacently assume they are free from such oppression. Cites a score of examples of censorship in America from religious groups to school boards. Congratulates the ACLU for combatting censorship.

A69 _____. "Why Not a Municipal Theatre?" *New York Times* 3 June 1951), II, 1-2.

Reports he is happy to see completion of a municipal music center, but wonders why a similar campaign has not been started to build a municipal theatre. Rice contrasts American theatre practices with those of Europe, and argues that a repertory theatre would contribute to the "cultural life of the country."

A70 _____. "A Letter." *New York Times* 4 November 1951, II, 3.

A remembrance in honor of the actress Mady Christians, whose death Rice blames on the McCarthy witch hunts.

A71 _____. "The Industrialization of the Writer." *Saturday Review* 35 (12 April 1952), 13-14, 62-63.

Rice argues here that as means of communication (film, radio, television) expanded, so too did corporate control. As a result, more writers are now salaried than at any other time, meaning that they have lost a measure of independence. Writing, like other forms of cultural production, is becoming increasingly standardized and mechanized. Individual craft is superseded by conformity of style; in consequence, there is less opportunity for the unorthodox writer to thrive. The exclusive dependence on salaried writing results in an "economic censorship" which breeds conformity and limits free speech. When the writer, like a frontline canary in WWI begins to droop and sicken, "look out for poison gas."

A72 _____. "What Stevenson Started." *New Republic* 128 (5 January 1953), 11-12.

Rice argues that in the current campaign between Richard Nixon and Adlai Stevenson the former addresses himself to the lowest common denominator in American voters while the latter's campaign is a "revelation" of respectful discourse with the people.

A73 _____. "Entertainment in the Age of McCarthy." *New Republic* 176 (April 13, 1953): 14-17. Reprinted as "Conformity in the Arts," a pamphlet published by the American Civil Liberties Union in 1953.

Rice recalls earlier visits with cultural commissars in the Soviet Union at which he stridently objected to censorship in Communist Russia. He now sees that, despite an appearance of freedom of expression in America, there remain serious obstacles to the expression of unpopular ideas in America. Pressure groups and church-affiliated organizations continue to exert undue pressure for artists to conform. Rice adduces examples of such pressure from his own career, citing the outcry against *Flight to the West*'s suggestion of abortion, while also analyzing film censorship and anti-communist sentiment that has blocked release of various forms of art and thought. He closes by arguing that Americans must reassert their constitutional rights to speak freely.

A74 _____. "Drama on Campus." *New York Times* 2 January 1955, II, 1, 3.

Tells of his two-month stay on the University of Michigan campus, where he gave lectures on censorship, playwriting, and theatre business. Found the unspoiled appetite for drama among the students enlightening and stimulating, especially their regard for non-realistic theatre. Thoroughly enjoyed the student production of *Dream Girl*. Despite the experience, he notes that drama is still the "poor stepchild" of the arts on American campuses.

A75 _____. "It's a Villain's World." *New York Times* 16 June 1955, I, 35.

In this report of Rice's 16 June address to the P.E.N. Congress in Vienna, the playwright is reported to have stated that the heroes of contemporary drama are "bewildered creatures, floundering themselves with wishful fantasies. . . . The recurrent themes of our plays are loneliness, rebellion, juvenile delinquency, emotional starvation, homosexuality, terror fantasies, sadism and schizophrenia."

A76 _____. "A Personal Memoir." *New York Times* 20 November 1955, II, 1, 3.

Rice's tribute to Robert Sherwood, whose *Abe Lincoln in Illinois* he credits with giving the foundering Playwrights' Company a "rousing start." The enduring leitmotif of Sherwood's drama, says Rice, is the reluctance of the sensual and self-centered man to assume responsibility that life thrusts upon him, and the gradual acknowledgement of moral obligations that the character learns.

A77 _____. "American Theatre and the Human Spirit." *Saturday Review* 38 (17 December 1955), 9. 39-41.

The essay seeks "to discover what ideological, cultural, and psychological trends are discernible in the American theatre today." The artist, says Rice, is not a thinker or innovator, but a "catalytic agent" for fusing and verifying what a culture knows and feels at a given time. After quickly summarizing the *zeitgeisten* of the Greek, Elizabethan, and early modern periods and their effects on the theatre, Rice turns to the contemporary world. He argues that in the wake of the Marxian, Darwinian, and especially Freudian revolutions, today's playwrights are infused with a sense of disillusionment and despair. They have turned to representing self-deluding, self-pitying characters who struggle to inform their lives with meaning. Playwrights should not be disparaged for the trend, as they are merely the chroniclers of their time. Should the modern world reintegrate itself, playwrights will be there to "celebrate the renascence of the human spirit."

A78 _____. "The Mind of the Playwright: A Conversation With Elmer Rice." *Esquire* 47 (April 1957), 66-67, 140.

The interview covers biographical information regarding Rice's years in the theatre, influences on his work (including painting), and the way Hollywood has ruined some of his plays. Rice also expresses his views on religion, saying it is his lack of belief in an afterlife which gives him the zeal to live in the world fully. Comments on the current state of the world, arguing that we live in a time of absolute disillusionment. The only response, he concludes, is to be realistic about life without being weighed down by social restrictions and taboos. Includes several photos.

A79 _____. "The Biography of a Play." *Theatre Arts* 43 November 1959), 59-64, 94-5.

Rice's reminiscences of the preparation for *Street Scene*, reprinted in *The Living Theatre*.

A80 _____. *The Living Theatre*. Harper and Brothers, 1959. Also published in London: William Heinemann Ltd., 1960.

After teaching a graduate seminar on modern drama at NYU in 1957, Rice revised and published his lectures. In the book he focuses on the theatre as a social institution, and on the relationship of the theatre's technical and human mechanisms to the production of dramatic literature. The text ranges in methodology from comparative analysis (using material on Japanese, Russian, and European drama gleaned from his travels abroad) to anecdotal history (his affiliation with the Playwrights' Company and the Federal Theatre Project, his lifelong animus against commercial theatre) to moral questioning (issues of censorship and so on). The book remains a lively account of American and international theatre of the twentieth century, as well a fine practical guide to life in the theatre.

A81 _____. "A Letter." *New York Times* 30 October 1960, II, 3.

Rice quotes ironically from a letter he had received stating that American audiences prefer cheap laughs and dramatic situations rather than provocative drama.

A82 _____. "Elmer Rice Views Theatre Real Estate Today--and Yesterday." *Dramatist's Bulletin* 2 (December 1961), 1-4.

In this interview Rice says that American theatres are still as he described them in *The Living Theatre* two years previously. Unlike theatres in Moscow, Berlin, Buenes Aires and Tokyo, American theatres are decrepit. Feels that perhaps Lincoln Center will spawn a new era when it is completed. [Followed by extended excerpt from *The Living Theatre*.]

A83 _____. *Minority Report: An Autobiography*. New York: Simon and Schuster, 1963.

Rice's autobiography focuses almost exclusively on his life in the theatre, refusing any mention of his first and third wives and only occasionally addressing the difficulties surrounding his marriage to Betty Field. The book covers events in Rice's boyhood and his early years in the legal profession, before recounting the legendary success of *On Trial*. Thereafter, the book concentrates on the genesis and outcome of his plays, his travels to Russia and the Orient, his life as a producer, director, theatre owner, and member of the Playwrights' Company and various writers' associations (P. E. N., etc.). The book ends with a "Credo and Coda" into which Rice distills his views on religion, writing, morals and politics.

A84 _____. "Author! Author!" Or, How to Write a Smash Hit the First Time You Try." *American Heritage* 16 (April 1965): 46-49, 84-86.

Rice's reminiscences of his decision to give up the bar for playwriting, and his subsequent success with *On Trial*. Most of the material is adapted from *Minority Report* (A83).

II. DRAMATIC PUBLICATIONS

The following is a list of Rice's plays. It includes texts in which Rice's plays have been individually published, collected, or anthologized. For unpublished plays, archival sources are cited.

ACCORDING TO THE EVIDENCE

According to the Evidence. (typescript) Library of Congress, Washington, D. C.

THE ADDING MACHINE

The Adding Machine. New York: Doubleday, 1923.

Anthologies
  Contemporary Plays. Ed. T. H. Dickinson and J. R. Crawford. Boston: Houghton Mifflin, 1925.
  Representative American Dramas, National and Local. Ed. Moses Montrose. Boston: Little, Brown and Co., 1926.
  Plays of Elmer Rice. London: Gollancz, 1933.
  Other Plays and "Not for Children": Being Four Plays by Elmer Rice. London: Gollancz, 1935.
  A Theatre Guild Anthology. New York: Random House, 1936.
  Modern American Drama. Ed. Harlan Hatcher. New York: Harcourt Brace Jovanich, 1941.
  British and American Plays, 1830-1945. Ed. Thomas Dickinson and Jack Crawford. New York: Oxford, 1947.
  Dominant Types in British and American Literature. Ed. William Davenport, Lowry Wimberly, and Harry Shaw. New York: Harper & Row, 1949.
  Seven Plays by Elmer Rice. New York: Viking, 1950.
  A College Treasury. Ed. P. A. Jorgenson and F. B. Shroyer. New York: Scribner, 1956.
  The Range of Literature. Ed. E. W. Schneider, A. L. Walker, and H. E. Childs. New York: American Book, 1960.
  Best American Plays (Supplementary Edition). Ed. John Gassner. New York: Crown, 1961.
  Twentieth-Century American Writing. Ed. William Stafford. New York: Odyssey Press, 1965.
  Three Plays. New York: Hill and Wang, 1965.
  The Making of Drama. Ed. Maurice Small and Maurice Sutton. Boston: Holbrook Press, 1972.
  The Design of Drama. Ed. Lloyd Hubenka and Reloy Garcia. New York: David McKay, 1973.
  The Disinherited: Plays. Ed. Abe Ravitz. Encino, CA: Dickensen Publishers, 1974.

AMERICAN LANDSCAPE

American Landscape. New York: Coward-McCann, 1939.

AS THE SPARKS FLY UPWARD

As the Sparks Fly Upward. (typescript) Elmer Rice Collection, Humanities Research Center, University of Texas-Austin. Library of Congress, Washington, D. C.

BETWEEN TWO WORLDS

Anthologies

Two Plays. New York: Coward-McCann, 1935.
Other Plays, and "Not for Children." (London: Gollancz, 1935).

BLACK SHEEP

Black Sheep. New York: Dramatist's Play Service, 1938.

THE BLUE HAWAII

The Blue Hawaii. (typescript) Elmer Rice Collection, Humanities Research Center, University of Texas-Austin. Library of Congress, Washington, D. C.

CLOSE HARMONY; OR, THE LADY NEXT DOOR (with Dorothy Parker)

Close Harmony: or, the Lady Next Door. New York: Samuel French, 1929.

COCK ROBIN (with Philip Barry)

Cock Robin. New York: Samuel French, 1929.

Anthology

Teatro norteamericano de vanguardia (Madrid: M. Aguilar, 1935).

COUNSELLOR-AT-LAW

Counsellor-at-Law. New York: Samuel French, 1931.
Counsellor-at-Law. Los Angeles: The Federal Theatre Project.

Anthologies

Famous Plays of 1932-33. London: Gollancz, 1933.
Seven Plays by Elmer Rice. New York: Viking, 1950.
Awake and Singing: 7 [sic] *Classic Plays from the American Jewish Repertoire.* Ed. Ellen Schiff. Mentor Books, 1994.

COURT OF LAST RESORT

Court of Last Resort: A Play in Ten Scenes. Newark, Del.: Proscenium Press, c. 1980.

Anthology

George Spelvin's Theatre Book. 6 (Summer 1984), 7-72.

Dramatic Publications 117

CUE FOR PASSION

    Cue for Passion. New York: Dramatist's Play Service, 1959.

DAY DREAM

    Day Dream. (typescript) Elmer Rice Collection, Humanities Research Center, University of Texas-Austin.

A DEFECTION FROM GRACE (with Frank Harris)

    A Defection from Grace. (typescript) Library of Congress, Washington, D. C.

A DIADEM OF SNOW

    A Diadem of Snow. The Liberator (April 1918), pp. 26-33.

    Anthology
    One-Act Plays for Stage and Study. 5th series. Ed. Elmer Rice. New York: Samuel French, 1929.

DREAM GIRL

    Dream Girl. New York: Coward-McCann, 1946.
    Dream Girl. Il Dramma 63 (15 June 1948): 9-40. Trans. Mino Roli.

    Anthologies
    Best Plays of the American Theatre, ed. John Gassner. New York:Crown, 1947.
    Seven Plays by Elmer Rice. New York: Viking, 1950.
    Three Plays. New York: Hill and Wang, 1965.
    Fifty Best Plays of the American Theatre. Ed. John Gassner and Olive Barnes. New York: Crown, 1969.

EXTERIOR (third part of *Sidewalks of New York*, copyright 1925)

    Exterior. The Scholastic 29 (November 14, 1936): 11-12.

    Anthology
    Three Plays Without Words. New York: Samuel French, 1934.

A FAMILY AFFAIR

    A Family Affair. (typescript) Elmer Rice Collection, Humanities Research Center, University of Texas-Austin. Library of Congress, Washington, D. C.

FIND THE WOMAN

    Find the Woman. (typescript) Library of Congress, Washington, D. C.

FLIGHT TO THE WEST

    Flight to the West. New York: Coward-McCann, 1941.

FOR THE DEFENSE

    For the Defense. New York, 1919.

THE GAY WHITE WAY

    Anthology
        One-Act Plays for Stage and Study. 8th series. Ed. Alice Gerstenberg. New York: Samuel French, 1934.

A GOOD WOMAN

    A Good Woman. (typescript). Elmer Rice Collection, Humanities Research Center, University of Texas-Austin.

THE GRAND TOUR

    The Grand Tour. New York: Dramatist's Play Service, 1952.

HELEN AND JOHN

    Helen and John. (typescript) Elmer Rice Collection, Humanities Research Center, University of Texas-Austin.

HELP! HELP!

    Help! Help! New York, 1919 [published by the author].

THE HOME-COMING (with Hatcher Hughes)

    The Home-Coming. (typescript) Library of Congress, Washington, D. C.

THE HOME OF THE FREE (published under Elmer L. Reizenstein)

    The Home of the Free. New York: Samuel French, 1934.

    Anthology
        The Morningside Plays, ed. Barrett H. Clark. New York: Frank Shay and Co., 1917.

THE HOUSE IN BLIND ALLEY

    The House in Blind Alley. New York: Samuel French, 1932.

THE HOUSE OF ARCHER

    The House of Archer. (typescript) Elmer Rice Collection, Humanities Research Center, University of Texas-Austin. Library of Congress, Washington, D. C.

Dramatic Publications

THE IRON CROSS

The Iron Cross. New York, 1915.
The Iron Cross. California: Proscenium Press, 1965 [a slightly revised version of the 1915 text].

IT IS THE LAW

It Is the Law. (typescript) Elmer Rice Collection, Humanities Research Center, University of Texas-Austin. Library of Congress, Washington, D. C.

JUDGMENT DAY

Judgment Day. New York: Coward-McCann, 1934.

Anthologies
Famous Plays of 1937. London: Gollancz.
Seven Plays by Elmer Rice. New York: Viking, 1950.
Other Plays, and "Not for Children." (London: Gollancz, 1935).

THE KINGDOM OF HEAVEN

The Kingdom of Heaven. (typescript) Elmer Rice Collection, Humanities Research Center, University of Texas-Austin. Library of Congress, Washington, D. C.

LANDSCAPE WITH FIGURES (first part of Sidewalks of New York 1925)

Anthology
Three Plays Without Words. New York: Samuel French, 1934.

THE LEFT BANK

The Left Bank. New York: Samuel French, 1931.

LIFE IS REAL

Life Is Real. (typescript) Elmer Rice Collection, Humanities Research Center, University of Texas-Austin.
Wir in Amerika. Germany, 1928.

LOVE AMONG THE RUINS

Love Among the Ruins. New York: Dramatist's Play Service, 1963.

A MATTER OF TIME

A Matter of Time. (typescript) Elmer Rice Collection, Humanities Research Center, University of Texas-Austin. Library of Congress, Washington, D. C.

THE MONGREL (adaptation based on the play by Hermann Bahr)
Note: Rice denied he ever adapted the play, claiming only that he had "done some tinkering with the dialogue." See James Allison, "A Study of Some Concepts of Social Justice in the Plays of Elmer Rice" (S79) for Rice's letter.

> *The Mongrel.* (typescript) Elmer Rice Collection, Humanities Research Center, University of Austin-Texas. Library of Congress, Washington, D. C.

MY COUNTRY IS THE WORLD

> *My Country is the World.* (typescript) Elmer Rice Collection, Humanities Research Center, University of Texas-Austin. Library of Congress, Washington, D. C.

A NEW LIFE

> *A New Life.* New York: Coward-McCann, 1944.

NOT FOR CHILDREN

> *Not for Children.* New York: Samuel French, 1951.
>
> Anthologies
> *Two Plays.* New York: Coward-McCann, 1935.
> *Other Plays and "Not for Children": Being Four Plays of Elmer Rice.* London: Gollancz, 1935.

ON TRIAL

> *On Trial.* New York: Samuel French, 1919.
>
> Anthologies
> *Best Plays of 1909-1919.* Ed. Burns Mantle and Garrison Sherwood. New York: Dodd, 1933.
> *Famous Plays of Crime and Detection*, ed. V. H. Cartmell and Bennett Cerf. Philadelphia: Blakiston, 1946.
> *Seven Plays by Elmer Rice.* New York: Viking, 1950.

ONE MUST EAT

> *One Must Eat.* (typescript) Elmer Rice Collection, Humanities Research Center, University of Texas-Austin. Library of Congress, Washington, D. C.

ORDEAL BY FIRE

> *Ordeal by Fire.* (typescript) Elmer Rice Collection, Humanities Research Center, University of Texas-Austin.

Dramatic Publications

THE PASSING OF CHOW-CHOW

    Anthology
        One-Act Plays for Stage and Study. 2nd series. Ed. Walter Eaton. New York: Samuel French, 1925.

PRELUDE FOR MARIONETTES

        Prelude for Marionettes. (typescript) Elmer Rice Collection, Humanities Research Center, University of Texas-Austin.

RUS IN URBE (second part of Sidewalks of New York, 1925)

    Anthology
        Three Plays Without Words. New York: Samuel French, 1934.

RETURN OF THE NATIVE

        Return of the Native. (typescript) Elmer Rice Collection, Humanities Research Center, University of Texas-Austin.

SEE NAPLES AND DIE

        See Naples and Die. New York: Samuel French, 1930.

    Anthology
    Famous Plays of 1932. London: Gollancz, 1932.
    Plays of Elmer Rice. London: Gollancz, 1933.
    Other Plays and "Not for Children." London: Gollancz, 1935.

THE SEVENTH COMMANDMENT

        The Seventh Commandment. (typescript) Elmer Rice Collection, Humanities Research Center, University of Texas-Austin. Library of Congress, Washington, D. C.

THE SIEGE OF BERLIN

        The Siege of Berlin. (typescript) Elmer Rice Collection, Humanities Research Center, University of Texas-Austin. Library of Congress, Washington, D. C.

THE SLAVES OF THE LAMP

        The Slaves of the Lamp. (typescript) Elmer Rice Collection, Humanities Research Center, University of Texas-Austin. Library of Congress, Washington, D. C.

STREET SCENE

        Street Scene. New York: Samuel French, 1929.

Anthologies

Six Plays. London: Gollancz, 1933

Contemporary Drama: American Plays. Ed. Bradlee Watson and Benfield Pressey. [c. 1931-1939].

Twentieth-Century Plays. Ed. Frank Chandler and Richard Cordell. New York: Nelson, 1934 (revised 1939, 1941).

Plays of Elmer Rice. London: Gollancz, 1933.

Other Plays and "Not for Children": Being Four Plays by Elmer Rice. London: Gollancz, 1935.

The Pulitzer Prize Winning Plays, 1918-1934. New York: Random, 1935 (Revised editions 1938, 1940).

Contemporary Drama: Nine Plays. Ed. Bradlee Watson and Benfield Pressey. New York: Scribner and Sons, 1941.

Twenty-Five Best Plays of American Theatre (Early Series). Ed. John Gassner. New York: Crown, 1941.

Pocket Book of Modern American Plays. Ed. Bennett Cerf. New York: Pocket Books, 1942.

Drama and Theatre: Illustrated by Seven Modern Plays. Ed. Albert Fulton. New York: Holt, 1946.

Twentieth-Century Plays. Ed. R. A. Cordell, 3d ed. New York: Ronald, 1947.

Twenty-Five Best Plays of Modern American Theatre. Ed. John Gassner. New York: Crown, 1949.

Seven Plays by Elmer Rice. New York: Viking, 1950.

Nine Modern American Plays. Ed. Barrett Clark and William Davenport. New York: Appleton-Century-Crofts, 1951.

Living Theatre. Ed. A. S. Griffith. New York: Twayne, 1953.

Famous American Plays of the 1920s. Ed. Kenneth McGowan. New York: Dell, 1959.

Contemporary Drama: European, English, Irish and American Plays. Ed. Bradlee Watson and Benfield Pressey. New York: Scribner and Sons, 1960.

Three Dramas of American Realism. Ed. J. E. Mersand. New York: Washington Square, 1961.

Three Plays. New York: Hill and Wang, 1965.

STREET SCENE (MUSICAL, book by Elmer Rice)

Street Scene. Music by Kurt Weill. Lyrics by Langston Hughes. New York, 1948.

THE SUBWAY

The Subway. New York: Samuel French, 1929.

Anthology
> *Teatro norteamericano de vanguardia* (Madrid: M. Aguilar, 1935).

TO THE STARS

> *To the Stars.* (typescript) Library of Congress, Washington, D. C.

TUCKER'S PEOPLE (based on Ira Wolfert's novel)

> *Tucker's People.* (typescript) Elmer Rice Collection, Humanities Research Center, University of Texas-Austin. Library of Congress, Washington, D. C.

TWO ON AN ISLAND

> *Two on an Island.* New York: Coward-McCann, 1940.

> Anthology
> *Seven Plays by Elmer Rice.* New York: Viking, 1950.

WAKE UP, JONATHAN (in collaboration with Hatcher Hughes)

> *Wake Up, Jonathan.* New York: Samuel French, 1928.

WE, THE PEOPLE

> *We, the People.* New York: Coward-McCann, 1933.

> Anthology
> *Other Plays, and "Not for Children."* (London: Gollancz, 1935).

THE WINNER

> *The Winner.* New York: Dramatist's Play Service, 1954.

III. UNPUBLISHED COLLECTED MATERIAL

The Library of Congress in Washington, D. C., the Billy Rose Collection of the New York Public Library at Lincoln Center, and the Elmer Rice Collection at the Harry Ransom Humanities Research Center at the University of Texas-Austin possess the largest collections of unpublished manuscripts by Rice.

Library of Congress, Washington, D. C.
> Non-circulating unpublished copyrighted manuscripts at the Library of Congress may be accessed through the Archives Reading Room. The collection includes the following:

> *A New Life* (c. D unpub. 84750 July 5, 1943)

According to the Evidence (c. D unpub. 18327 May 21, 1914). Under E. Riezenstein.
The Adding Machine (c. D unpub. 46667 Nov. 29, 1922)
American Landscape (c. D unpub. 59263 Sep. 13, 1938)
As the Sparks Fly Upward (c. D unpub. 42574 May 22, 1956)
Black Sheep (unpub. 42672 Oct. 26, 1923)
Between Two Worlds (c. D unpub. 30244 June 29, 1934)
Blue Hawaii (c. D unpub. 45587 Oct. 20, 1924)
Cock Robin (c. D unpub. 80791 no date)
Counsellor-at-Law (c. D unpub. 43632 Sep 3 1931)
Court of Last Resort (c. D unpub. 63830 Sep. 1, 1965)
Cue for Passion (c. D unpub. 47847 Oct. 22, 1958)
Defection from Grace (with Frank Harris) (c. D unpub, B 2980 no date)
A Diadem of Snow (c. D unpub. 38977 Dec. 8, 1917). Under E. Reizenstein.
Dream Girl (c. D unpub. 94249 July 14, 1945)
Family Affair (c. D unpub. 37033 Nov. 11, 1916). Under E. Reizenstein
Find the Woman (c. D unpub. 35693 Nov. 15, 1918). Under E. Reizenstein
Flight to the West (c. D unpub. 72382 Nov. 14, 1940)
For the Defense (c. D unpub. 34572 Nov. 22, 1919)
The Grand Tour (c. D unpub. 29045 no date)
Helen and John (c. D unpub. 35572 July 19, 1928)
Help! Help! (c. D unpub. 21015 July 3, 1919)
The House of Archer (c. D unpub. 27309 July 14, 1921)
Home of the Free (c. D unpub. 10342 March 23, 1917)
Home-Coming (with Hatcher Hughes) (c. D unpub. 20914 June 7, 1917)
The House in Blind Alley (c. D unpub. 13523 April 14, 1916)
Iron Cross (c. D unpub. 34225 Oct. 12, 1915). Under E. Reizenstein.
It Is the Law (with Hayden Talbot) (c. D unpub. 10380 March 13, 1922)
Judgment Day (c. D unpub. 302444 June 29, 1934)
Kingdom of Heaven (c. D unpub. 14578 May 9, 1918). Under E. Reizenstein.
The Left Bank (c. D unpub. 50096 Sep. 30, 1930)
Life Is Real (c. D unpub. 16637 April 6, 1926)
Love Among the Ruins (c. D unpub. 27932 June 14, 1951)
A Matter of Time (c. D unpub. 39124 Nov. 20, 1917). Under E. Reizenstein.
The Mongrel (C. D unpub. 1C 69850)
My Country Is the World (c. D unpub. 90718 Oct. 6, 1944)
Not for Children (c. D unpub. 27312 June 12, 1934)
On Trial (c. D unpub. 29045 Aug. 27, 1914). Under E. Reizenstein.
One Must Eat (c. D unpub. 43670 Dec. 29, 1917). Under E. Reizenstein
Return of the Native (c. D unpub. 42575 May 22, 1956)

See Naples and Die (c. D unpub. 40055 Aug. 17, 1928)
The Seventh Commandment (with Frank Harris) (c. D unpub. 34367 no date) under E. Reizenstein.
Sidewalks of New York (c. D unpub. 18929 April 28, 1925)
Slaves of the Lamp (c. D unpub. 63831 Sep. 1, 1965)
Soft Music (with Dorothy Parker) (c. D unpub. 69172 no date)
Street Scene (c. D unpub. 35572 July 19, 1928)
Street Scene (musical) (c. D unpub. 6104 Nov. 22, 1946)
The Subway (c. D unpub. 45587 Oct. 20, 1924)
The Siege of Berlin (c. D unpub. 63690 May 19, 1939)
To the Stars (c. D unpub. 80024 no date)
Tucker's People (adapted from Ira Wolfort's novel) (c. D unpub. 64716 no date)
Two on an Island (c. D unpub. 67272 Dec. 7, 1939). Under E. Reizenstein.
Wake Up, Jonathan (w/ Hatcher Hughes) (c. D unpub. 43293 Dec. 15, 1920)
We, the People (c. D unpub. 55008 Nov. 30, 1932)
The Winner (c. D unpub. 35907 January 13, 1954)

The Billy Rose Collection, New York Public Library at Lincoln Center, New York.

This non-circulating collection contains extensive materials which include holdings in the Hallie Flanagan and Robinson Locke Collections, typescripts of plays, nonfictional material by Rice, published interviews and reviews. An exhaustive current list of holdings is available from the Billy Rose Collection staff. The following is an abbreviated list.

1. Call number MWEZ + n.c. 6446

    Portfolio of loose newspaper clippings, many undated, with no author entry and in poor condition. Contains reviews, letters from Rice to various New York newspapers, and an occasional article by Rice.

2. Call number MWEZ X n.c. 25, 361

    Box contains sheaves of newspaper clippings (primarily reviews of plays), and halftones of Rice's letters to editors (through 1959).

3. Call number MWEZ X n.c. 16, 441A

    Sheaf of photographs of Rice in conjunction with Playwrights' Company: Robert Sherwood, Maxwell Anderson, S.N. Behrman, Sidney Howard.

4. Call number MWEZ X n.c. 20, 313: The Hallie Flanagan Collection
    Clippings and halftones related to Rice's activities as regional director of the Federal Theatre Project, and his resignation as regional director.

5. Call number NAFR x, Ser. 2; volume 288, pp. 35-38: The Robinson Locke Collection.
    Contains a single article, *"On Trial: The Greatest Dramatic Novelty of the Year,"* published in *Current Opinion*, July 1915.

6. Call number Envelope 1891: The Locke Collection
    Same as above.

7. Call number MWEZ + n.c. 2313
    Material related to Federal Theatre Project: pressbooks for Orson Welles's *Macbeth* and other plays. Clippings on Sidney Ross, V. Meyerhold, Herman Rosse, Michael Bohnen; also, articles on the Shakespeare Fellowship of America and the Westchester Playhouse. Rice is represented by only a few articles related to his resignation from the Federal Theatre Project.

8. Call number MWEZ X n.c. 17, 829; n.c. 17, 830: The Arthur Jasspe Gift
    Photostats of miscellaneous articles by Rice ("Sex in the American Theatre," "Introduction to *Two Plays*"), an interview with *Esquire*, and clippings related to Rice's dealings with the Playwright's Company.

9. Call number MWEZ X n.c. 19, 312: The Edward Goodman Collection
    Clippings regarding Rice's resignation as regional director of the Federal Theatre Project in 1936.

10. Call number MWEZ + n.c. 28, 524, #4
    "Four Dramatists of Freedom," an article on Rice and three other playwrights in *Rockefeller Center Magazine*, October 1942, pp. 18-19, 26-28. [Note: Library reports material lost.]

11. Call number NBLA +
    Article by Rice entitled "New York: Raw Material for the Drama" in *Theatre Magazine* vol. 49, March 1929, p. 26-28.

Unpublished Collected Material 127

12. Call number NBLA
     Photocopy of article by Rice, "The Playwright as Director," from *Theatre Arts*, v. 13, May 1929 (355-60).

13. Call number * PYP
     Photocopy of article by H. A. Gilbert, "The Winner of the Pulitzer Prize Award," from *B'nai B'rith Magazine*, v. 43, July 1929 (329-30).

14. Call number NBLA
     Article by Moses J. Montrose, "Elmer Rice," from *Theatre Guild Magazine*, v. 7, 1930 (14-17, 64).

15. Call number NBLA+
     Article by Joseph Freeman, "Elmer Rice," from *New Theatre*, September 1934 (6-8).

16. Call number MWA+
     Article by Joseph Mersand, "Elmer Rice: Realist of the Drama," from *Player's Magazine* November 1939 (7-8).

17. Call number NAFA
     Article by Ralph Collins, "The Playwright and the Press: Elmer Rice and His Critics," from *Theatre Annual*, 1948-49 (35-58).

Elmer Rice Collection, Ransom Humanities Research Center, University of Texas—Austin

This non-circulating collection is the largest single collection of Rice's manuscripts and correspondence. The collection includes, in addition to the manuscripts noted in Section I of the Primary Bibliography: acting drafts, prompt books, and translations of plays; Rice's business and personal correspondence; photographs and theatre programs; royalty statements and contracts; Rice's correspondence related to his affairs with the A.C.L.U.; a collection of letters to Bertram Bloch and Frank Harris; and Rice's notebooks and appointment books. A current list of holdings is available from the Center staff, and there is a descriptive bibliography available from U.M.I. Dissertation Service by Donald Gene Bristow (S151). The following lists only significant unpublished materials, all of which are found in boxes 1-46.

Box 6
     Motion picture scenario of *Counsellor-at-Law* (two scripts).

Box 11
> Motion picture story treatment and screenplay drafts of *Earth and High Heaven*.

Box 14
> Radio/television script for *The Grand Tour*.

Box 15
> Scenario and motion picture manuscript of *Holiday Inn*.

Box 33
> Two manuscripts for a proposed operetta, *The Pearl of Persia*.

Box 40
> Treatments, scenarios, and manuscripts for film and television versions of *Street Scene*.

Annotated Secondary Bibliography: Reviews

This chronologically-arranged secondary bibliography of reviews focuses on Rice's theatrical writings. For reviews of published non-dramatic writings, see the Primary Bibliography. Reviews refer to currently running productions.

1914–1918

R01 Price, William Thompson. "Some Plays of the Month Technically Considered." *American Playwright* 3.8 (15 August 1914): 300-03.
 On Trial seems to the uninformed viewer to violate every dramatic principle in existence. Actually, it is an important play that will catapult "Almer Reitzenstein" to a career of artistic freedom and experiment. His use of the flashback will create greater objectivity in the delineation of character because it is not dependant on sequence.

R02 No byline. "*On Trial* Proves Interesting." *New York Times* 20 August 1914.
 The play shows great ingenuity and provides great excitement for the audience.

R03 No byline. "*On Trial*." *Nation* 99 (27 August 1914): 260-61.
 A conventional story rendered in novel form. The flashback, in addition to creating a method to render reality scrupulously, may also indicate the increased influence of the cinema on live drama.

R04 No byline. "First Guns of the Dramatic Season." *Current Opinion* 57 (14 October 1914): 248-49.
 On Trial is the most interesting play of the season, shocking audiences with its use of film techniques on the stage. The

stunning experiment has the effect of increasing the plays's realism.

R05 No byline. "The Play." *New York Times* 18 October 1914.
>Compliments Hans Roberts in role of the secretary in *On Trial*.

R06 No byline. "*On Trial*." *Dramatist* 6.1 (October 1914): 498-99.
>The play fails whenever it attempts innovation, but works well when it remains conventional melodrama. The jacknife stage is an encumbrance that shatters illusion, and the flashback technique is an abject imitation of film. The plays's success will be passing.

R07 Hamilton, Clayton. "Chronological Sequence in the Drama." *Bookworm* 40 (October 1914): 181-83.
>*On Trial* succeeds as art for art's sake, there being no plot to it. The play reveals great technical proficiency by turning the plot around. A recent article by the same critic "probably" gave Rice the idea for the inversion.

R08 Pollack, Channing. "*On Trial*." *Green Book Magazine* (October 1914): 886-88.
>The story burns a candle at both ends by putting the trial scene first. Rice's bold experiment joins the drama to film and makes for a significant work of theatre.

R09 No byline. "*On Trial*: the Play of the Month." *Hearst's* 26.5 (November 1914): 640-47.
>Plot synopsis and excerpts along with production photos.

R10 No byline. "Mr. Reizenstein's Success With *On Trial*." *Green Book Magazine* 12 (November 1914): 901-3.
>Reviews use of flashback technique. Includes photo of Rice.

R11 Mantle, Burns. "The Stage." *Munsey* 53 (November 1914): 346.
>The secrecy surrounding the production of *On Trial* has lead more theatre managers to hide the openings of new plays. As for the play, it interests audiences despite the fact that its story is conventional.

R12 No byline. "A Play Written Backwards." *Everybody's Magazine* 31 (1914): 700-702.
>One of the great successes of the season. Rice's application of cinematic techniques to the stage is highly effective and makes

up for the trite story. An engrossing play, even if the ending is ludicrous.

R13 Eaton, Walter Pritchard. "On Trial." *American Magazine* (15 January 1915): 42, 87.
The play depends on trick and surprise, but pulls it off so well that it should be a popular success.

R14 Cather, Willa. "On Trial." *McClure's* 44.3 (January 1915): 20-21.
The play contains worn-out characters and is purely conventional, despite its use of film techniques.

R15 No byline. "London Likes *On Trial*." *New York Times* 30 April 1915: 5.
Reviews of the Lyric Theatre production compliment the strong melodrama and thrilling plot twists of the play.

R16 No byline. "*On Trial* in London." *New York Times* 16 May 1915: 4.
The play has received as enthusiastic a reception as anything in London this season.

R17 No byline. "*On Trial*—Greatest Novelty of the Year." *Current Opinion* 59 (July 1915): 24-7.
Overview of the play and of Rice's immediate success, along with production photos and excerpts.

R18 No byline. "Plays." *New York Times* 23 April 1917: 7.
Announcement for Columbia University production of *Home of the Free*.

R19 No byline. "Mr. Hornblower Goes to the Play." *Theatre Magazine* 194 (April 1917): 213-14.
The Iron Cross is a conventional peace tract presented almost exclusively as dramatic narrative. Edward Nicander stands out as the satiric Karl. Rice is perhaps too compassionate towards the Austrians.

R20 No byline. "Mr. Hornblower Goes to the Play." *Theatre Magazine* 208 (June 1918): 353-56.
Home of the Free reveals a bright, satiric style and provides for a startling curtain.

1919-1923

R21 Woollcott, Alexander. "*For the Defense* is Tense." *New York Times* 20 December 1919: 14.
A well contrived and suspenseful melodrama which uses the flashback effectively.

R22   Reid, Louis. "The Dramatic Mirror." *Dramatic Mirror* 1 January 1920.
      For the Defense is a taut evening of theatre, but individual performances are not strong.

R23   No byline. "The Latest Fashion in Melodrama." *Life* 75 (January 1920): 75.
      For the Defense is a good sex melodrama with an unusual villain, which should make it popular.

R24   No byline. "Mr. Hornblow Goes to the Theatre." *Theatre Illustrated Magazine* 31 (February 1920): 100.
      The ingenuity of the plot in *For the Defense* is crafty, but the play succeeds only because of the acting.

R25   Broun, Heywood. "*Wake Up, Jonathan*" *New York World* 18 January 1921.
      A premeditated attempt to reap financial reward by serving up cheap theatrical tricks.

R26   Woollcott, Alexander. "Mrs. Fiske Returns." *New York Times* 18 January 1921: 1.
      Mrs. Fiske saves *Wake Up, Jonathan*, a trite and insipid comedy which develops some interest and a deal of amusement in the last act.

R27   Reid, Louis. "Mrs Fiske Returns in Inferior Play." *Dramatic Mirror* 22 January 1921.
      Wake Up, Jonathan is "pure hokum," but Mrs. Fiske plays her part well.

R28   Woollcott, Alexander. "First Nights." *New York Times* 23 January 1921: 1.
      Compares *Wake Up, Jonathan* to listening to the recitation of multiplication tables. Focuses on Mrs. Fiske's talent, referring to the play itself as pretentious and condescending.

R29   No byline. "Dramatic and Musical." *New York Clipper* 26 January 1921: 19.
      Wake Up, Jonathan is a tasteful comedy in which Mrs. Fiske and her supporting cast shine.

R30   Firkins, O. W. "Drama From a Christmas Stocking." *The Weekly Review* 4 no. 90 (2 February 1921): 112-13.
      The chief fault of *Wake Up, Jonathan* is Rice's contempt for probability and the laws of nature.

R31   Lewissohn, Ludwig. "Native Plays." *Nation* 112 (2 February 1921): 112.

>   *Wake Up, Jonathan* is a weak play cluttered by sentimental melodrama.

R32 Benchley, Robert. "Hokum: Plain and de Luxe." *Life* 77 (3 February 1921): 172.

>   Lauds Mrs. Fiske for trying to save *Wake Up, Jonathan* from a trite script.

R33 No byline. "Mr. Hornblow Goes to the Theatre." *Theatre Illustrated Magazine* 33 (April 1921): 261.

>   *Wake Up, Jonathan* is a decent though not superior play, and a good vehicle for Mrs. Fiske.

R34 Corbin, John. "Back to the Legitimate." *New York Times* 30 November 1922: 2.

>   *It Is the Law* is a return to straight, legitimate crime melodrama that exceeds as a spine tingler. "Tense, rapid and compelling."

R35 No byline. "Dramatic and Musical." *New York Clipper* 6 December 1922: 20.

>   *It Is the Law* succeeds as a competent drama.

R36 No byline. "Mr. Hornblower Goes to the Play." *Theatre Magazine* 263 (February 1923): 19.

>   In *It Is the Law* the "father of the inverted drama" returns to the format of *On Trial*. This play is more farfetched, but remains an entertaining melodrama weakened by the presence of an unbelievable villain.

R37 No byline. "*Adding Machine* Replaces Poor Zero." *New York Times* 20 March 1923: 1.

>   The play is the best example of the new expressionism yet experienced in New York. The graveyard scene is gratuitous and vulgar, but the work generally succeeds in conveying an illusion of reality via the unreal.

R38 Broun, Heywood. "*The Adding Machine*." *New York World* 20 March 1923.

>   The value of the play lies in its experimentation with dramatic form, thought it is not a success in achieving its goal of breaking free of the materialistic fetters of prose drama, which makes stiff symbols of the figures on the stage and robs them of the illusion of life.

R39 Hammond, Percy. "*The Adding Machine*." *New York Tribune* 20 March 1923.

A seemingly significant play that remains insoluble and which does not take the audience into its confidence.

R40 Woollcott, Alexander. "*The Adding Machine.*" *New York Herald* 20 March 1923.
>The form of the play is novel and exciting, but serves mainly to reveal the author's ordinary mind and lack of subtle thought.

R41 No byline. "*The Adding Machine.*" *New York Times* 25 March 1923.
>A very advanced play, "deliberately and depravedly modern." The play's faults are found in its modern form, not the playwright's writing.

R42 Reid, Louis R. "Dramatic and Musical." *New York Clipper* 28 March 1923: 14.
>*The Adding Machine* is interesting and different, and the Theatre Guild is to be congratulated for producing the work of an American playwright.

R43 Lewisohn, Ludwig. "Creative Irony." *Nation* 116 (4 April 1923): 399.
>*The Adding Machine* succeeds at synthesizing the expressionist method better than O'Neill's *The Hairy Ape*. Although Rice's worldview might infuriate the spectator, you cannot withdraw from its power and completeness. Mr. Zero exemplifies the modern man who has "slavery in his soul." The collaboration between dramatist, producer and designer is imaginative, and the actors give the play a strange eloquence.

R44 Benchley, Robert. "Drama: Financial Advice." *Life* 81 (12 April 1923): 20.
>Lauds *The Adding Machine* and chastises the audiences for laughing at inappropriate times in the play.

R45 Young, Stark. "Marketing Expressionism." *New Republic* 34 (April 1923): 164-65.
>*The Adding Machine* "makes clear for the dullest spectator what expressionism is" as a theatrical method. Criticizes the play for its lack of a central idea and its indebtedness to European sources. Accuses Rice of exploiting expressionism's methods without connecting it to significant content, of writing "a play not so much about life as about expressionism."

R46 Seidenberg, Roderick. "*The Adding Machine.*" *Freeman* 164 (2 May 1923): 184-85.

Though the play reveals a dramatic flair and a talent for characterization, it suffers by imitating expressionism too closely. A "concoction of strident modernity," expressionism creates only a trivial and contemptuous mood without the saving grace of irony.

R47 Pollack, Philip. "Letter to the Editor." *Freeman* 166 (16 May 1923): 231-32.
Defends *The Adding Machine* from charges of plagiarism of German sources. The play achieves an overwhelming truth.

R48 No byline. "*The Adding Machine*." *Theatre Magazine* 37 (May 1923): 19.
The play begins in realistic form, but moves quickly to expressionism. Rice perhaps chisels too long and deeply at Zero's psyche, and the play at times lapses into tedium. But this is an important play for an American dramatist.

R49 Farrar, John. "To See or Not to See." *Bookman* 57 (May 1923): 319-20.
The Adding Machine is a more successful attempt at expressionism than Thomas Lawson's *Roger Bloomer*. After Scene Four, however, the play goes downhill, and Shrdlu is an excrescence.

R50 Wilson, Edmund. "The Theater." *Dial* 74 (May 1923): 526-27.
The first half of *The Adding Machine* is first-rate tragic satire, but the psychological weakness of Mr. Zero—his concern for status in heaven—weakens the play.

R51 No byline. "*The Adding Machine*." *Theatre Magazine* 37 (June 1923): 30-32+.
Excerpts from the play with accompanying production photographs.

R52 Farrar, John. "To See or Not to See." *Bookman* 58 (September 1923): 58.
The Adding Machine is a striking piece of expressionist theatre. However, scene five is offensive and other scenes read better than they play.

1924–1928

R53 Wright, Ralph. "Drama: Expressionism." *New Statesman* 22 (22 March 1924): 699-700.
As seen in the London Stage Society's production of *The Adding Machine*, expressionism is a continuance of melodrama. The technique produces good satiric effect in Rice's play, but loses its edge in the Elysium Fields scene. The ending of the play is

muddled as real characters are sacrificed to the abstractions necessary to expressionism.

R54 No byline. "News of the London and Paris Stages." *New York Times* 23 March 1924: 3
    Reporting on the London performance, the critic states that the first act of *The Adding Machine* was interesting, but the play as a whole was more an "interesting experiment ... than a commercial proposition."

R55 Broun, Heywood. "Close Harmony." *New York World* 1 December 1924.
    A humorous play that nevertheless possesses deep emotion and thought. An accurate portrayal of contemporary suburban life.

R56 Woollcott, Alexander. "Close Harmony." *New York Sun* 1 December 1924.
    The play seldom resorts to tricks and achieves moments of human intercourse wrought with great tact and intuition.

R57 Young, Stark. "Suburban Harmonies." *New York Times* 2 December 1924: 1.
    Close Harmony contains fine material composed with skill, courage and genuine stage instinct. The performance, however, dragged due to unbroken tempo of speeches, which usually came one after the other in the same time, the same distance apart, and from the same mental rhythm.

R58 Young, Stark. "Rudolph Schildkraut." *New York Times* 16 December 1924: 2.
    Rice's adaptation of *The Mongrel* loses the German version's social commentary, yielding, in combination with Winifred Lenihan's direction, a play "on an old-fashioned model. Only Schildkraut's performance stood out.

R59 Krutch, Joseph Wood. "Too Much Main Street." *Nation* 119 (17 December 1924): 686-87.
    Close Harmony follows a weak and insignificant protagonist into the bland social environment of suburbia in order to record the banal thoughts and actions of middle class life. Not only a bad play, but evidence of work that is leading American literature down a blind alley.

R60 No byline. "*The Mongrel*: Play of the Month." *Living Age* (3 January 1925): 70-76.
    Excerpts from the play along with production photographs. The play is attributed to Bahr, with no mention of Rice's name.

R61 Skinner, Richard. "*The Mongrel.*" *Independent* 114 (10 January 1925): 51.

Unlike O'Neill's *Desire Under the Elms*, Rice's adaptation of Bahr's story leaves room for the nobler elements of life which O'Neill ignores.

R62 J. B-W. "Drama: *The Adding Machine.*" *New Statesman* 30 (21 January 1928): 462-3.

Rice presents a good view of the "Americanization" of all culture in an industrial age. Zero, however, fails to interest us because the play lacks a sense of fate: his character is therefore nought. The Court Theatre production is a crude version of expressionism.

R63 No byline. "Mr. Hornblow Goes to the Play." *Theatre Magazine* 40 (February 1925): 62, 64.

Bahr's story, from which *The Mongrel* was adapted, must have been awfully thin. Schildkraut sometimes plays with fine realism, but the play is without substance.

R64 No byline. "Parisian Stage." *New York Times* 4 December 1927.

The Paris production of *The Adding Machine* suffers from Gaston Baty's aimless direction and the play's own lack of profundity.

R65 Jennings, Richard. "*The Adding Machine* at the Court Theatre." *Spectator* (7 January 1928): 47.

The play contains some excellent satire and racy humor, but Rice's use of expressionist method does not arouse empathy for Zero. In addition, British actors are puzzled by expressionism, and do not play it well.

R66 Atkinson, Brooks. "Who Killed *Cock Robin?*" *New York Times* 13 January 1928: 6.

The play is novel, attractive and uneven, with a humor that is entertaining but "unblended" and generic. Production makes for an agreeable evening.

R67 Morgan, Charles. "Mr. Freeman of *Cock Robin.*" *New York Times* 28 January 1928: 6.

Primarily a biography on Howard Freeman, currently playing in Rice's play.

R68 Krutch, Joseph Wood. "Heart to Heart." *Nation* 126 (1 February 1928): 130.

Cock Robin keeps its plot within the laws of probability and its characters produce a solid illusion of life. The plot unraveling is ingenious and the play is the best mystery of the season.

R69 Bellamy, F. R. "*Cock Robin.*" *Outlook* 14 March 1923: 423.
An enjoyable detective story with a highly satisfactory denouement. Play shows a good combination of humor and mystery.

R70 Brown, John Mason. "*Cock Robin.*" *Theatre Arts* 12 (March 1928): 172.
The play is stuck between satire and a murder mystery, languishing because it is wholly neither. The direction is monotonous.

1929-1933

R71 No byline. "Elmer Rice's Play Given at N.Y.U." *New York Times* 4 January 1929: 4.
The Passing of Chow-Chow performed at the University Playhouse at Washington Square.

R72 Anderson, John. "Street Scene." *New York Evening Journal* 11 January 1929.
The play builds engrossing trivialities into a rich and compelling drama. The play recreates frankly and unblinkingly the life and atmosphere of New York. A play of great feeling and compassion.

R73 Atkinson, Brooks. "On a Sidewalk of New York." *New York Times* 11 January 1929: 4.
Street Scene's unflinchingly honest and authentic characterizations and episodes (derived from New York street life) are to be praised. Despite its slight and unoriginal story, the play is "as vital, as fascinating, as comic, as the streets along which New York people live."

R74 Atkinson, Brooks. "Affairs on the West Side." *New York Times* 20 January 1929: 1.
Street Scene depicts the characters, settings and essences of New York street life accurately, unsentimentally and without judgement. Rice's casting and directing and Jo Mielziner's scenic design are also to be commended.

R75 Skinner, Richard. "The Play." *Commonweal* 9 (23 January 1929): 348-49.

Street Scene has extraordinary sweep and power. Its gripping illusion creates a mood of great intensity, producing a "surging drama of frightened, awestruck people." Realism is here used not to particularize a theme but to draw out its universal themes. Though the drama is brutal, it is also honest and true.

R76 Krutch, Joseph Wood. "Cross Sections." *Nation* 128 (30 January 1929): 142.

The Adding Machine was one of few successful expressionist plays, but since its arrival Rice has been more careful not to allow his characters to become abstractions. In *Street Scene* he renders characters as individuals, and achieves a startling power.

R77 Young, Stark. "*Street Scene*." *New Republic* 57 (30 January 1929): 296-98.

The set and writing are clever, and the directing is good. But although the play is entertaining, it is theatrical rubbish because its action is not believable. The last act takes the sting out of the play's realism and makes the spectator less fearful of reality.

R78 Carb, David. "Seen on Stage." *Vogue* 73 (2 March 1929): 114.

Street Scene has a bare, melodramatic plot but this fails to detract from the vitality of the play. Every scene has veracity and is filled with convincing dialogue. The first act is especially entertaining and absorbing.

R79 No byline. "*Street Scene*." *Catholic World* 128 (March 1929): 720-22.

Discarding Rice's earlier expressionistic style, the play is completely realistic. Its themes are dignified by being universal, and its characters exalted because they struggle to learn how to bring down the walls they put up to separate themselves from their own salvation.

R80 No byline. "The Editor Goes to the Play: *Street Scene*." *Theatre Magazine* 49 (March 1929): 50.

The play is gripping, holding audiences riveted as its action grows to a powerful conclusion. Rice presents real people with defects of character and real emotions. A spontaneous success.

R81 Clark, Barrett. "Broadway Brightens Up a Bit." *Drama Magazine* 19 (March 1929): 170.

Street Scene is the likely candidate for the Pulitzer. It is like a picture exhibition or a symphonic poem to one part of the city's life. There is no sentimentalizing in the play.

R82 Clark, Barrett. "*The Subway*." *Drama Magazine* 19 (March 1929): 171.

    The play pales in comparison to *Street Scene* and should have remained at the bottom of Rice's storage trunk. Sophie never comes across as anything more than a sentimental abstraction.

R83 Colum, Padraic. "*Street Scene*." *Dial* 84.3 (March 1929): 244-46

    The play contains a single intellectual idea, that of living our lives without making others miserable. However, the idea is not sufficiently illustrated or emphasized.

R84 Littell, Robert. "Brighter Lights." *Theatre Arts Monthly* 13.3 (March 1929): 164.

    Street Scene continues Rice's bold theatrical experimentation and produces a remarkable play with a wonderful set. The piece brings out the terrible loneliness of New York life.

R85 No byline. "The Play That Is Talked About." *Theatre Magazine* 49 (April 1929): 26-7+.

    Overview of *Street Scene* with cast list, production photos and excerpts.

R86 No byline. "The Editor Goes to the Play." *Theatre Magazine* 49 (April 1929): 47.

    The production of *The Subway* at the Cherry Lane Theatre on 25 January looks as if it transplants two characters from *Street Scene*, even though it was written in 1923. There are moments of real drama in *The Subway*, but is rambling.

R87 Woollcott, Alexander. "Elmer the Unexpected." *Collier's* 83 (4 May 1929): 15, 66.

    Street Scene will end up the most successful play on Broadway for the year and be awarded the Pulitzer. As he did when he broke in with *On Trial* in 1914, Rice has confounded the myth of Broadway by maintaining his reputation as a playwright. The history of the creation and production of *On Trial* was repeated as Rice struggled to get backing for *Street Scene*.

R88 Krutch, Joseph Wood. "The Pulitzer Prize." *Nation* 128 (5 June 1929): 680-81.

    The choice of *Street Scene* for the Pulitzer is not surprising since it is a good play that also captured popular audiences. O'Neill's *Dynamo* is more moving, but it would never be popular.

R89 No byline. "Elmer Rice Play in London." *New York Times* 15 July 1929.

1929-1933

London production of *The Subway* at the Lyceum Club well received. The brief American run was due to its inadequate staging.

R90 Young, Stark. "Quinteros and Rice." *New Republic* 60 (16 October 1929): 243-44.

Compares *See Naples and Die* with Serafin and Joaquin Quinteros's *A Hundred Years Old*. Rice's play exhibits skill, but its whimsical tone is inappropriate for its theme.

R91 Atkinson, Brooks "Elmer Rice Experiments With Comedy." *New York Times* 27 September 1929: 4.

While parts of *See Naples and Die* are quite enjoyable—amusing lives, sardonic incidents, and one or two of the performances—the comedy is scattered and the plot too contrived. Rice's first foray into comedy is hardly successful.

R92 Krutch, Joseph Wood. "Holiday." *Nation* 129 (16 October 1929): 409-10.

See Naples and Die looks pale alongside the still-running *Street Scene*, but it is a diverting play because of its extravagant improbability.

R93 No byline. "At Stanford This Summer." *Drama* 20 (October 1929): 20.

The production of *The Adding Machine* at the Tributary Theatre contained an admirable rhythm that contributed to exciting drama. Production photos included.

R94 Cour, Philip. "Street Scene and Other Paris Plays." *New York Times* 17 November 1929: 6.

The Paris production is a box office success in which French critics found ingenious inventiveness of form and a melodramatic effectiveness. But the plays overall lacks imagination in its emotional representation.

R95 No byline. "Stockholm Hails *Street Scene*." *New York Times* 29 November 1929: 5.

Swedish premiere met with a full house and great approval.

R96 No byline. "The Editor Goes to the Play." *Theatre Magazine* 50 (November 1929): 70.

See Naples and Die has the mood of a romantic operetta, but is faulted for the non-stop wisecracking of its chief characters. The play shows an American who refuse to talk seriously. Extravagant comedy is not Rice's metier.

R97 Sherriff, R. C. "Street Scene and Stage Scene." *Theatre Arts Monthly* 14.3 (February 1930): 164-66.

What accounts for the fabulous success of *Street Scene*? The realities of everyday life are more intensely interesting than what the imagination can conceive. Rice's play holds its audience until the murder plot interrupts as a theatrical trick.

R98   Trask, C. Hooper. "*Street Scene* in Berlin." *New York Times* 16 March 1930: 4.

The play is fundamentally American and its audience appeal depends on its recognizably American scenes. The German production was played with too much gusto and the German press found it to be "out of date naturalism."

R99   No byline. "*Street Scene* Hailed at London Premiere." *New York Times* 10 September 1930: 2.

London premiere has all the ingredients of a triumph, with unanimously favorable reviews focusing on its realism and novelty. The play is overflowing with life and novelty.

R100   Jennings, Richard. "The Theatre: *Street Scene*." *Spectator* 27 September 1930: 407.

The London production at the Globe Theatre created an appropriate atmosphere for the themes of the play. Rice's characters are like photographs snapped in a moment of time, yet he compresses a good deal of personality into these types.

R101   Morgan, Charles. "Mr. Rice's Play in London." *New York Times* 28 September 1930: 4.

Focuses on *Street Scene*'s murder story as a narrative flaw. The murder is too prominent to be woven with complete success into the general texture of the street scene; yet it cannot stand alone as the drama's subject. More psychological depth is required.

R102   Atkinson, Brooks. "And as for Freedom." *New York Times* 6 October 1931: 3.

The characters and dialogue in *The Left Bank* are intelligent and the theme handled with humor and understanding. The directing and performances are sensitive and honest, creating Rice's "maturest play" and the "modern American theatre at its best."

R103   Atkinson, Brooks. "Left Bank Culture." *New York Times* 18 October 1931: 1.

Defends *The Left Bank* against charges of dullness, responding that it favors extremely literate dialogue, honest characterization, and unadorned truth over theatrical pyrotechnics.

R104 Chatfield-Taylor, Otis. "Latest Plays." *Outlook* 159 (21 October 1931): 248.

The Left Bank is an example of stark realism characterized by a fine impartiality. There is little action, but intelligent talk and a good cast see the play through.

R105 Krutch, Joseph Wood. "Realism and Drama." *Nation* 133 (21 October 1931): 440-41.

Rice has the keenest eye for significant detail among contemporary playwrights. Sometimes this leads him, as in *The Left Bank*, to render his dramas too pictorially. When they become static, they lose force and power.

R106 Young, Stark. "Mr. Rice and Mr. Laughton." *New Republic* 68 (21 October 1931): 264-5.

The Left Bank is well directed by Rice, but the writing is formulaic and there is little new thought on the play's old theme. The dialogue consists mainly of statements.

R107 Atkinson, Brooks. "Elmer Rice Applying Pattern of *Street Scene* to a New York Lawyer's Office." *New York Times* 7 November 1931: 2.

Although *Counsellor-at-Law* is far too long and unsifted, Rice's capacity for observation makes this an engrossing play. Muni's performance is forceful and inventive, and is supplemented by Rice's pithy and revealing dialogue. The character portraits produce an animated play.

R108 Beebe, Lucien. "Mr. Rice Has Great Aversion for the Fraudulent Bohemian." *New York Herald Tribune* 8 November 1931: 1.

The Left Bank makes for competent drama, but Rice is too serious in his intellectual pretention. Rice himself says the play attacks, not real people, but caricatures of American types. He also enjoyed directing the play, and looks forward to one day producing his own work as well.

R109 Chatfield-Taylor, Otis. "Latest Plays." *Outlook* 159 (25 November 1931): 407.

Muni is nothing short of brilliant in *Counsellor-at-Law*. Rice has trouble realistically depicting snobs, but the play as a whole succeeds.

R110 Skinner, Richard. "*Counsellor-at-Law*." *Commonweal* 25 November 1931.

The story carries no important themes and exists simply as the tale of a not very important man. Nothing binds the characters together, making for clever portraiture but little cohesiveness.

R111   Wyatt, Euphemia Van Rensselaer. *"The Left Bank."* Catholic World 134 (November 1931): 210-11.
>Rice's realism in this play, as opposed to *Street Scene*'s, is unsavory and tiresome.

R112   Carb, David. "Seen on Stage." *Vogue* 78 (1 December 1931): 102.
>*The Left Bank* views American expatriates with only a tourist's eye, and the plot is too reminiscent of Greenwich Village dramas of the last decade.

R113   Krutch, Joseph Wood. *"Counsellor-at-Law."* Nation 133 (2 December 1931): 621-22.
>Comparing the play to Behrman's *Brief Moments* shows that Rice's skills are found in his depiction of atmosphere and character through language and gesture, while Behrman is better writing pure comedy.

R114   Young, Stark. "Three More Plays." *New Republic* 69 (2 December 1931): 69-71.
>*Counsellor-at-Law* succeeds because Rice does not strive for weighty truths. It is better than *Street Scene*, partly owing to Muni's bravura performance.

R115   No byline. "Ex-Lawyer." *Theatre Guild Magazine* 9 (December 1931): 6-8.
>*Counsellor-at-Law* has Rice's usual photographic sharpness, but the play is too long. Rice's direction and Muni's performance deserve credit.

R116   DeCasseres, Benjamin. *"The Left Bank."* Arts and Decoration 36.2 (December 1931): 76.
>This is Rice's best play to date, even thought it is somewhat unoriginal. Entertaining, with a fine performance by Kathleen Alexander.

R117   Fergusson, Francis. "A Month of the Theatre." *Bookman* 36 (December 1931): 302.
>*The Left Bank* should be seen despite Rice's ideas because the direction and casting are exemplary.

R118   Hutchens, John.   "Anchors Aweigh."   *Theatre Arts Monthly* 15.4 (December 1931): 975.
>*The Left Bank* is an elegantly simple play of extreme humanity. Rice shows again he is not content with existing theatrical conventions.

R119 No byline. "*Counsellor-at-Law*." *Dramatist* 23.1 (January 1932): 1446-48.

>The theme of the conflict between a man's life and his reputation is a solid one, but the play is talky and tedious. Rice is not adept at dramatizing his conflicts, choosing instead to have them discussed.

R120 No byline. "*The Left Bank*." *Theatre Guild Magazine* 19 (January 1932): 4.

>A most satisfying play, considering it is mainly dialogue. Capable performances and writing.

R121 No byline. "That Bauble Success." *Theatre Guild Magazine* 19 (January 1932): 18-19.

>Excerpts and production photos from *Counsellor-at-Law*.

R122 Field, Louise Munsell. "Our Laggard Theatre." *North American Review* 233 (January 1932): 151.

>*Counsellor-at-Law* is thoroughly delightful. Though the story is weak, the deftness and veracity of characters compensates for the lack of plot.

R123 Hutchens, John. "Greece to Broadway." *Theatre Arts Monthly* 16.1 (January 1932): 21-22.

>*Counsellor-at-Law* is reminiscent of *Street Scene* in its vigorous description and breadth of observation, but here the accumulated detail saps the play's energy and produces a tiring picture of reality.

R124 Wyatt, Euphemia Van Rensselaer. "*Counsellor-at-Law*." *Catholic World* 134 (January 1932): 470-71.

>Though unremarkable in terms of character and story, the play holds one's attention because of Rice's sharp attention to detail and his shrewd direction.

R125 No byline. "No. 81-284 at the Play." *New York Times* 27 March 1932: 2.

>Reviewer and fellow inmates vigorously applauded *Counsellor-at-Law* for its true-to-life characterizations, particularly that of George Simon. Audience appreciated Rice's accurate portrayal of the grimness of life.

R126 Verschoyle, Derek. "*See Naples and Die*." *Spectator* 2 April 1932: 476.

>Not a model of dramatic composition, the play still engages the audience by its extravagances. Olive Blakeney's performance is a marvel.

R127 Barratt, Louise Bascom. "*Counsellor-at-Law*." *Life* (May 1932): 43.

Like Marlene Dietrich, Muni is a delight for the theatrical palate.

R128 No byline. "*Counsellor-at-Law* Returns With Muni." *New York Times* 13 September 1932: 2.

Brief report on Paul Muni's return to cast and on new cast members.

R129 Atkinson, Brooks. "Literary Manners and Morals in Elmer Rice's Comedy Entitled *Black Sheep*." *New York Times* 14 October 1932: 6.

Finds theme and writing thoroughly conventional and acting "jangled." The play would have been better left unproduced. When Rice moves away from themes of social problems, the work suffers.

R130 Garland, Robert. "*Black Sheep*." *New York World-Telegram* 14 October 1932.

A thoroughly dispirited play that should have sent the audience home early.

R131 Lockridge, Richard. "*Black Sheep*." *New York Sun* 14 October 1932.

Rice has succumbed to the "conflict between the Artist and the Conventions" and produced the worst play of his career.

R132 Creighton, Peet. "The Up-Turn." *Theatre Arts Monthly* 16.5 (December 1932): 961-2.

Black Sheep is Rice's least interesting produced play, rendering reality with the lifelessness of commercial photography.

R133 Atkinson, Brooks. "Elmer Rice's *We, the People*, in Which the Causes for Revolution Are Described." *New York Times* 23 January 1933: 5.

The play is a bristling indictment of America's political system, and Rice himself is a "revolutionary." Despite overburdening the play and sacrificing clarity with a plethora of social causes and muddling character interrelationships, the performance is vigorous in its angry attack on social complacency.

R134 Brown, John Mason. "*We, the People*." *New York Evening Post* 23 January 1933.

The play left the audience cold, its proletarian themes lost on the patrician spectators at the Empire Theatre. A weak imitation of Coward's *Cavalcade*.

R135 Garland, Richard. "*We, the People*." *New York World-Telegram* 23 January 1933.

>   An over-written play chastising the very economic system which has made Rice wealthy.

R136 Lockridge, Richard. "*We, the People.*" *New York Sun* 23 January 1933.
>   A courageous and well-written play that, unfortunately, will not draw sufficient audiences to keep it alive because theatregoers have their own opinions and do not like being preached to.

R137 No byline. "*We, the People.*" *Time* 21 (30 January 1933): 22.
>   A "potent squawk," the play is written strongly and "at the top of its lungs." Crude but exciting theatre.

R138 Atkinson, Brooks. "*We, the People.*" *New York Times* 5 February 1933: 2.
>   The play raises the question of the place and function of the propaganda play. Even though not to current tastes, and despite obvious flaws in construction, however, the play shows Rice trenchant and grimly forceful in expressing his passions.

R139 Krutch, Joseph Wood. "The Prosecution Rests." *Nation* 136 (8 February 1933): 159-61.
>   As a sociological drama, *We, the People* is a disappointment. The play will not hold those who do not want to hear its message. The contemporary drama of protest must find a suitable method for drawing in its audience.

R140 Skinner, Richard. "*We, the People.*" *Commonweal* 27 (8 February 1933): 411.
>   Rice legitimately treats social ills in his drama and critics are wrong to fault him for his melodramatic tendencies. Rice has many objective facts to support his image of America in decline, and has every artistic right to dramatize them. However, he errs by directing his attack against deliberate hypocrisies, when it is actually a state of blindness and numb consciousness that leads people to act as they do.

R141 Parker, Robert Allerton. "Two Playwrights, With a Difference." *Literary Digest* 115 (11 February 1933): 15-16.
>   *We, the People* and Noel Coward's *Design for Living* are both successes. Overview of critical responses to Rice's play, focusing on flaws.

R142 "The Drifter." "Drama." *Nation* 136 (15 February 1933): 172.
>   Rice's forceful and unrelenting attack against complacency in *We, the People* has audiences expressing themselves vocifer-

ously. Rice minces no words in this stirring and effective attack on contemporary life.

R143   Young, Stark. "*We, the People.*" *New Republic* 74 (15 February 1933): 18019.

Rice's ideas are less bourgeois here than in *The Left Bank*. The script confronts topical issues directly, and the episodic structure provides moments of real drama. Rice is able to motivate the audience's indignation, and this serves to help one discover empathy for the characters.

R144   No byline. "*We, the People.*" *World Tomorrow* 16.8 (22 February 1933): 176.

The play gives a clear picture of contemporary life with all its social inequities and injustices. The ending sacrifices drama for propaganda, but the play remains a penetrating picture of the American scene.

R145   Chaffee, Edmund. "*We, the People.*" *Christian Century* 1.7 (22 February 1933): 231.

A powerful indictment of the present situation in America. Rice should be commended for his evenhanded treatment of religion and the character of the priest.

R146   No byline. "Returning to *We, the People.*" *Literary Digest* 115 (4 March 1933): 19.

Propaganda plays are not currently popular, but Rice's play can be defended as such. [Atkinson's defense of the play is excerpted.]

R147   Carb, David. "Seen on Stage." *Vogue* 81 (15 March 1933): 73.

We, the People is grim, humorless and violent with a black vs. white mentality when it comes to capitalism and the proletariat. A sprawling play containing a number of scenes that should be eliminated.

R148   DeCasseres, Benjamin. "*We, the People.*" *Arts and Decoration* 38.5 (March 1933): 58.

Rice at his Marxist worst. A play in which "Art is Art and Art is Propaganda." A lumbering play filled with platitudinous drivel.

R149   Smith, Alfred E. "*We, the People.*" *New Outlook* 161 (March 1933): 10.

The play is a propaganda piece which attempts to justify the hopelessness and despair of the disenfranchised. The radical intent of the play is not realized, and audiences should let Rice know that, having been given an education and success in America, he should "direct his energy to better purposes than inciting his less fortunate fellow citizens to violence."

R150 Wyatt, Euphemia Van Rensselaer. "*We, the People.*" *Catholic World* 139 (March 1933): 717.

Even though the play is biased, it is interesting and undergirded with real emotion. Helen's willingness to succumb to Collins' entreaties, however, is an unfair depiction of women.

R151 No byline. "London Sees Rice Play." *New York Times* 11 April 1933: 3.

The production of *Counsellor-at-Law* at the Picadilly conveyed the bustle of American law. *The London Times* admires the play for its lively pace and interesting story.

R152 Vershoyle, Derek. "Stage and Screen." *The Spectator* 20 April 1933: 618.

Counsellor-at-Law is excellently written and researched.

R153 McCarty, Barclay. "Three Designs for Living." *Theatre Arts Magazine* 17 (April 1933): 258-60.

We, the People is not quite successful aesthetically or as a work of social commentary. Although written with vitality and sincerity, it is not creative enough to instill sympathy in an audience not concerned with social problems. In the third act Rice swerves from his story and disrupts the play's unifying idea.

R154 Morgan, Charles. "The London Letter." *New York Times* 6 May 1933: 5.

Although the opening scene of the London production of *Counsellor-at-Law* moved too fast and developed too slowly, the play eventually captured the audience with its narrative energy.

R155 McKenna, Kenneth. "Character Acting of Acid Sharpness." *Stage* (May 1933): 20-21.

We, the People, despite containing fifty characters spread out across twenty scenes, succeeds at getting great performances from American actors. Rice has melded their diversity into a swift-moving drama. Whatever disunity remains in the play serves as a reflection of the American culture it represents. Rice should be congratulated for showing how rugged individualism needs to be replaced by collective responsibility.

1934–1938

R156 Atkinson, Brooks. "Elmer Rice on the Attempted Assassination of a Dictator in *Judgment Day*." *New York Times* 13 September 1934.

Despite early moments of excitement and humor, the play is a workmanlike melodrama which runs into excess and confusion.

R157 Brown, John Mason. "*Judgment Day.*" *New York* Post 13 September 1934.

The play is unintentionally funny and so old fashioned that audiences felt they were in the distant past.

R158 Gabriel, Gilbert. "*Judgment Day.*" *New York American* 13 September 1934: 2.

Rice's parable is a bold protest and rousing accusation against fascism.

R159 Garland, Robert. "Nazi Regime Target of *Judgment Day.*" *New York World Telegram* 13 September 1934: 2.

The play indulges in no end of shouting. Being hysterically opposed to Hitler does not make a play.

R160 Hammond, Percy. "*Judgment Day.*" *New York Herald Tribune* 13 September 1934.

A moving and emotional experience, though Rice lets his enthusiasm for justice overwhelm his dramatic technique.

R161 Lockridge, Richard. "*Judgment Day.*" *New York Sun* 13 September 1934: 1.

A play to make your sympathies and hair stand on end. Loud and violent, the play is compelling.

R162 Garlin, Sender. "Change the World." *Daily Worker* 18 September 1934: 5.

Judgment Day fails because it does not expose fascism as the last stage of a decaying capitalism. Rice continues to promote bourgeois ideology even while he critiques it.

R163 No byline. "Tyrants Taken for Ride in Melodrama *Judgment Day.*" *Newsweek* 4 (22 September 1934): 28.

Rice's indictment of tyranny is loud, hysterical and laced with strong language and emotions. The vigor of Rice's passion is appreciated by audiences.

R164 Atkinson, Brooks. "*Judgment Day.*" *New York Times* 23 September 1934.

Reports that opinion regarding the play is polarized between those appreciating its social awareness and those who find it bombastic.

R165 Skinner, Richard. "*Judgment Day.*" *Commonweal* 20 (28 September 1934): 509.

    The play is marred by Rice's black and white juxtapositions of good and evil, and could use more subtlety of expression. Still, this is melodrama at its best, even though the antagonists are villains rather than the more dangerous zealots.

R166 Krutch, Joseph Wood. "Joseph Wood Krutch Says." *Nation* 139 (29 September 1934): 20.

    In *Judgment Day* Rice gives the audience nonstop resounding excitement.

R167 Parker, Robert Allerton. "Elmer Rice Rowels His Critics." *Literary Digest* 118 (29 September 1934): 20.

    Judgment Day is the only play of the season to energize critical debate. The play is obviously in response to the Reichstag fire, and makes for gripping melodrama.

R168 Skinner, Richard. "The Play." *Commonweal* 29 (September 1934): 509.

    Judgment Day brims with hate and anger toward the injustices taking place in Europe. The play contains exaggerations, but the emotional effects are staggering.

R169 Krutch, Joseph Wood. "Tempest in Teapots." *Nation* 139 (3 October 1934): 392.

    Judgment Day is fine melodrama and treats an important theme, but this is not sufficient to make it an important play. Rice is prone to sermonizing.

R170 Mannes, Marya. "Vogue's Spolight." *Vogue* 84 (15 October 1934): 51.

    Judgment Day is profoundly arrogant in the way it reduces a serious theme, totalitarianism, to crude melodramatic caricature. The characters are puppet-like, and the play contains too much sordid reality without a balance of beauty.

R171 Atkinson, Brooks. "Elmer Rice's *Between Two Worlds* Takes Place on an Ocean Liner." *New York Times* 26 October 1934: 2.

    The play is over-scrupulous and descriptive. Although desultory in its character development, the play contains good conversation that is pithy and stimulating.

R172 Wyatt, Euphemia Van Rensselaer. "The Drama." *Catholic World* 140 (October 1934): 89-90.

    Judgment Day is a loud play that kept audiences thumping and clapping with excitement.

R173 No byline. "New Plays." *Time* (5 November 1934): 32.

Between Two Worlds has no purpose, plan or development. It is satisfying only as social commentary.

R174 Krutch, Joseph Wood. "The Grand Canal." *Nation* 139 (14 November 1934): 574.

Between Two Worlds is pure discussion about social purpose, without a hint of dramatic flair.

R175 Gruber, Ide. "All Around Town." *Golden Book* 20 (November 1934): 506.

Judgment Day has plenty of detail, but it overwhelms the play. The cast, however, is capable.

R176 Mannes, Marya. "Vogue's Spotlight." *Vogue* 84 (15 December 1934): 51.

Between Two Worlds is an example of photographic realism, and contains some appalling but humorous characters. The play is not boring, but cannot seem to make up its mind to be realistic or an obvious fiction.

R177 No byline. "Broadway in Review." *Theatre Arts Monthly* (December 1934): 900-902.

Between Two Worlds is exciting and provocative.

R178 No byline. "*Between Two Worlds*." *Stage* 12.28 (December 1934): 28-29.

Made of good parts, but the play overall does not develop its themes quickly enough. The conflict of Western capitalist sexual mores as opposed to those of the Communist east shows that perhaps life in Russia is not so grim after all.

R179 Alexander, Leon. "Two Authors Between Two Worlds." *New Theatre* (December 1934): 19-20.

Though Rice still belongs to the "breed of *Nation* liberals," *Between Two Worlds* shows greater clarity of social thought. Rice is too timid, however, to move beyond exposing capitalism to where he can summon the masses to a true revolution.

R180 Isaacs, Edith. "Playhouse Gates." *Theatre Arts Magazine* 18 (December 1934): 900-902.

Between Two Worlds is "Russian" in its implied drama. The play keeps heart and mind active, especially in scenes where Schildkraut is featured.

R181 Wyatt, Euphemia Van Rensselaer. "*Between Two Worlds*." *Catholic World* 140 (December 1934): 342-43.

The play never realizes its potential, though Schildkraut's acting is sensational.

1934–1938 153

R182 No byline. "Elmer Rice Play a Mirth Provoker." *New York Times* 25 November 1935: 8.

    The London premiere of *Not for Children* is a curious hybrid play that amuses the audience for more than three hours. The play-within-a-play, reminiscent of Pirandello or Shaw, is stimulating and provocative, but the play is unlikely to receive further production.

R183 Verschoyle, Derek. *"Not for Children." Spectator* 29 November 1935: 336.

    The production at the Fortune Theatre in London was presented as a satire on theatre and a disquisition on dramatic criticism. Rice dissects the nature of dramatic illusion on stage, but the play is too long and the satire diluted.

R184 Morgan, Charles. *"Not for Children." New York Times* 22 December 1935: 3.

    The London performance was a "devil of dullness" because it loses itself in Pirandellian mystification. Rice, however, infuses the play with intellectually vivacious dialogue, though his wit is too dry for the audience.

R185 Morgan, Charles. "Far from the WPA's Most Madding Strife: Mr. Rice's *Not for Children* Gets a Mild Spanking in London." *New York Times* 29 December 1935: 2.

    This piece skillfully juggles planes of illusion and is at times successfully farcical, but the wit is generally too complex for the audience. Rice's presentation of man as an economic unit is a misapplication of his art.

R186 Smith, Hugh. "The News From Dublin." *New York Times* 29 December 1935: 1.

    The Gate Theatre's production of *Not for Children* maintains an appropriate pace for a play of ideas. The cast, notably Hilton Edwards and Merriel Moore, were fine in a satisfying production.

R187 No byline. "Still Not for Children." *New York Times* 1 March 1936: 2.

    The Los Angeles production was received with laughter, applause, and some bewilderment. Although amusing, even profound as a theatrical satire, it does not hang together as a play and is likely to find a diminishing audience.

R188 No byline. "Melodrama by Rice Praised in London." *New York Times* 20 May 1937: 1.

Judgment Day rings true, lending this gripping production a poignancy and effectiveness that help make it one of the best plays seen in London in a long time.

R189   Fleming, Peter. "Totalitarian Justice on the Stage." *Spectator* (28 May 1937): 987-88.

Judgment Day, playing first at the Cottage Theatre before moving to the West End, deserves attention because Rice avoids the pitfalls of dogma and never subordinates his drama to it. Though first licensed in 1933, the play still thrills audiences with its condemnation of totalitarianism.

R190   Morgan, Charles. "*Judgment Day*: Notes, Mainly Favorable, On the English Production of Mr. Rice's Play." *New York Times* 20 June 1937: 7.

A political play applicable to tyrants of Right and Left, a suspenseful and brave rejection of the rationales by which tyrants justify their tyranny. It lacks, however, full ironic insight and hence the stature of high tragedy.

R191   Ormsbee, Helen. "Elmer Rice, Absent Four Years, Back on Broadway with Play." *New York Herald Tribune* 27 November 1938: 1.

In *American Landscape* Rice forces the audience to go back to past to ask questions. A play with a strong sense of form and great craftsmanship.

R192   Darlington, W. A. "*Judgment Day*." *New York Times* 3 December 1938: 7.

The play has substance and audiences have lauded the performances.

R193   Anderson, John. "Mr. Rice's New Play." *New York Evening Journal* 5 December 1938: 1.

American Landscape shows Rice wiser and more moderate than in past plays, but as drama the play's noble efforts fall short.

R194   Atkinson, Brooks. "Elmer Rice Speaks for the Democratic System in *American Landscape*." *New York Times* 5 December 1938: 2.

A diffuse drama, possibly suffering from a poor first night performance. Possesses ambitious design and exalted purpose, but the result is a tepid drama.

R195   Brown, John Mason. "*American Landscape*." *New York Post* 5 December 1938: 2.

The play is a sincere sermon which defends great principles, but Rice avoids deeper problems in favor of easy dramatic responses.

R196 Coleman, Robert. "*American Landscape.*" *New York Daily Mirror* 5 December 1938.

A worthy theme, but the play too often takes on aspects of pageant and forsakes drama.

R197 Lockridge, Richard. "*American Landscape.*" *New York Sun* 5 December 1938: 1.

Rice succeeds brilliantly at handling perilous material, creating a moving and rich allegory.

R198 Mantle, Burns. "*American Landscape.*" *New York News* 5 December 1938: 2.

A courageous experiment containing a "challenging patriotism," the play nevertheless has trouble accommodating the role of the ghosts.

R199 Watts, Richard Jr. "*American Landscape.*" *New York Herald Tribune* 5 December 1938: 1.

There is sincerity and earnest patriotism in the play, but it is "curiously superficial" and unpersuasive.

R200 Whipple, Sidney. "*American Landscape.*" *New York World Telegraph* 5 December 1938: 1.

Play has little dramatic power and is filled with garrulous characters.

R201 Atkinson, Brooks. "Elmer Rice Takes the Long View Toward Democracy in *American Landscape.*" *New York Times* 11 December 1938: 1.

Although philosophically strong the play is a weak drama, suffering from too many characters, a structural division of audience focus between farm and factory, and a deus ex machina ending that does not solve the human problem of will that Rice delineates.

R202 No byline. "New Play in Manhattan." *Time* 12 December 1938: 31-32.

American Landscape attempts to be a sermon, but achieves only a fitful eloquence.

R203 Krutch, Joseph Wood. "Prodigal's Return." *Nation* 147 (24 December 1938): 700.

American Landscape is lifeless and prosaic. Though the theme is worthy the play never goes beyond being a simple essay.

R204 Young, Stark. "*American Landscape.*" *New Republic* 97 (28 December 1938): 230.
>A tedious play that is banal and over-explicit. Even Rice's directing is flat.

R205 Vernon, Grenville. "*American Landscape.*" *Commonweal* 30 (December 1938): 273.
>The play requires a fantastic touch, and Rice is no fantasy writer. The theme is admirable, but the style is inadequate.

1939–1943

R206 Wyatt, Euphemia Van Rensselaer. "*American Landscape.*" *Catholic World* 148 (January 1939): 472-73.
>The framework of the play gives Rice the chance to give all voices a hearing. He is a writer of cultivated wisdom, and a lack of box office success is not a sufficient criterion for judging the play.

R207 Gilder, Rosamond. "Hell's Paving Stones." *Theatre Arts Monthly* 23.3 (February 1939): 86-89.
>*American Landscape* has an able cast but the ghosts are not used to dramatic effect and the characters are flat symbols.

R208 Angoff, Charles. "*American Landscape.*" *North American Review* 247 (Spring 1939): 155-56.
>An intellectual farina that bulges with college debating-team speeches and mere recitations. The speeches never become an integral part of the drama, and the play as a whole shows that Rice does not feel strongly enough about the play's themes to treat them creatively.

R209 Atkinson, Brooks. "Lincoln's Prairie Years." *New York Times* 23 October 1939: 1.
>Robert Sherwood's *Abe Lincoln in Illinois* is a profoundly moving portrait of America's spiritual heritage, thanks in part to Rice's "illuminating" direction.

R210 No byline. "*Two on an Island* Opens: Betty Field and John Craven in Elmer Rice's Play in Boston." *New York Times* 16 January 1940: 4.
>Boston received this "gay new play" warmly in its pre-New York tryout.

R211 Atkinson, Brooks. "Elmer Rice's *Two on an Island* is a Fable of Young People in Manhattan." *New York Times* 23 January 1940: 2.

> This "pleasant fable," while skillfully produced, presents a skin-deep view at an ambling pace. Actress Betty Field gives the whole play a "captivating radiance."

R212 Brown, John Mason. "Elmer Rice's New Play, *Two on an Island*." *New York Post* 23 January 1940.

> Rice provides an entertaining guide to the City, and though the play lacks drama the inspired conversation and good acting keep it afloat.

R213 Lockridge, Richard. "Elmer Rice's *Two on an Island* Opens at Broadhurst." *New York Sun* 23 January 1940.

> The play reveals a good deal of sympathy and tenderness. Even though it is essentially a diffuse compilation of irrelevancies, it shows genuine feeling and provides some good love scenes.

R214 Mantle, Burns. "*Two on an Island* Little Old Story of Little Old New York." *New York Daily News* 23 January 1940.

> The theme is old but Rice's appealing characters and the acting of Betty Field deliver a fresh take on the subject.

R215 Watts, Richard Jr. "Manhattan Idyll." *New York Herald Tribune* 23 January 1940.

> *Two on an Island* shows Rice's eye for humor and his sympathetic sensibility, and reveals the playwright in a "romantic and optimistic mood."

R216 Whipple, Sidney. "*Two on an Island* a Pleasant Comedy." *New York World Telegram* 23 January 1940.

> The play is unpretentious and ingeniously structured. Rice reveals a more tolerant view of life in a play that is not profound but still pleasant.

R217 Atkinson, Brooks. "Polished Rice." *New York Times* 28 January 1940: 2.

> *Two on an Island* is a tame play, though a pleasant and discursive little story imaginatively designed by Jo Mielziner, expertly directed by Rice, and enchantingly acted by Betty Field and John Craven.

R218 Krutch, Joseph Wood. "Drama." *Nation* 150 (3 February 1940): 136.

> *Two on an Island* re-establishes Rice as the best contemporary playwright for capturing the accent of modern urban life. Meilzner's set complements the production, and helps establish Rice as a top comic writer.

R219 Atkinson, Brooks. "Two Plays About the Young People Who Adopt Manhattan as Foster Parent." *New York Times* 4 February 1940: 1.

Two on an Island chronicles a young couple's adventures in Manhattan with affectionate humor and a reporter's eyes and ears, but is disappointingly superficial.

R220 No byline. "New Play in Manhattan." *Time* 35 (5 February 1940): 41.

Two on an Island shows Rice "unembattled," creating a picturesque play that is slick rather than sincere. The picture of New York is exhaustive, but never alive. Likens the play to Rice's novel *Imperial City*.

R221 Nathan, George Jean. "Two on a Theme." *Newsweek* 15 (5 February 1940): 34.

Two on an Island shows Rice forsaking his favorite drama of social significance for a popular success, at which the playwright succeeds shamelessly. Although the set and production are first-rate, this is "way beneath his earlier dramatic level."

R222 Vernon, Grenville. "*Two on an Island.*" *Commonweal* 31 (9 February 1940): 348.

The play reveals much that is engaging, but it needs drastic cutting. An intense, rather than deep play, it is the most enjoyable work Rice has written in years.

R223 Gilder, Rosamond. "Brain and Brawn." *Theatre Arts Monthly* 24.3 (March 1940): 167-68.

Two on an Island is an engaging comedy in which Rice deliberately produces sketchy characters in order to allow the actors, especially Luther Adler as Ormont, to shine.

R224 Wyatt, Euphemia Van Rensselaer. "*Two on an Island.*" *Catholic World* 150 (March 1940): 729-30.

The play lacks any idealism, and nothing more lacking in charm can be imagined than the character of Adler. The play is insincere and unworthy of Rice.

R225 No byline. "*Flight to the West* Opens: New Rice Play Receives an Ovation in Princeton." *New York Times* 15 December 1940: 5

The play opened at the McCarter Theatre to long applause and close to a dozen curtain calls. Cast, especially Paul Henreid, were excellent and the set quite effective.

R226 Atkinson, Brooks. "Elmer Rice's *Flight to the West* Dramatizes the Passenger List of an Atlantic Clipper." *New York Times* 31 December 1940: 1.

The play is one of Rice's most stirring dramas. The vigorous dialogue reflects human agony as well as the bitter truths of the times. The play expresses passionate convictions and profoundly moving human feeling. Cast brilliantly and acted straightforwardly, Rice deserves credit for direction as well. The most absorbing play of the season.

R227 Brown, John Mason. "*Flight to the West* Staged at Guild." *New York Post* 31 December 1940.
Though interesting as discussion, the play is insufficiently dramatic. A good intellectual forum of topical issues.

R228 Lockridge, Richard. "Elmer Rice's *Flight to the West* Opens at Guild Theatre." *New York Sun* 31 December 1940.
A faulty, but deeply moving play. Engrossing thought and discussion, but little action.

R229 Mantle, Burns. "*Flight to the West* Adds a Tense Drama to the Broadway List." *New York Daily News* 31 December 1940.
Rice shows an exalted integrity in the play by moderately tempering his arguments.

R230 Watts, Richard Jr. "Journey by Clipper." *New York Herald Tribune* 31 December 1940.
Flight to the West is a contemporary and passionate play that nevertheless becomes monotonous. There are moments of great emotion when Rice delineates the mental state of his characters as they are caught in the torrent of history.

R231 Whipple, Sidney. "*Flight to the West* New Propaganda Play." *New York World Telegram* 31 December 1940.
The audience is already prepared to agree with the principles of the play, and so the themes are rendered too obvious.

R232 Freedley, Morris. "*Flight to the West*." *New York Morning Telegraph* 1 January 1941.
Although the first act is electrifying, the play bogs down in a morass of talk and melodrama.

R233 Gibbs, Walcott. "Forum in the Sky." *New Yorker* 16 (11 January 1941): 31.
Rice's anti-Nazi play is exhaustive and passionate, but is expressed in the rhetoric of the crusader and in a dramatic form lacking necessary dramatic suspense.

R234 Marshall, Margaret. "*Flight to the West*." *Nation* 152 (11 January 1941): 53.
After a slow opening the play finds an appropriate pace to lead it to its satisfying denouement. The writing, however, never

rises above average anti-fascist commentary. At times, Rice indulges in the demagoguery he opposes.

R235 Ormsbee, Helen. "Rice Moves His Trip on Clipper Up a Year for Wartime Play." *New York Herald Tribune* 12 January 1941: 1, 3.
> Discusses why Rice chose to treat serious material in *Flight to the West*, and finds complexity in characters.

R236 No byline. "*Flight to the West.*" *Time* (13 January 1941): 57.
> More recitation than drama, the play is propagandistic and undramatic.

R237 O'Hara, John. "Rice to the West." *Newsweek* 17 (13 January 1941): 52.
> *Flight to the West* represents Rice at his polemical worst. The characters spout unrealistic nonsense in long, periodic sentences. The play also lacks action.

R238 Vernon, Grenville. "*Flight to the West.*" *Commonweal* 33 (17 January 1941): 328.
> The work contains praiseworthy sentiments, excellent acting and effective staging. For all that it remains a melodrama rather than a fully-fleshed out drama.

R239 Atkinson, Brooks. "*Flight to the West.*" *New York Times* 19 January 1941: 1
> The play is absorbing and the acting and writing moving, dealing with "shattering realities" of the day. The outstanding drama of the season on Nazi fanaticism. Although Rice's effects are powerful, they could be more poetic. However, Henreid's Nazi is portrayed with superb insight and "trenchant exactitude."

R240 Allen, Kelcey. "*Flight to the West.*" *Women's Wear Daily* (January 1941).
> The play is an inspired commentary on the present historical situation, told with great bravado and courage.

R241 Young, Stark. "Three Flights." *New Republic* 104 (January 1941): 84-5.
> Though full of serious intention, the play fails to establish a single tone or dramatic mood. The playwright lacks creative imagination and has nothing original to say. The language is trite and banal. American playwrights must find a way to universalize the theme of the war, while at the same time making their characters genuine created images of the present time. Mielziner's sets and Eleanora Mendelssohn's performance are the only standouts.

R242 No byline. "*Flight to the West.*" *Stage* 1 (February 1941): 28-9.

A rare instance of a contemporary calamity being successfully transposed into dramatic terms. Imaginative and sensitive, played on a wonderful set. (Includes production photos.)

R243 Wyatt, Euphemia Van Rensselaer. "*Flight to the West.*" *Catholic World* 152 (February 1941): 595-96.

Rice shows himself again unwilling to shut his eyes to shadows, and writes with vigor and conviction about pressing issues. Rice is masterful at blending subjective and objective action, and this allows him to escape charges of defeatism.

R244 Gilder, Rosamond. "Crime, Women and Song." *Theatre Arts Monthly* 25.3 (March 1941): 184-85.

Flight to the West concentrates significant action in compelling language to produce effective theatre.

R245 Anderson, John. "Paul Muni Gives Richer Performance in Fine Revival of Elmer Rice's Play." *New York Journal American* 25 November 1942.

This production of *Counsellor-at-Law* is superior to the original because Muni's performance has matured and the play moves faster.

R246 Kronenberger, Louis. "Mr. Muni Resumes His Law Practice." *New York "PM"* 25 November 1942.

Counsellor-at-Law is still a lively and unpretentious play after eleven years.

R247 Lockridge, Richard. "Rice's *Counsellor-at-Law* Is Revived at Royale Theatre." *New York Sun* 25 November 1942.

The play is not quite what is used to be and comes across as too leisurely and less tense.

R248 Mantle, Burns. "*Counsellor-at-Law* Revived to Repeat First Success." *New York Daily News* 25 November 1942.

Almost as stimulating as the first production, the revival is more refined and Muni's performance more polished.

R249 Nichols, Lewis. "*Counsellor-at-Law.*" *New York Times* 25 November 1942: 2.

This revival with Paul Muni in the role he originated twelve years earlier, is as "taut" and "tidy" as the original. The evening is Muni's, and it is a "good evening in the theatre."

R250 Pihodna, Joseph. "Old Fave Returns." *New York Herald Tribune* 25 November 1942.

Some of *Counsellor-at-Law* shows its age, but Muni knows how to capture the play's high moments.

R251 Rascoe, Burton. "Paul Muni is Starred in *Counsellor-at-Law*." *New York World Telegraph* 25 November 1942.

The play allows Muni to submerge himself into his role more successfully than anything else he has tried. Rice's revisions in this production, however, make the play less taut than the original.

R252 Waldorf, Wilela. "Paul Muni Reappears in Rice's *Counsellor-at-Law*." *New York Post* 25 November 1942.

The play is still the best vehicle for Muni's talents.

R253 No byline. "Old Play in Manhattan." *Time* 40 (7 December 1942): 55.

The new *Counsellor-at-Law* keeps its engaging hokum and Muni's brilliant performance intact.

R254 Kerr, Walter. "*Counsellor-at-Law*." *Commonweal* 37 (11 December 1942): 206.

The revival of the play retains the original's entertainment value. Muni's performance is especially noteworthy, in part because he delivers in a low murmur the "few unnecessary blasphemies" that remain in the play.

R255 Gassner, John. "Upswing in the Theatre." *Current History* 3.17 (January 1943): 455-58.

The revival of *Counsellor-at-Law* provides a vivid portrait of reality without many larger implications. Simon is not an endearing character, and the play as a whole lacks the profundity of a contemporary play like Wilder's *The Skin of Our Teeth*.

R256 Gilder, Rosamond. "Old Indestructible." *Theatre Arts Monthly* 27.1 (January 1943): 16-17.

Praises Muni's realistic acting in revival of *Counsellor-at-Law*.

R257 "M. T. W." "*Counsellor-at-Law*." *Catholic World* 164 (February 1943): 453.

The revival may be better than the original, since audiences are not as shocked by the subject matter. Muni is still wonderful and has a fine supporting cast.

R258 No byline. "*Counsellor-at-Law*." *Independent Woman* 22 (May 1943): 155.

The revival has the same audience appeal as the original. Rice still does not draw effective female characters, as seen by Simon's wife.

R259 Barnes, Howard. "Hospital Scene." *New York Herald Tribune* 16 September 1943.

A New Life is more tricky than profound, and a tedious show with only flashes of intensity.

R260 Chapman, John. "With Wife's Help, Elmer Rice Bears a Baby in *A New Life*." *New York Daily News* 16 September 1943.

An earnest but unconvincing play with uneven and stilted writing.

R261 Garland, Robert. "*A New Life* Presented at Royale Theatre." *New York Journal American* 16 September 1943.

Field is wonderful, but the play plods along, weighed down by meager attempts at social significance.

R262 Kronenberger, Louis. "A Visit From a Lame Stork." *New York "PM"* 16 September 1943.

A New Life is a halting play which does not announce its theme until after the birth scene. Clumsy and garrulous, though Field is superb.

R263 Morehouse, Ward. "Elmer Rice's Nine-Scene Drama *A New Life* Begins Playwright's Season." *New York Sun* 16 September 1943.

This hollow and talky piece is a great disappointment, though it is Betty Field's best role to date.

R264 Nichols, Lewis. "Elmer Rice Discussed *A New Life* in the Drama Which Opened Last Night." *New York Times* 16 September 1943.

Though Rice is an excellent draftsman, this play fails because its characters are stereotyped and the action too pat.

R265 Rascoe, Burton. "*A New Life* a Bright Little Thing, Though Mr. Rice Gets Profound Again." *New York World Telegram* 16 September 1943.

A pleasant but unexciting play that thinks it is more profound than it is. Rice is a capable craftsman, not a thinker.

R266 Waldorf, Wilela. "Elmer Rice's *A New Life* at Royale." *New York Post* 16 September 1943.

Not one of Rice's more inspired works. The themes of class struggle and a woman's labor pains do not mesh well, and Rice still has not learned to draw effective portraits of the plutocrats he loves to chide.

R267 Rascoe, Burton. "*A New Life* Illustrates Deplorable Trend." *New York World Telegraph* 18 September 1943: 1.

>The play shows another good dramatist trying too hard to become a "Deep Thinker" providing audiences with "Great Messages." Prefers *On Trial*.

R268 No byline. "Two More on the Aisle." *Newsweek* 22 (27 September 1943): 96.

>*A New Life* is a strange and tedious diffusion of ideas. The peepshow version of the birth scene might impress audiences, but as a whole the play fails to move the spectator.

R269 Young, Stark. "The Ham Hangs High." *New Republic* 109 (27 September 1943): 426-27.

>*A New Life* is drawn all in black and white and therefore stultifying as theatre. Rice, in his twenty-fourth play, is still impervious to the values of life and art. Even the birth scene lacks genuine effect. Betty Field's performance was quite convincing.

R270 Phelan, Kappo. "*A New Life*." *Commonweal* 38 (1 October 1943): 585.

>The play is nine sterile scenes which make no sense, a cheap and outmoded attack on capitalists.

R271 Marshall, Margaret. "Drama." *Nation* 157 (2 October 1943): 157.

>*A New Life* is supposed to be serious but is actually comic in its ineptitude. Women's natural functions do not qualify for dramatic material, and the play as a whole strikes a low, rather than moral, tone.

R272 Gilder, Rosamond. "A New Season, *A New Life*." *Theatre Arts Monthly* 27.11 (November 1943): 641-44.

>Rice is to be praised for daring to dramatize issues of importance. However, he is too drawn to a reportorial style and does not invest his characters with life. The experimental birth scene is tedious and fails utterly to express the experience of childbirth. In the denouement, Rice fails to bring the opposing characters into direct confrontation, thus attenuating his message.

R273 Wyatt, Euphemia Van Rensselaer. "*A New Life*." *Catholic World* 158 (November 1943): 187.

>The portrayal of parenthood is pleasant but the theme of class tension is not effectively drawn out.

1944–1948

R274 Barnes, Howard. "Dream Show." *New York Herald Tribune* 15 December 1945.

    A comedy of "sustained delight" replete with wit and substance. Not a simple play, but Rice's writing keeps the action fluid and interesting.

R275 Chapman, John. "*Dream Girl* a Dream of a Play." *New York Daily News* 15 December 1945.

    A captivating comedy which includes Field in every scene.

R276 Garland, Robert. "Elmer Rice's *Dream Girl* Opens at Coronet." *New York Journal American* 15 December 1945.

    A thoroughly satisfactory blending of Rice's comic writing and Field's acting. Great gaiety and gusto mixed with wit and caustic social commentary.

R277 Morehouse, Ward. "Elmer Rice Writes a Deft and Delightful Comedy in *Dream Girl*." *New York Sun* 15 December 1945.

    Rice returns to hit-writing by mingling realism and fantasy and by using an ingenious set. A solid hit.

R278 Nichols, Lewis. "Elmer Rice Discusses *A New Life* in the Drama Which Opened Last Night at the Royale." *New York Times* 15 December 1945: 2.

    The plot follows a set formula, draws characters in a casual, even caricaturist fashion. The play is staged and, in some cases, performed well, but is generally disappointing.

R279 Rascoe, Burton. "Elmer Rice Writes Bright Comedy." *New York World Telegraph* 15 December 1945.

    Rice, the most vocal critic of America and American theatre produces in *Dream Girl* a witty and charming comedy that celebrates bourgeois values. An unusually literate play which teaches that reality and illusion must be properly balanced.

R280 Waldorf, Wilela. "Elmer Rice's *Dream Girl* Stars Betty Field—And How!" *New York Post* 15 December 1945.

    Though the play is often confusing and a rather elementary representation of the female psyche, Field's performance guarantees a hit and a later motion picture version.

R281 Kronenberger, Louis. "A Jolly Night With the Rice's." *New York "PM"* 16 December 1945.

Following Thurber's lead, Rice produces a female version of the "Walter Mitty" stories. After a slow opening, the play picks up pace. Field is the best actress on Broadway.

R282 Nichols, Lewis. "Glad Tidings: *Hamlet* and *Dream Girl* Arrive in Time to Help Brighten the Season." *New York Times* 23 December 1945: 1.

The play is funny, with scenes containing just the right amount of burlesque to be winning. Field's performance is outstanding although some of the scenes could bear a little cutting.

R283 No byline. "*Dream Girl*." *Time* 46 (24 December 1945): 77-8.

The first entertaining night of the new season, the play shoots for pure fun and hits the mark. Field shows verve and versatility.

R284 No byline. "The Play is a Dream." *Newsweek* 26 (24 December 1945): 88.

Dream Girl is a thoroughly delightful comedy, with Field handling a variety of roles in her daydream sequences.

R285 No byline. "*Dream Girl*." *Life* 19 (31 December 1945): 36-8.

Rice's merriest play yet. [Photos of Rice and Betty Field, along with production photos, are included.]

R286 Young, Stark. "*Dream Girl*." *New Republic* 113 (31 December 1945): 903.

The play contains scenes and themes of great variety, and Field's ability to play with versatility make the play a success. Rice's writing is "gentle" and shows flashes of charm and witty affection.

R287 Krutch, Joseph Wood. "Drama." *Nation* 162 (12 January 1946): 54.

Dream Girl will probably not remain one of Rice's greatest successes, but by keeping the fantasy theme simple the play achieves a moderate success. Rice must have co-written the work with Field, because she is so natural in the part.

R288 Phelan, Kappo. "*Dream Girl*." *Commonweal* 43 (15 February 1946): 456-57.

The play is funny, psychologically apt and amusing. However, a serious tone is sometimes called for. Rice's innovations are brilliant in both script and set. The only modern play in which soliloquy is effective.

R289 Gassner, John. "Theatre Arts." *Forum* 105 (February 1946): 564.

Dream Girl is "sentiment masking as modernism." By conventional standards it is a good play, but when it pretends to experimental art it fails.

R290 Gilder, Rosamond. "Matter and Art." *Theatre Arts Monthly* 30.2 (February 1946): 78-79.

Dream Girl deals only with the surface of the protagonist's psychological being. Still, Betty Field provides a tour de force of rapid shifts in mood and feeling.

R291 Wyatt, Euphemia Van Rensselaer. "*Dream Girl.*" *Catholic World* 162 (February 1946): 454-55.

Polished entertainment which allows the spectator to bask in Rice's wit and Field's fine acting.

R292 Atkinson, Brooks. "The New Play." *New York Times* 10 January 1947: 2.

The musical version of Street Scene has a superb cast and "simple and honest" lyrics. The maturity of Kurt Weill's compositions and Rice's script create a magnificent musical.

R293 Barnes, Howard. "Bravo." *New York Herald Tribune* 10 January 1947.

Street Scene is an uneven but exciting folk drama, akin to *Porgy and Bess*. Though the music has an uneven texture, this is an important modern opera which should have been done long ago.

R294 Chapman, John. "Musical *Street Scene* a Splendid and Courageous Sidewalk Opera." *New York Daily News* 10 January 1947.

A work of great integrity which refuses to be bound by limitations of Broadway musical. Excellent lyrics and effective music propel this work of great imagination.

R295 Garland, Robert. "The Play." *New York Journal American* 10 January 1947.

The musical version of *Street Scene* fails to synchronize into a unified whole and thus never realizes its potential as an "American *opera comique*." The score is brilliant.

R296 Hawkins, William. "*Street Scene* Has Operatic Touch." *New York World Telegram* 10 January 1947.

If one ignores the work's designation as a dramatic musical and views it as an opera, the piece is intensely interesting. Both the score and the singers' performances are outstanding.

R297 Morehouse, Richard. "*Street Scene* Offered at Adelphi." *New York Sun* 10 January 1947.

A highly impressive folk opera with great singing. A credit to the work of the Playwright's Company.

R298 Watts, Richard Jr. "Elmer Rice's *Street Scene* Is Not Helped by Music." *New York Post* 10 January 1947.

Rice's play was wonderful as a meticulously drawn portrait of real life, but is unsatisfying as a musical. Weill's score obscures the emotional effects of the play.

R299 Kronenberger, Louis. "*Street Scene* Set to Music Is Still Lively Theatre." *New York "PM"* 12 January 1947.

Though unlike the original production, the musical retains the interest of the audience. As a "folk opera," the production highlights atmospheric music and strong lyrics.

R300 Lardner, John. "Theatre." *New Yorker* 22 (18 January 1947): 44.

The musical version of *Street Scene* is not a dramatic musical, but an opera complete with recitative. It contains an ambitious score and a good book, but it is not as energizing as the original play.

R301 Atkinson, Brooks. "New York to Music: Mr. Rice's *Street Scene* and Mr. Weill's Score." *New York Times* 19 January 1947: 1.

Under Charles Friedman's versatile direction, this musical version of Rice's Pulitzer Prize-winning play is a masterpiece of stage expression. The "comic and fantastic" score by Kurt Weill, perceptive text by Rice, and lyrics by Langston Hughes combine to make this the finest musical since *Oklahoma*.

R302 No byline. "Street Opera." *Newsweek* 29 (20 January 1947): 84.

The musical of *Street Scene* is better understood as an opera. The music and singing are so good and the production so professional that the original impact of the play is not diminished. A gamble that has paid off handsomely.

R303 No byline. "*Street Scene* the Musical." *Time* 49 (20 January 1947): 69.

More folk opera than musical, the piece succeeds despite Weill's often heavy-handed score. Though the songs and dances distract one from the play, Rice's script retains enough vitality to see the performance through.

R304 Brown, John Mason. "Saying It with Music." *Saturday Review of Literature* 30 (1 February 1947): 24-26.

The musical version of *Street Scene* sways uncertainly between opera and dramatic realism. The drama retains its power when it is spoken as dialogue, but the music is too operatic when it should derive from popular music. The result is that the operatic and the realistic contradict each other.

R305 Wyatt, Euphemia van Renneslaer. *Street Scene.*" *Catholic World* 164 (February 1948): 453.

> The musical is highly significant in the history of American drama. One cannot remember the play now without also hearing Weill's music. Rice's story grows emotionally with the musical and dance accompaniment.

R306 "J. S." "Cherry Lane Revives *The Adding Machine.*" *New York Times* 18 November 1948: 2.

> The Cherry Lane revival of the play is a successful production, capably directed and performed, which nevertheless will not appeal to casual theatre-goers. The play remains esoteric even after twenty-five years.

1949–1953

R307 Atkinson, Brooks. "Betty Field and Elliot Nugent Play Leading Parts in Elmer Rice's *Not for Children.*" *New York Times* 14 February 1951: 2.

> This revival is well-performed, but the script is aimlessly boring. Contains a few bits of amusing satire, but most of it is ponderous and unwieldy.

R308 Chapman, John. "*Not for Children* Is the Greatest Theatre Curiosity Since Jo-Jo." *New York Daily News* 14 February 1951.

> The play is without sense or intention, except perhaps as an expression of whimsy.

R309 Coleman, Robert. "*Not for Children* Satire on Theatre's Faults." *New York Daily Mirror* 14 February 1951.

> The play is a novel satire with some biting moments, but the force of the play is lost in stage trickery. Obviously indebted to Pirandello, Rice's play carries its metaphysical jokes too far.

R310 Guernsey, Otis Jr. "Full of Nots!" *New York Herald Tribune* 14 February 1951.

> *Not for Children* is a frustrating and baffling attempt at surrealism which is so convoluted that it defies explanation.

R311 Hawkins, William. "*Not for Children* Opens at Coronet." *New York World Telegram* 14 February 1951.

> The play is formless and without resolution. One cannot fathom what Rice had in mind when he wrote this arbitrary and shapeless play.

R312 McClain, John. "New Elmer Rice Play Not For Adults Either." *New York Journal American* 14 February 1951.
>A confused and adolescent work of theatre. Understands why director must come out to explain the play [nb: the critic sees Bromberg's apologia as existing outside Rice's script, as an actual attempt to intervene and explain the play].

R313 Watts, Richard Jr. "Elmer Rice Looks at Theatre." *New York Post* 14 February 1951.
>*Not for Children* contains an entertaining premise, but its satire lacks true satiric sense. Rice's self-mockery is not comic, and his attacks on theatre are not timely since the kind he mocks went out of style twenty years ago.

R314 Gibbs, Walcott. "The Mighty Fall." *New Yorker* 27 (24 February 1951): 66.
>*Not for Children* has no discernible subject or theme, just a great deal of arch literary conversation without purpose.

R315 No byline. "*Not for Children*." *Newsweek* 37 (26 February 1951): 49.
>Rice should have left the script in his trunk, and the Playwrights' Company should have shown better judgment. The performers are confused and uncomfortable with the script.

R316 No byline. "*Not for Children*." *Time* 57 (26 February 1951): 50.
>A foolish play that should not have been produced. Rice's two-hour prank is filled with cliched satire.

R317 Kerr, Walter. "*Not for Children*." *Commonweal* 53 (9 March 1951): 541-42.
>The play has no point to it and becomes hopelessly entangled in order to obscure its poverty of ideas. An idle and self-indulgent work.

R318 No byline. "*Not for Children*." *Theatre Arts Monthly* 25.4 (April 1951): 19.
>The hopelessly entangled plays-within-plays expresses through form the inseparability of illusion and truth in the theatre. However, the humor is juvenile and the themes tired.

R319 Atkinson, Brooks. "Judy Holliday Acts in Rice's *Dream Girl* Put On at the City Center." *New York Times* 10 May 1951: 1.
>Every aspect of this revival — humorous dialogue, sensitive direction, and first-rate supporting cast — contributes in making this one of the most pleasant offerings of the year.

R320 Chapman, John. "Judy Holliday Shifts Characters and Plays a Wistful *Dream Girl*." *New York Daily News* 10 May 1951.
>Holliday's performance is a success, though Rice's revised version of the play needs cutting.

R321 Coleman, Robert. "*Dream Girl* Is Off-Beat Without Betty Field." *New York Daily Mirror* 10 May 1951.
>The original play was developed for Field, and Holliday's performance is too broad to recapture its comic touch.

R322 Garland, Robert. "A Disappointing Play and Performance." *New York Journal American* 10 May 1951.
>Holliday does not do the revival of *Dream Girl* justice, and the lack of Rice's original direction leaves the play trite and tiring.

R323 Guernsey, Otis Jr. "Not Born Yesterday." *New York Herald Tribune* 10 May 1951.
>The new production of *Dream Girl* has its bright moments, but an erratic performance by Holliday and foggy production in a too-large house make this a dispiriting evening.

R324 Hawkins, William. "Judy Holliday Proves Some *Dream Girl*." *New York World Telegram* 10 May 1951.
>Holliday plays this demanding role well, making the character tender rather than funny.

R325 Watts, Richard Jr. "Revival of Elmer Rice's *Dream Girl*." *New York Post* 10 May 1951.
>This version lacks the dexterity of acting and directing that made the original so successful. Reviews of the original were probably overstated, as the script now seems plodding and labored.

R326 Kerr, Walter. "*Dream Girl*." *Commonweal* 54 (25 May 1951): 165.
>Holliday is not well-suited to Rice's script or the cavernous City Center Theatre. Her range is too narrow to attempt the versatility needed for the role.

R327 Wyatt, Euphemia Van Rensselaer. "*Dream Girl*." *Catholic World* 173 (July 1951): 306-7.
>Even though Holliday attempted to play up the farce values of the play, the production is lacking in vigor.

R328 Atkinson, Brooks. "*The Grand Tour*." *New York Times* 11 December 1951: 2.
>The first half of the play is much more original and entertaining than the second, which gets bogged down in tawdry writ-

ing. The leading players do well, but the supporting cast is generally very weak. A disappointing show.

R329 Chapman, John. "*The Grand Tour*." *New York Daily News* 11 December 1951.

    The play would have succeeded better as a novel. Its complications are undramatic and unexciting.

R330 Coleman, Robert. "*The Grand Tour* an Amiable but Spotty Drama." *New York Daily Mirror* 11 December 1951.

    When the play strives for humor it succeeds, but when it becomes melodramatic it falters. The large Beck Theatre is not an appropriate venue for this intimate play.

R331 Hawkins, William. "*The Grand Tour* Best at Its Simplest." *New York World Telegram* 11 December 1951.

    Most of the play is witty, but its plot complexities bog the action down. Clarity is lost in the second half of the play.

R332 Kerr, Walter. "The Play." *New York Herald Tribune* 11 December 1951.

    Rice, who used to discuss ideas with his audiences, merely chats with them in *The Grand Tour*. The play is too casual and unanimated, revealing Rice in a reminiscent and garrulous mood.

R333 McClain, John. "Does Not Justify Noble Effort." *New York Journal American* 11 December 1951.

    The Grand Tour is confused and talky, though the actors bring energy to their tedious roles.

R334 Watts, Robert Jr. "A Trip to Europe With Elmer Rice." *New York Post* 11 December 1951.

    The Grand Tour, although sincere, achieves only the level of wistful romance. The play lacks variety and depth and is sparse in its emotional effects.

R335 Gibbs, Walcott. "*The Grand Tour*." *New Yorker* 27 (22 December 1951): 49-50.

    The play covers a good deal of ground, but apart from revealing that Rice has traveled extensively, there is little to recommend the play.

R336 No byline. "*The Grand Tour*." *Newsweek* 38 (24 December 1951): 43.

    The opening scenes contain great freshness, but this dissipates in the second act. The result is a pedestrian drama containing gravid sentiment but little emotion.

R337   Kerr, Walter. "*The Grand Tour.*" *Commonweal* 55 (28 December 1951): 299.

   A gentle excursion into small talk without the warmth of character and wit of dialogue Rice usually provides.

R338   Nathan, George Jean. "Mr. Nathan Goes to the Play." *Theatre Arts Monthly* 36.2 (February 1952): 73.

   The Grand Tour is excessively verbose and trite, made worse by poor performances.

1954–1958

R339   Atkinson, Brooks. "Joan Tetzel and Tom Helmore Starred in Elmer Rice's play *The Winner*." *New York Times* 18 February 1954: 1.

   Although the acting, direction, design and even writing are thoroughly competent, the story line is predictable and insubstantial. Below the level of Rice's best work.

R340   Chapman, John. "Elmer Rice's *The Winner* Infirm." *New York Daily News* 18 February 1954.

   The scenes in the law court are vivid, but when the play strives for comedy it falters. The plot wanders and Rice's conclusions are unsatisfying.

R341   Coleman, Robert. "Elmer Rice's *The Winner* Opens at the Playhouse." *New York Mirror* 18 February 1954.

   This comedy of values begins by looking promising, but ends up only half a winner. Rice does not pursue his themes rigorously.

R342   Hawkins, William. "Elmer Rice Drama Comes to Playhouse." *New York World Telegraph* 18 February 1954.

   A loquacious play, but only the courtroom scenes come alive.

R343   Kerr, Walter. "*The Winner.*" *New York Herald Tribune* 18 February 1954.

   Rice's tone is ambiguous and the audience does not know if the play is comedy or melodrama. Spectators are constantly readjusting to Rice's changing attitudes toward his characters.

R344   McClain, John. "Play Mild Success." *New York Journal American* 18 February 1954.

   Despite a slow beginning, *The Winner* picks up pace in the second half and proves mildly successful as a melodrama.

R345 Watts, Richard Jr. "Troubles of a Girl and Her Money." *New York Post* 18 February 1954.
>Rice continues to slump with *The Winner*. He asks provocative moral questions but deals with them superficially.

R346 Gibbs, Walcott. "*The Winner*." *New Yorker* 30 (27 February 1954): 78-80.
>Rice's dialogue is unrealistically garnished and too arch and all the characters are repugnant. The courtroom scene picks up speed, but by then it is too late.

R347 No byline. "*The Winner*." *Newsweek* 43 (1 March 1954): 71.
>The play is notable only because it marks Rice's fortieth year in the theatre. His status as one of the finest American writers is not justified here. The story is pedestrian, and though the trial scenes are expertly crafted, the rest of the play is monotonous and pointless.

R348 Hewes, Henry. "Lessons for Losers." *Saturday Review of Books* 37 (6 March 1954): 25.
>Eva is an unsympathetic heroine in *The Winner*, and the dialogue of the play is better suited to the artificialities of drawing room comedy. As serious commentary on urban existence the play has merit.

R349 No byline. "*The Winner*." *America* 90 (20 March 1954): 664.
>Rice has lost his zing and this play cannot sustain the interest of the audience.

R350 No byline. "*The Winner*." *Theatre Arts Monthly* 38.4 (April 1954): 16.
>The play shows an old pro providing sprightly dialogue and humor to hackneyed themes.

R351 Atkinson, Brooks. "Fantasy Minus Sting: *Adding Machine* Adds Up to Enjoyment." *New York Times* 10 February 1956: 1.
>Much of what was startlingly original about the play in 1923 has become commonplace by 1956. But the play, revived at the Phoenix Theatre, continues to be engrossing. The writing is vigorous and alive, and the production well-acted and directed.

R352 Aston, Frank. "Rice Borrows From *Hamlet*." *New York World Telegram* 26 November 1958.
>Despite dialogue that is sometimes too high-toned, Rice has produced in *Cue for Passion* an interesting drama.

R353 Atkinson, Brooks. "Modern Hamlet Legend: Elmer Rice's *Cue for Passion* Arrives." *New York Times* 26 November 1958: 2.

1954-1958

The play is a modernization of the Hamlet legend in which differences from the original remind viewers that they are more civilized, tepid, rational, and prosaic than Hamlet and his contemporaries. The production is well-staged and acted.

R354 Chapman, John. "Elmer Rice's *Cue for Passion* Gives Hamlet New Complex." *New York Daily News* 26 November 1958.

Rice's modern Hamlet is merely a spoiled brat without heroic resonance, and the play is verbose.

R355 Coe, Robert Allen. "*Cue for Passion*." *Dramatist* 16 (26 November 1958): 6.

A tedious reworking of Shakespeare's masterpiece.

R356 Coleman, Robert. "Windy Reworking of *Hamlet* by Rice." *New York Daily Mirror* 26 November 1958.

The drama of *Cue for Passion* is obscured by cascades of polysyllabic rhetoric that the actors cannot handle. Modern playwrights should not try to improve on Shakespeare.

R357 Kerr, Walter. "*Cue for Passion*." *New York Herald Tribune* 26 November 1958.

A modified success, but Rice's teeter-totter tends to bring Shakespeare down while Freud goes up, and vice versa.

R358 McClain, John. "Rice Scores Again in Absorbing Drama." *New York Journal American* 26 November 1958.

Cue for Passion contains full characterizations and provocative themes. Rice's writing is thoughtful and at times humorous.

R359 Watts, Richard Jr. "Hamlet in Southern California." *New York Post* 26 November 1958.

Cue for Passion is a taut and compelling drama with excellent casting and acting. No slavish imitation of *Hamlet*, but a true reworking of its themes into modern idioms.

R360 Tynan, Kenneth. "*Cue for Passion*." *New Yorker* 34 (6 December 1954): 116-17.

A literary curiosity, the play owes more to Freud than to Shakespeare. Tony is a weak character because he is never in jeopardy and does not represent a larger community. Rice's psychiatric themes are reductionist.

R361 Atkinson, Brooks. "*Cue for Passion*." *New York Times* 7 December 1958: 1.

The differences between our civilization and Shakespeare's necessitated that Rice write with more directness, economy and less flourish in the play than one finds in *Hamlet*. The result is a superb production and a fascinating lesson for students of writing and culture.

R362   No byline. "Shakespeare and Freud." *Newsweek* 52 (8 December 1958): 66.

Though the *Hamlet* plot in *Cue for Passion* is carried off to a marked degree, the play is strongest when Rice adds his own psychiatric insights to the Shakespearean themes. The play's occasional verbosity is saved by a good cast.

R363   No byline. "*Cue for Passion.*" *Time* 72 (8 December 1958): 77-8.

The play is interesting enough to hold attention, but there is too little Shakespeare and too much Freud in it. The action becomes a blueprint of human behavior, rather than a rich tapestry of possibilities.

1959–1963

R364   No byline. "*Cue for Passion.*" *Theatre Arts Monthly* 43.2 (February 1959): 21-22.

The play provides a fascinating character study of its protagonist, but overall is too self-consciously literate and verbose.

R365   Wyatt, Euphemia Van Rensselaer. "*Cue for Passion.*" *Catholic World* 188 (February 1959): 418.

Though the character of Horatio is tiresome in his psychoanalyzing, the play is exciting from start to finish.

R366   No byline. "*Street Scene* (musical)." *Musical America* 79 (October 1959): 29-30.

The revival has quickly closed.

R367   Gellert, Roger. "Religion and Sex." *New Statesman* 6 October 1961: 530.

The production of *The Winner* at the Pembroke Theatre was improbable and choked with coincidences. Though of dubious morality, the play was nevertheless good natured and engaging.

R368   No byline. "Play by Elmer Rice in World Premiere." *New York Times* 5 May 1963: 6.

Love Among the Ruins was staged by the Stagers company at the University of Rochester. Robert Hogan directs the play, with Rice in attendance.

1964–1974

R369 Gussow, Mel. "Rice's Social Consciousness: W.P.A. Theater Offers *The Adding Machine*." *New York Times* 5 December 1970: 1.

    Although effectively acted and directed, this production suffers from the obsolescence of its innovations. Nevertheless, the Workers of the Players Art are to be praised for staging this historically significant work at their new Bowery playhouse.

1974–1995

R370 Goldman, Rowena. "Fringe." *Drama* 138 (October 1980): 56.

    The production of *The Adding Machine* at the Gate Theatre reveals similarities between Rice's dialogue and characters and those of Ionesco.

R371 Gussow, Mel. "*Counsellor* Sets Precedents." *New York Times* 26 July 1977.

    The revival of Rice's 1931 realist masterpiece still retains the vigor of character found in the original.

R372 Eder, Richard. "*Counsellor-at-Law*." *New York Times* 8 September 1977.

    The play still captures the rhythms of life in a modern office.

R373 Jaques, Damien. "Rep Puts New Relevance into *Dream Girl* Comedy." *Milwaukee Journal* 25 October 1993.

    The production turns the play into a "contemporary theatre piece that resonates with feminism." The blending of outrageous fantasy and sobering reality seems appropriate for current American culture.

R374 Joslyn, Jay. "*Dream Girl* Among Best Rep Plays." *Milwaukee Sentinel* 26 October 1993.

    With a proper tongue-in-cheek approach to Rice's text, the play remains bright and sprightly.

R375 Spencer, Gordon. "Women in Transition: Rep Enacts Stories of Growth." *Shepard Express* 11 November 1993.

    Dream Girl is fine play with a clever theme, loaded from the outset with humorous possibilities. Along with other shows in the 1993 season, Rice's play dramatizes the processes of growth in interesting female characters.

R376 Fricker, Karen. "In Kentucky, a Director's Derby." *Variety*, 6-12 February 1995.

Anne Bogart's production of *The Adding Machine* gives the play a mediated, postmodern book while revivifying its stark image of life.

Annotated Secondary Bibliography: Books, Articles, Sections

The following secondary bibliography of books, articles, and sections concentrates on Rice's career in the theatre.

1914–1918

1919–1923

S01 Mantle, Burns, ed. *The Best Plays of 1920-21*. Boston: Small, Maynard & Co., 1921.
     The Theatre Guild's production of *The Adding Machine* was among the most successful shows of the year.

S02 No byline. "The Cold Gray Dawn." *New York Times* 25 March 1923: 1.
     Brief discussion of expressionism, stating that the claims that *The Adding Machine* qualifies as expressionism would be laughed out of Germany. Calls the play a laudable attempt, and the faults of the play are blamed on Rice's own lack of depth as a playwright.

S03 Corbin, John. "Expressionism and the Cartoon." *New York Times* 1 April 1923: 1.
     Sees the merit of *The Adding Machine* in its having familiarized its audiences with the techniques of expressionism. The symbolism of the play, however, is unimaginative.

S04 Parker, Robert Allerton. "Expressionism: Good, Bad, and Indifferent." *The Independent* 110 (14 April 1923).
     Expressionism is not more appropriate for delineating the inner significance of incidents, since realist playwrights do this

without sacrificing clarity and objectivity. *The Adding Machine* reveals a "volcanic scorn of sane and sober craftsmanship" and thus denies the audience the slow revelation of the playwright's vision. Expressionism is pretentiously modernist, yet nothing in it is new.

S05 Farrar, John. "To See or Not to See." *Bookman* 57 (May 1923): 319-20.

Criticizes *The Adding Machine* for satirizing other cultural views of heaven. Points to possible sources for Rice's representation of Elysium.

S06 Rice, Elmer. "*The Adding Machine.*" *Theater: Illustrated Magazine* 37 (June 1923): 30-47.

Playscript and production photos.

1924–1928

S07 Dukes, Ashley. *The Youngest Drama: Studies of Fifty Dramatists.* Chicago: Charles L. Sergel, 1924.

Expressionism was the only proper vehicle for conveying the subjective states of a "nobody" like Mr. Zero in *The Adding Machine*. What the style loses in dialogue it makes up for in the depiction of mental attitude.

S08 Dickinson, Thomas H. *Playwrights of the New American Theater.* New York: Macmillan, 1925. [Reprinted 1967]

In "The Mystery of Form," *On Trial* is assessed as an example of the virtues of chronological displacement. With the emerging view of people as a repository of unconscious memories, dreams and passions, such experimentation is necessary and welcome. Expressionism, too, as used in *The Adding Machine*, will allow the externals of events to be torn away to reveal the more important internal realities of modern life.

S09 Montrose, Moses J. *The American Dramatist.* Boston: Little, Brown & Company, 1925.

Brief mention of Rice as following O'Neill's lead in theatrical experimentation.

1929–1933

S10 Krutch, Joseph Wood. "Drama: Cross Section." *Nation* 128 (30 January 1929): 142.

Expressionism, the logical extreme of the naturalistic method, reduces individual characters to types and symbols. In

Street Scene Rice allows the characters to be both individuals and abstractions. Although naturalism ultimately is unimportant as a dramatic method, Rice shows an enviable mastery over the form.

S11 Atkinson, Brooks. "Honor Where Honor Is Due." *New York Times* 19 May 1929: 1.

Advocates *Street Scene* for the Pulitzer Prize in drama. The play is the most finely-wrought chiaroscuro of middle-class life that an American dramatist has drawn. Praises the play's realism, its intuitive grasp of character and its loose, fluid format.

S12 No byline. "Pulitzer to Street Scene." *Town Crier* 1 July 1929: 1.

Congratulates Rice on his ability to manipulate such a large cast and unwieldy plot.

S13 Brown, John Mason. *Dramatis Personae*. New York: Viking, 1929.

Brief mention of the Guild Theatre's production of *The Adding Machine*, and of Rice as a "theatre propagandist."

S14 Mantle, Burns. *Best Plays of 1928-1929*. New York: Dodd, Mead 1929.

Street Scene was the sole successful play in January.

S15 No byline. "Sumner Assailed as Paid Vice Hunter: Elmer Rice, Playwright, Attacks Censorship Advocate in Debate at Luncheon." *New York Times* 25 January 1931: 25.

Rice's speech at the National Republican Club turned into an attack on Sumner's prudery and a statement against censorship.

S16 No byline. "Leading Churchmen Scored on Theatre: Elmer Rice Assails Cardinal Hayes and Dr. Manning for Views on Stage Decency." *New York Times* 19 February 1931: 20.

In an address to the Columbia University Writer's Club, Rice attacked the "hysterical ranting" on decency in the theatre. Opposing the Mastick censorship bill, Rice argued that the current theatre emphasizes plays of ideas.

S17 Krutch, Joseph Wood. "The Kinds of Comedy." *Nation* 131 (2 December 1931): 621-22.

Contrasts Rice's realism with S. N. Behrman's more stylized work. Rice is a great mimic of the language and gestures of contemporary types, which helps him to create admirable atmosphere.

S18 Mantle, Burns. *Best Plays of 1930-31*. New York: Dodd, Mead, 1931.

Mentions revival of *Cock Robin* at the Pasadena Community Playhouse.

S19   Levin, Meyer. "Elmer Rice." *Theatre Arts Monthly* 16.2 (February 1932): 54-62.
Contrasts Rice with O'Neill, distinguishing the latter as an "artist's artist" and the former as the "public's artist." Rice's career has gone through three phases of commercial plays (up to *The Adding Machine*): "art" plays (up to *Street Scene*) and plays that compound surface realism, romantic content, melodramatic plot and expressionistic characterization. Rice is both more humane and more American than O'Neill, and his work shows a gradual deepening of purpose.

S20   Mantle, Burns. *The Best Plays of 1931-32*. New York: Dodd, Mead, 1932.
The Left Bank was the first dramatic success of the season.

S21   Atkinson, Brooks. "Some Reasons Why Men Suffer." *New York Times* 5 February 1933: 1.
In *We, the People* Rice vigorously proclaims his baleful political mood. The play may not be to Broadway taste, but its bluntly propagandistic view is nevertheless powerful. The conclusion dramatizes with great eloquence Rice's "grim force" as a playwright.

S22   Parker, Robert Allerton. "Returning to *We, the People*." *Literary Digest* 115 (4 March 1933): 19.
Review of current critical views of the play.

S23   Mantle, Burns. *The Best Plays of 1933-34*. New York: Dodd, Mead, 1933.
Otto Kruger's performance in *Counsellor-at-Law* was the outstanding success of the season. *We, the People*, on the other hand, finds Rice too wedded to his convictions and prejudices. The play deserved greater success.

1934–1938

S24   Ross, George. "Elmer Rice Back from Europe, Defers for a Couple of Years His Soviet Theatre Plan." *New York World-Telegram* 23 May 1934: 2.
Disparages Rice's plans to create a "superior bolshevik theatre" and comments on success of London production of *Counsellor-at-Law*.

S25   Atkinson, Brooks. "Elmer Rice's Judgment Day in the Service of Justice—The Season's First Bombshell." *New York Times* 23 September 1934: 1.

[Note: After his earlier unfavorable review, Atkinson was sent by Rice a copy of Douglas Reed's *The Burning of the Reichstag*, upon which Rice modeled his trial scenes. Rice and Atkinson then wrote simultaneous views of the play. For Rice's response see A33.]

The play is turgid and barnstorming in style, though it will arouse debate and opinion. Rice's roaring attack on Hitlerism is not as subtle as Reed's. The play also requires less clumsy staging and direction.

S26   Freeman, Joseph. "Elmer Rice." *New Theatre* (September 1934): 7.
Predicts that Rice will move away from merely liberal sentiments expressed in *We, the People* to more overtly Marxist analysis in *Judgment Day*.

S27   Krutch, Joseph Wood. "Tempests in Teapots." *Nation* 139 (3 October 1934): 391-92.
Reviews *The Bride of Torozko* with *Judgment Day*. Rice's play is good melodrama, but not serious drama. Takes Rice to task for his published defense of the play.

S28   Garland, Robert. "Elmer Rice Needs Another *Street Scene*." *New York World-Telegram* 3 November 1934: 1.
Counters Rice's recent attacks on theatre critics by pointing out past positive reviews of his early plays. Feels Rice is too smitten with Russian theatre, which is not the theatre for Broadway.

S29   Kunitz, Joshua. "The Theatre." *New Masses* 20 November 1934: 26.
Rice would enjoy large and receptive audiences if he would turn away from liberal dogma and compose true Marxist dramas.

S30   Coe, Kathryn and William Cordell, eds. *The Pulitzer Prize Plays*. New York: Random House, 1935.
Brief biographical portrait of Rice.

S31   Mantle, Burns. *Best Plays of 1934-35*. New York: Dodd, Mead & Co., 1935.
Plot summaries and critical reception of *We, the People* and *Judgment Day*.

S32   No byline. "Mr. Rice Quits in Row Over WPA Drama." *New York Times* 24 January 1936: 15.
Reports on issues related to Rice's resignation.

S33   No byline. "Politics Charged to the WPA by Rice." *New York Times* 25 January 1936: 7.

Report of Rice's press conference, at which he accused the government of "partisan politics" in the running of the WPA theatre program.

S34 No byline. "Mr. Rice Resigns." *Nation* 142 (12 February 1936): 174.
Rice's resignation is an embarrassment to the administration. Questions policy of linking relief and cultural objectives in this manner.

S35 No byline. "More Red Propaganda From the Raw Deal." *New York Evening Herald* 18 March 1936: 1.
Commenting on Rice's interest in Russian theatre, the article argues that theatre is a powerful communist propaganda machine that promotes class hatred in New York as well as in Moscow.

S36 *The Theatre Guild Anthology*. New York: Random House, 1936.
Brief biographical portrait of Rice.

S37 Lawson, John Howard. *The Theory and Technique of Playwriting*. New York: G. P. Putnam's Sons, 1936.
We, the People contains a poor climax, because the final speech is an abstract statement which is never wedded to action. *Judgment Day*, though containing a vital and exciting climax, reveals Rice's weakness as a thinker, as it shows that he sees history not as a process of social forces but as the expression of the immutable morality of individuals.

S38 Mantle, Burns. *Best Plays of 1935–36*. New York: Dodd, Mead and Co., 1936.
Brief mention of Pasadena Playhouse production of *Not for Children*.

S39 Drew, Elizabeth. *Discovering Drama*. New York: W. W. Norton, 1937.
Rice is grouped with Odets and Galsworthy as writers who expose, not the eternal troubles of mankind, but the "suffering which a man-made social system imposes on him."

S40 Quinn, Arthur Hobson. *A History of the American Drama: From the Civil War to the Present Day*. New York: F. S. Crofts and Co., 1937.
Recognizes that Rice has caused more differences of critical opinion than any playwright writing before 1920. *On Trial* offered hope for a revival of melodrama, but Rice's experimentation in *The Adding Machine* led him to a "sordid analysis of human life." *Street Scene* is his best play, while *The Subway* deals with

issues too dark for concern. Rice's later work is primarily bad melodrama, and his dwindling critical reputation is deserved.

S41 No byline. "Five Playwrights Organize Own Production Unit." *New York Herald Tribune* 8 March 1938: 1.
Description of the Playwrights' Company.

S42 No byline. "How Elmer Rice Wrote New Play." *New York Sun* 10 June 1938: 2.
Recounts genesis of *We, the People*.

S43 Morehouse, Ward. "Elmer Rice: He's One of the Big Five." *New York Sun* 17 December 1938: 1.
Background to formation of the Playwright's Company.

S44 Denlinger, Sutherland. "Elmer Rice Still Out of Theatre." *New York World-Telegram* 14 December 1938: 1.
Interview with Rice. Although with *American Landscape* he has returned to the theatre, he has not returned to the commercial theatre he left. Denies turning his back on the Left, and praises Roosevelt for putting America back on track. Also expresses support of the Federal Theatre Project and the WPA.

S45 Krutch, Joseph Wood. "Prodigal's Return." *Nation* 147 (24 December 1938): 700-701.
Reviews Philip Barry's *Here Come(s) the Clowns* and Rice's *American Landscape*. The latter is filled with lifeless dialogue.

S46 Young, Stark. "Ars Longa." *New Republic* 97 (28 December 1938): 230-31.
American Landscape reviewed with Philip Barry's *Here Come(s) the Clowns*. Rice's play is tedious, banal, and over explicit.

S47 Gassner, John. "Bounded in a Nutshell." *One-Act Play Magazine* 2 (December 1938): 594-96.
Bemoans the current season as a total loss, but calls the new Playwrights' Company a triumph. *American Landscape* and Odets's *Rocket to the Moon* are the only two significant serious plays of the year. Although the Company might be better named "the Liberal's Company," it is to be congratulated for its fine productions. *American Landscape*, in particular, deserves recognition for its deep convictions and progressive vision, and for its evocation of a new passion for democracy.

S48 Brown, John Mason. *Two on the Aisle*. New York: W. W. Norton, 1938.

Reprints reviews from 1929–1938, including that of *We, the People*.

S49 Flexner, Eleanor. *American Playwrights 1918–1938: The Theatre Retreats From Reality*. New York: Simon and Schuster, 1938.

In the chapter, "New Realism," *Street Scene* is judged a superlative example of the form, while *We, the People* utilizes a panoramic style that will later influence George Sklar, John Wexley and others.

S50 Mantle, Burns. *Best Plays of 1937–38*. New York: Dodd, Mead and Co., 1938.

Mentions San Francisco Federal Theatre Project's production of *Judgment Day* and Chicago revival of *See Naples and Die*.

S51 Mantle, Burns. *Contemporary American Playwrights*. New York: Dodd, Mead and Company, 1938.

Rice's playwriting has grown in assurance and technique. An overview of his career follows, stressing his independent nature.

1939–1943

S52 Darlington, W.A. "More on *Judgment Day*." *New York Times* 3 December 1939: 6.

The public's perception of this play as political propaganda has perhaps prevented it from getting the audience it deserves, but its high production quality and its direct relevance to events of the day will earn it a larger following.

S53 Block, Anita. *The Changing World in Plays and Theatre*. Boston: Little, Brown and Company, 1939.

In "The Social Conflict," *The Adding Machine* is distinguished from plays by Ernst Toller because it does not advance a "positive social philosophy."

S54 Bricker, Herschel, ed. *Our Theatre Today*. New York: Samuel French, 1939.

Rice appears sporadically in anecdotes relating to the sale and production of Broadway scripts.

S55 Chandler, Frank W., ed. *Twentieth-Century Plays: American*. New York: Thomas Nelson and Sons, 1939.

Brief autobiographical portrait of Rice accompanying text of *Street Scene*.

S56 Krutch, Joseph Wood. *The American Drama Since 1918: An Informal History*. New York: Random House, 1939: 226-283.

"The Drama of Social Criticism" places Rice's work in context with the plays of Howard Lawson and Clifford Odets, as well as recent work by the Federal Theatre Project. Admires Rice for producing work which is theatrically stimulating, keenly observed and socially relevant, but faults him for his dependence on melodrama. Traces a curve of maturity in Rice's work that reaches its apex in *Street Scene* and dwindles thereafter.

S57 Mersand, Joseph. *Traditions in American Literature: A Study of Jewish Characters and Authors*. New York: Modern Chapbooks, 1939.

Rice is the interpreter of New York City life, with *Street Scene* his most convincing portrayal. His study of law has contributed to his success as a playwright. Rice combines a passion for justice with an accuracy of observation. When he presents a picture of America disintegrating, audiences and critics desert him.

S58 Montrose, Moses J. *Representative American Dramas: National and Local* [revised edition]. Boston: Little, Brown and Co., 1939.

Substantial biographical portrait of Rice.

S59 Flanagan, Hallie. *Arena: The History of the Federal Theatre*. New York: Benjamin Blom, 1940. [Rptd. 1965]

Brief mention of Rice's affiliation with the Federal Theatre Project.

S60 Sobel, Bernard, ed. *The Theatre Handbook and Digest of Plays*. New York: Crown Publishers, 1940.

Bibliography of primary works through *American Landscape*, along with an entry stating that Rice is not primarily an innovator in American drama but an important social realist.

S61 Hughes, Charlotte. "Elmer Rice, Apparently at Rest." *New York Times* 17 January 1941: 1, 3.

Sums up Rice's problems while simultaneously producing *Flight to the West* and running the Plymouth Theatre. Rice is a "one man storm center" who insists with great integrity on utilizing the immediate social world for his plays.

S62 Chandler, Frank W. and Richard Cordell, eds. *Twentieth-Century Plays: American* [revised edition]. New York: Thomas Nelson and Sons, 1941.

Reprint of S55.

S63   Mantle, Burns. *Best Plays of 1940–41*. New York: Dodd, Mead and Co., 1941.

   Brief mention of Pasadena Playhouse productions of *Not for Children* and *Two on an Island*. Refers to *A New Life* as "the first serious drama of the season."

S64   Mersand, Joseph. *The American Drama: 1930–1940*. New York: Modern Chapbooks, 1941.

   Repeats almost verbatim material in *Traditions in American Literature* (S57).

S65   Mantle, Burns. *Best Plays of 1942–43*. New York: Dodd, Mead and Co., 1943.

   Brief mention of revival of *Counsellor-at-Law*.

S66   Nathan, George Jean. *The Theatre Book of the Year 1942–1943: A Record and an Interpretation*. New York: Alfred Knopf, 1943.

   Plot summary and review of 1942 revival of *Counsellor-at-Law*. Wonders why Muni's present performance is lauded more so than its original.

1944–1948

S67   Nathan, George Jean. *The Theatre Book of the Year 1943–1944: A Record and an Interpretation*. New York: Alfred Knopf, 1944.

   A New Life reveals Rice's "dramaturgical schizophrenia" because it attempts to inject political and economic dicta into simple melodrama. In less ostentatious hands the play might have succeeded; under Rice's hard striving the work comes to nothing.

S68   Croissant, Albert. *El Teatro American: Un Analisis Critico*. Trans. Rafael Trujillo. Pasadena, CA: Keystone Press, 1945.

   Surveying Rice's output through *Flight to the West*, the author praises Rice's mastery of detail which, though sometimes sordid, contributes to both realistic effects and a drama which embodies universal themes of justice and liberty.

S69   Nathan, George Jean. *The Theatre Book 1945–1946: A Record and an Interpretation*. New York: Alfred Knopf, 1946.

   Though most critics found *Dream Girl* enchanting, the play actually reduces Georgina to the "matrimonial will" of Redfield and thus leaves her weak and passive.

S70   Gagey, Edmond M. *Revolution in American Drama*. New York: Columbia UP, 1947.

Brief analysis of *Two on an Island* as an example of the "Bagdad-on-the-Hudson" theme, and of *The Left Bank* as a "distinctive part of the American scene in the twenties and early thirties."

S71 Mersand, Joseph. *Revolution in American Drama.* New York: Columbia University Press, 1947.

Rice, as a liberal rather than a radical thinker, moved away from the objectivity of his social dramas (such as *Street Scene*) toward a theatre of social propaganda in *We, the People*. In the latter, he recalls in simple human terms the suffering of the thirties and creates a stirring indictment against free enterprise gone wrong. The venture into propaganda drama by an established Broadway playwright constituted a significant development in American theatre. Later works (*Two on an Island*, *The Left Bank*) return to the objective stance of his early plays, and continue to act as sharply observed portraits of contemporary American life.

S72 Nathan, George Jean. *The Theatre Book of the Year 1946–1947: A Record and an Interpretation.* New York: Alfred Knopf, 1947.

After a slow start, the musical version of *Street Scene* shows a fresh and unpretentious approach to American folk opera. Sometimes overdramatic, the work nevertheless captures the flavor of works like *Porgy and Bess*.

1949–1953

S73 Collins, Ralph. "The Playwright and the Press: Elmer Rice and His Critics." *Theatre Annual: 1948–1949*: 35-58.

The article seeks to test the effect newspaper reviews have on the life of a play. Collins chooses Rice as a model because of his longevity in the theatre, the variety of his work, and his frequent battles with reviewers. After considering more than a dozen plays covering almost three decades, Collins concludes that the reviewers, while capable of unerringly picking out very bad or very good plays for damning or praise, consistently misconstrue the slightly bad or moderately good work. He calls for reviewers to become less impressionistic, and to base their responses on the entire canon of an author's work and on the cultural contexts in which the plays are produced.

S74 Morehouse, Ward. *Matinee Tomorrow: Fifty Years of Our Theatre.* New York: McGraw-Hill, 1949.

Brief accounts of the productions of *On Trial*, *The Adding Machine* and *Street Scene*, the last of which is referred to as "relentlessly observant."

S75   Rice, Vernon. "It All Happens at Once to Elmer Rice." *New York Post* 3 December 1951: 2.

Recounts Rice's legal difficulties with the television program Celanese Theatre over its production of *Counsellor-at-Law*.

S76   Downer, Alan S. *Fifty Years of American Drama: 1900–1950*. Chicago: Henry Regnery Company, 1951 [Reprinted 1966].

In "From Romance to Reality," *Street Scene* is analyzed for its contribution to American realism. The play is actually constructed as "domestic symphony" with all the details of life arranged harmoniously within a commonplace frame. In "Beyond the Fourth Wall," *The Adding Machine* is praised for its unsentimental use of expressionist stage techniques. The play is not so much an explicit attack on the social order as it is a study of its victims. So, while the social criticism is not new, the presentation of it achieves a new freshness.

S77   Hughes, Glenn. *A History of the American Theatre 1700–1958*. New York: Samuel French, 1951.

Rice's affiliation with the Federal Theatre Project represented an attempt to blend radical politics with mainstream bureaucracy.

S78   Nathan, George Jean. *The Theatre Book of the Year 1950–1951: A Record and an Interpretation*. New York: Alfred Knopf, 1951.

Not for Children is a throwback to the days of clever plays-within-plays. However, the tricks no longer awe audiences or provoke them, so Rice should have left the play in his desk.

S79   Allison, James A. "A Study of Some Concepts of Social Justice in the Published Plays of Elmer Rice." Unpublished Dissertation (Denver University). *ADD* W1953 (1953).

Non-verifiable source.

S80   Nathan, George Jean. *The Theatre in the Fifties*. New York: Alfred Knopf, 1953.

The Grand Tour fails because Rice creates a character who speaks in cliches without knowing this about herself. Rice seems to believe too that merely talking about poetic subjects creates poetry. But the play, though it begins happily, becomes a complicated mishmash of outworn themes. Rice's discontent with the critics, voiced after the failure of *Not for Children* and now this play, could be assuaged if he would only produce a decent play.

1954–1958

S81 Gassner, John. *Theatre in Our Times*. New York: Crown Books, 1954.
  Passing reference to *The Adding Machine* as an example of American expressionism.

S82 Sievers, W. David. *Freud on Broadway: A History of Psychoanalysis and the American Drama*. New York: Hermitage House, 1955.
  In "O'Neill's Allies in Analysis," Rice's work is analyzed from strictly a Freudian perspective. Notes that Rice read Freud at the beginning of his career and has remained interested by also reading Jung, Adler, Ferenczi and Stekel. Argues that plays from *Wake Up, Jonathan* through *The Adding Machine*, *The Subway*, *Dream Girl* and *The Grand Tour* as noteworthy because Rice shows he is aware of the importance of psychoanalytic theory even while he does not accept its therapeutic application. Rice is praised for his facility in handling stream of consciousness as a means to dramatize suppressed states of mind and for having the courage to treat themes of sexual frustration in his plays.

S83 Lumley, Frederick. *Trends in Twentieth-Century Drama*. London: Barrie and Rockliff, 1956.
  Rice is estimated to follow only O'Neill in American drama. His plays reveal a fine grasp of debate and rhetoric, especially in *Judgment Day*. The later work falls off considerably, as Rice creates mere pastiches of his early work. Still, he must be assessed as a master of the social purpose play.

S84 McCarthy, Mary. *Sights and Spectacles*. New York: Farrar, Straus, 1956.
  In "Three Plays With Music" the musical version of *Street Scene* is described as not having aged "except where Rice tried to rejuvenate it."

S85 Oppenheimer, George. *The Passionate Playgoer: A Personal Scrapbook*. New York: Viking, 1958.
  Excerpts from John Anderson's (R72) review of *Street Scene*, as well as Rice's description of theatre critics (S73).

1959–1963

S86 Morehouse, Ward. "Playwriting's Old Pro." *Theatre Arts* 43 (April 1959): 17-20.

Reminiscences of Rice's career from *On Trial* to *Cue for Passion*, along with an interview. Rice "links the theatre of Charles Frohman and Belasco with that of Rodgers and Hammerstein," and can recall many forgotten American dramatists. He complains that contemporary students and audiences do not appreciate the work of anyone other than O'Neill from the early part of the century.

S87 Hewitt, Barnard. *Theatre U. S. A. 1665–1957*. New York: McGraw-Hill, 1959.

The Adding Machine is discussed as an experimental play, while *Street Scene* is admired as Rice's best play and one of the high points in American dramatic realism.

S88 Dusenbury, Winifred L. *The Theme of Loneliness in Modern American Drama*. University of Florida Press, 1960.

In "Socioeconomic Forces," *Street Scene* is analyzed alongside O'Neill's *The Hairy Ape* and Anderson's *Winterset* as examples of plays in which loneliness is a function of a debilitating and alienating economic order. The crowded tenement setting in Rice's play is implicitly critiqued as the source of loneliness dramatized in the characters. Sam and Mrs. Maurrant are the loneliest characters, while only Rose sees lucidly the impossibility of overcoming alienation by dependence on someone else.

S89 Broussard, Louis. *American Drama: Contemporary Allegory from O'Neill to Williams*. Norman: Oklahoma University Press, 1962.

In "Elmer Rice and John Howard Lawson" the author places in context the arrival of expressionistic and "allegorical" dramas by the two playwrights. Rice's antipathy to comparisons between *The Adding Machine* and works of German expressionism is noted, but the author argues that evidence for influence is too overwhelming. He congratulates Rice, nevertheless, for developing a unique union of form and content in the play.

S90 Weales, Gerald. *American Drama Since World War II*. New York: Harcourt, Brace & World, 1962.

In "The Playwrights of the Twenties and Thirties" the author argues that Rice's work is fatuous and "quite ordinary." However, mention is made only of plays written after 1945.

S91 Himelstein, Morgan Y. *Drama Was a Weapon: The Left-Wing Theatre in New York, 1929–1941*. New Brunswick: Rutgers UP, 1963.

An overview of Rice's reputation among Marxist critics during the period of social plays. In most cases, Marxist reviewers were both enticed by and afraid of Rice. On the one hand his plays were critical of the existing socioeconomic system; however, his liberal solutions defused the need for revolutionary reform. After Rice's "retirement" from the stage in 1934, Marxist intellectuals tried unsuccessfully to wean Rice to their cause.

1964-1974

S92   Mendelsohn, Michael J. "The Social Critics On Stage." *Modern Drama* 6.3 (December 1963): 277-285.

"Social protest plays" are distinguished from "problem plays" in that the former "looks at contemporary society with hostile eyes" and goes beyond calling attention to society's problems by issuing calls for action. Rice is discussed alongside Lawson and Odets and is termed a liberal, rather than a radical playwright. In most of his social plays the criticism of society is implicit, and in his climax as a professional leftist, *We, the People*, the politics overwhelm the art and Rice gets too caught up in his message.

S93   Hoffmann, Frederick J. "Mr. Zero and Other Ciphers: Experiments on the Stage." In *Essays in the Modern Drama*, ed. Morris Freedman. Boston: D. C. Heath, 1964. Reprinted from *The Twenties* by F. J. Hoffmann (New York: Viking, 1955).

The Adding Machine represents the most remarkable illustration of expressionistic comedy in American drama. Its theatrical techniques lead to the thesis of the play, that Zero is a type who does not progress or grow but only repeats his failures in new ways. This form of expressionism was useful for social satire, especially as against standardization in work and morality. Rice was especially adept at using expressionist staging and writing to criticize the prevailing economic order, as seen in Sophie's suffering and suicide in *The Subway*.

S94   Rabkin, Gerald. *Drama and Commitment: Politics in the American Theatre of the Thirties*. Bloomington: Indiana University Press, 1964.

In "Elmer Rice and the Seriousness of Drama," Rabkin argues that Rice, whose work is unique in its inconsistency and its alteration between seriousness and conventionality, is the playwright who most forced the issue of whether or not American drama could claim the virtue of seriousness. *Not for Children* expresses Rice's "belligerently anti-theatrical attitude" and his disillusionment with the theatre. Yet Rice was a brilliant compromiser capable of mediating between the exigencies of the popular stage and his desire to write meaningful political theatre. A "seismographic" reader of American culture, Rice's plays of the twenties and thirties address the sense of dehumanization prevalent in the country. Rice never integrated Marxist theory into his critique of America, but remained forever a liberal humanist. A talented craftsman and committed social activist, Rice nevertheless seldom transcended craft with real dramatic vision.

S95   Hogan, Robert. *The Independence of Elmer Rice*. Carbondale: Southern Illinois University Press, 1965.

Hogan argues that, along with O'Neill, Rice is the first American dramatist "whom we could call modern or excellent." Attempting to avoid treating the plays as a journalist-critic or as an academic critic interested only in literary merit, Hogan strives for a "theatrical criticism" that accounts for Rice's brilliant theorizations about the drama as well as for his sometimes awkward execution in some of the plays. He traces Rice's career through the "potboilers," the "realist" plays, and the plays of "social conscience," covering over forty plays, almost half of them closely. Hogan closes with a ranking of the plays and an account of his experience directing *Love Among the Ruins*.

S96   Lewis, Allan. *American Plays and Playwrights of the Contemporary Theatre*. New York: Crown, 1965.

In "The Tired Deans," Rice along with Behrman is presented as the "respected but tired elder statesmen of the Broadway stage." Rice's recent offerings (*Dream Girl*, *The Winner*, *The Grand Tour*, and *Cue for Passion*) reveal this once committed writer no longer fighting for social causes but retreating into personal psychological studies. In his prime, Rice was a courageous experimenter with expressionism and documentary theatre. Never a profound or original thinker, Rice nevertheless adapted current ideas even when they were unpopular. The McCarthy years quieted rebellious thinkers like Rice, and unfortunately new social causes have arrived too late for Rice to become involved with them: "[H]e would have written, otherwise, a stirring tribute to the fighters for civil rights." Further, Rice's tireless advocacy for free speech makes his entire career as a writer an enduring monument.

S97   Taubman, Howard. *The Making of American Theatre*. New York: Howard-McCann, 1965: 177-78.

Under "New Voices in the 1920s" Rice is judged an "uneven" dramatist who sought honorably to report the real turbulence of the world. *Street Scene*, though shot through with sentimentality, maintains a high level of probity.

S98 Hogan, Robert. "Rice: The Public Life of a Playwright." *Modern Drama* 8.4 (February 1966): 426-39.

Rice, along with O'Neill, represent the first American dramatists producing excellent work. Rice remains next to O'Neill the most distinguished American playwright, yet his work and legacy are largely ignored today. The essay argues that because of Rice's lifelong dedication to social causes and his desire to improve the quality and availability of American drama, he should be acknowledged more widely. More than merely a weather vane for American theatrical and social culture for half a century, Rice has also directed that culture in better directions through his uncompromising work.

S99 Kronenberger, Louis, ed. *The Best Plays of 1958-59*. New York: Dodd, Mead and Company, 1966.

Excerpts from *Cue for Passion*. Notes that the character of Tony is an "Oedipus uncomplex Hamlet," and that the consequences of his actions take a therapeutic rather than tragic turn.

S100 Laufe, Abe. *Anatomy of a Hit: Long-Run Plays on Broadway from 1900 to the Present Day*. New York: Hawthorn Books, 1966.

Aligns *Street Scene* with Williams's *The Glass Menagerie* in that both present characters who are victims of frustration. Rice uses the Maurrant-Sankey love plot to emphasize the theme of oppression. The musical version was likely ahead of its time.

S101 Valgemae, Mardi. "Rice's *The Subway*." Explicator 25 (March 1967), Item 62.

Argues against the socioeconomic readings of Sophie's suicide given by Hogan (S95) and Rabkin (S94), insisting that her language and actions as she prepares to throw herself in front of the train "owe more to the gospel according to Freud than to Marx." Sophie is not committing suicide out of despair, nor is she being metaphorically raped by modern technology; instead, she reflects a high pitch of erotic desire to which she submits willingly.

S102 Anderson, Robert. "In Memorium: Elmer Rice." *New York Times* 21 May 1967: 3.

Praises Rice as one of a generation of playwrights who, in the twenties and thirties, "made American playwriting respectable world literature." Wonders whether Rice's plays will stand the test of time.

S103 Bolton, Whitney. "Theatre Poorer Without Elmer Rice." *New York Morning Telegraph* 24 May 1967: 2.

    Reports on memorial service for Rice at Plymouth Theatre, which drew five hundred mourners. Quotes Rice's aphorism, "I don't despair . . . I try again."

S104 *American Theatre*. Stratford-upon-Avon Studies 10. New York: St. Martin's Press, 1967.

    Brief mention of *Street Scene* in chapter entitled "Realism in the Modern American Drama."

S105 Mathews, Jane De Hart. *The Federal Theatre, 1935–1939: Plays, Relief and Politics*. Princeton: Princeton UP, 1967.

    Covering Rice's affiliation with the FTP, Mathews documents his role in advocating a subsidized theatre and overseeing the auditions for actors and directors. The book also recounts Rice's support for the Living Newspaper, and his subsequent resignation when its production of *Ethiopia* was censored.

S106 Napieralski, Edmund. *Elmer Rice: A Critical Evaluation of His Full-Length Published Plays*. Unpublished Dissertation (Loyola University). *ADD* X1967 (1967).

    Non-verifiable source.

S107 Brown, Jared Allen. "The Theatrical Development of Social Themes in Selected Plays by Elmer Rice.". Unpublished Dissertation (University of Minnesota). *DAI* 41 (1968): 2109-A.

    Rice is praised as one of America's outstanding social dramatists, whose lifelong commitment to social causes may have, paradoxically, retarded his development as a playwright. His plays are most successful when they portray social injustice without proposing corrective action, contain elements of moral ambiguity, and offer instances of humor and sophisticated theatricality.

S108 Elwood, William R. "An Interview With Elmer Rice on Expressionism." *Educational Theatre Journal* 20.1 (March 1968): 1-7.

    In this interview conducted in 1965, the interviewer seeks to know if Rice had been influenced by German expressionism in *The Adding Machine* and *The Subway*. Rice says he know nothing about German expressionism, beyond having seen a review of Kaiser's *From Morn Til Midnight*. He suggests that a common social and psychological environment existed for both German and American playwrights of the time, which produced similar work among them without direct influence. Rice also discusses and compliments the recent Phoenix Theatre production of the play, and argues that *The Subway* is more an example of expressionism than is *The Adding Machine*.

S109 Gassner, John. *Dramatic Soundings*. New York: Crown, 1968.

Rice has never achieved the level of O'Casey, but *Street Scene* remains a credible slice of life, and *The Adding Machine* is a testament to theatrical resourcefulness.

S110 Taylor, William, ed. *Modern American Drama: Essays in Criticism*. DeLand, FL: Everett/Edwards, Inc., 1968.

The speech rhythms of *Street Scene* ring true because Rice is not afraid to include vulgarisms and trite expressions. *Street Scene* represents a symphonic presentation of life by its use of dialect and offstage sound for ambience.

S111 Dukore, Bernard and Daniel Gerould. "Explosions and Implosions: Avant-Garde Drama Between World Wars." *Educational Theatre Journal* 21 (March 1969): 6-15.

The Adding Machine represents an exemplary expression of the quest for salvation in a technologized world.

S112 Roney, Edmund Burke. *The Effect of Directing and Producing on the Playwriting of Elmer Rice*. Unpublished Dissertation (Stanford University). *DAI* 30/03 (September 1969): 1265A.

When Rice began directing in 1929 he was already established as a writer. His work, it is argued here, declined after this time, possibly due to his new interest in directing and producing. This comes about because Rice forsook his verbal skills for more visualization, and because he began to "write good theatre" rather than good plays.

S113 Herron, Ima Honaker. *The Small Town in American Drama*. Dallas: Southern Methodist University Press, 1969.

Rice's attack on machine society in *The Adding Machine* anticipated a return to rural themes in later American drama.

S114 Durham, Frank. *Elmer Rice*. New York: Twayne Publishers, 1970.

This overview focuses on Rice's published plays and treats them chronologically. Durham recognizes in Rice a "kind of one-man history of American playwriting from 1914 until the 1960's." Crediting Rice with superior technical skill and craftsmanship, Durham also criticizes him for his affinity for potboilers and his unwillingness to cut and condense his longer works. In reference to the explicitly political plays, Durham argues that Rice was no revolutionist, but a utopianist who fought against those who betrayed the liberal principles of the Declaration of Independence and the Bill of Rights.

S115 Nathan, George Jean. *Passing Judgments.* Rutherford: Farleigh Dickinson Press, 1970 [Rpt. of 1935 volume].
    Rice's trips to Russia and his slavish adherence to Communist theatre has not benefitted the writing of plays like *American Landscape.*

S116 Smiley, Sam. *The Drama of Attack: Didactic Plays of the American Depression.* Columbia: University of Missouri Press, 1972.
    Rice is proposed as a model for writers who "engaged in multiform social commitment." Because he strove to reach audiences with a low common intellect, Rice sometimes oversimplifies his writing. *Judgment Day*, for example, is effective with audiences but is pushed toward didacticism.

S117 Valgemae, Mardi. *Accelerated Grimace: Expressionism in the American Drama of the 1920s.* Carbondale: Southern Illinois UP, 1972.
    Traces Rice's experience with forms of expressionism and analyzes *The Adding Machine* and *The Subway* from this perspective.

S118 Bobin, Jane F. *Prize-Winning American Drama: A Bibliographic and Descriptive Guide.* Metuchen, NJ: Scarecrow Press, 1973.
    Provides a cast list, plot summary, and production credits for *Street Scene*, along with a critical overview of Rice and short bibliography.

S119 Usigli, Rodolfo. "Elmer Rice, o de la sencillez de los grandes." In *Conversaciones y Encuentros.* Organizacion Editorial Novaro, 1973.
    An interview published after Rice's death, covering his views on Continental theatre, American actors, and the trials of a theatre manager.

S120 Wilson, Garff B. *Three Hundred Years of American Theatre and Drama: From "Ye Bear and Ye Cubb" to "Hair."* Englewood Cliffs, NJ: Prentice-Hall, 1973.
    The Adding Machine is acknowledged as an effective expressionist drama directly influenced by German sources. *The Subway* is termed a "realistic tragedy," but Rice's later plays stirred more anger in the playwright than in the audiences he sought to arouse.

S121 Bungert, Hans. "Rice: *The Adding Machine*" in *Das Amerikanische Drama*, ed. Paul Goetsch. Düsseldorf: August Bagel Verlag, 1974.

Given Rice's use of both expressionistic elements and realist techniques, the play presents a "de-Europeanized" version of expressionism which points toward the complex sociocritical protest plays of the 1930s.

S122 Weaver, Richard Alden. *The Dramaturgy of Elmer Rice*. Unpublished Dissertation (University of Missouri-Columbia). *DAI* 34/11 (May 1974): 7381A.

The study sets out to discover the theories which helped determine Rice's mindset and then to evaluate the effect of these theories on his drama. Under "theories of life" Rice's political, social and economic theories are studied, while under "theories of art" the significant aesthetic ideas are evaluated. The author concludes that Rice was essentially a mild socialist with distinctly pro-American biases, a humanist and free thinker whose work "reflects his own time."

S123 Soudek, Ingrid. *A Contrastive Study of Ernst Toller's "Die Maschinenstürmer" and Elmer Rice's "The Adding Machine."* Unpublished Dissertation (University of Michigan). *DAI* 35 (November 1974): 2956A.

Both plays address the problem of human obsolescence in the age of automation, but while Toller's conclusions are reached through a materialist critique of socioeconomic factors Rice's play approaches the issue from a metaphysical perspective. Rice is thus a determinist and a cynic who attempted to cash in on serious expressionism in order to create a box office hit.

S124 Palmieri, Anthony Francis. *Elmer Rice: A Playwright's Vision of America*. Unpublished Dissertation (University of Maryland-College Park). *DAI* 35 (December 1974): 3477A.

Attempts to come to grips with totality of Rice's work from a specifically literary perspective, offering descriptive and interpretive accounts of each play. Argues that changes in Rice's plays can be accounted for by reference to shifting climates of opinion in American culture. (For the published version, see S141).

S125 Goldstein, Malcolm. *The Political Stage: American Drama and Theater and the Great Depression*. New York: Oxford UP, 1974.

Traces Rice as a member of the "independent" theatre movement of the early 1930s. Rice commanded a hearing during this period not so much because of the quality of his work but because of his passionate attacks against social injustice.

Counsellor-at-Law successfully continues the themes and style of *Street Scene*, but in *We, the People* Rice attempts a pageant drama that precludes him from studying characters in depth.

S126 Williams, Jay. *Stage Left*. New York: Scribner and Sons, 1974.
Passing references made to Rice's work with the Theatre Guild and the Federal Theatre Project. *We, the People* is described as anticipating Roosevelt's New Deal politics.

S127 Soudek, Ingrid Worth. *A Contrastive Study of Toller and Rice*. Unpublished Dissertation (University of Michigan).
Second listing. See S123.

S128 Weaver, Richard A. "*The Adding Machine*: Exemplar of the Ludicrous." *Players* 49 (1974): 130-33.
By delineating Zero as a ludicrous character Rice is able to create both empathy and disdain for him.

1975–1984

S129 Graves, Richard Claude. *The Critical Response to the Produced Full-Length Plays of Elmer Rice*. Unpublished Dissertation (University of Denver). *DAI* 36/07 (January 1975): 4114A.
Restricted to Rice's plays produced in New York City, the study maintains that Rice was an innovative but flawed playwright who could rise to great statements of political importance even if he could not always write great plays. Rice is criticized for investing his plays with too much anger and for his tendency to reduce complex dilemmas to simple arguments and solutions. His work, however, made critics treat American drama as a serious art form.

S130 Kaes, Anton. "Elmer Rice's *The Adding Machine*." *Studien zur Deutschen Literatur* 43 (1975): 121-34.
Analyzes the subjective theatricality of the play, noting that Zero's mood shifts are captured by lighting and sound effects.

S131 Kaes, Anton. *Expressionismus in Amerika*. Tübingen: Max Niemeyer Verlag, 1975.
Expanded version of S130, incorporating The Adding Machine into the traditions of German expressionism. Zero's innate slave mentality negates Rice's social criticisms in the play, as does the burlesque humor. However, although American expressionism in general trivialized the original intentions of the European avant-garde, American versions of the form are, paradoxically, more entertaining and able to communicate to broader audiences.

S132 Zeller, Loren. "Two Expressionistic Interpretations of Dehumanization: Rice's *The Adding Machine* and Muñiz's *El Tintero*." *Essays in Literature* 2.2 (Fall 1975): 245-255.

    Muñiz's contemporary play, though similar to Rice's early work, was not directly influenced by it. A number of thematic parallels can be found, and both playwrights make use of similar expressionistic techniques. In terms of tone, however, while Rice does not create empathy for Zero, Muñiz depicts a character with whom we are meant to identify.

S133 Bauland, Peter. "Expressionism in Modern American Drama." *Amerikanisches Drama Und Theater Im 20. Jahrhundert*. Ed. Alfred Weber and Siegfried Neuweiler. Gottingen: Vandenhoeck and Ruprecht, 1975.

    The Adding Machine is among the most interesting American adaptations of expressionism. Rice's sense of humor distinguishes this play from the dour German expressionists, and this has helped it to retain its freshness.

S134 Weiand, Hermann J., ed. "Elmer Rice" in *Insight IV: Analyses of Modern British and American Drama*. Frankfurt am Main: Hirschcraben-Verlag, 1976.

    An analysis of *The Adding Machine* in which the author argues that the play is a satirical comedy on the theme of technological alienation and which makes extensive use of expressionistic techniques. The play, unlike most expressionist work, retains an "exceptional vitality" because it is not marred by pseudo-profundity or narrow social or political concerns. Rice does a fine job of balancing our empathy with Zero and our scorn for him. The real attack is on the "soul of mass-man" as it develops from mass culture.

S135 Avery, Lawrence G., ed. *Dramatists in America: Letters of Maxwell Anderson, 1912-1958*. Chapel Hill: University of North Carolina UP, 1977.

    Includes letters to Rice regarding the founding and operations of the Playwrights' Company, Rice's direction of Anderson's plays, and personal correspondence.

S136 Choudhuri, A. D. *The Face of Illusion in American Drama*. Atlantic Highlands, N.J.: Humanities Press, 1979.

    In "*The Adding Machine*: Machine Creates Illusion," the author argues that the play is not primarily concerned with socioeconomic issues but with "human wastage, loss of human potential, increase in human misery, and overall destruction of happiness in life." Rice reveals a sound philosophy which "encouraged a realistic understanding of the mechanism of social life, and a perceptive insight into the idealistic urge of individuals." This combination makes *The Adding Machine* an effective vehicle for exposing how technology creates only an illusion of happiness.

S137 Bruning, Eberhard. "Relations Between Progressive American and German Drama in the Twenties and Thirties." in *Three Epoch-Making Literary Changes: Renaissance, Enlightenment, Early Twentieth Century.* Ed. Bela Kopeczi and Gyorgy Vajda. Stuttgart: Bieber, 1980
    Non-verifiable source.

S138 Driver, Tom. *Romantic Quest and Modern Query: A History of the Modern Theatre.* New York: Delta Books, 1980.
    The Adding Machine is the purest example of expressionist theatre written in American drama. The play is full of bitter irony and excellent satire.

S139 Dorsey, John T. "The Courtroom Scene in Four Plays by Elmer Rice." *Journal of the College of International Relations (Japan).* 1 (February 1980): 221-31.
    Non-verifiable source.

S140 Greenfield, Thomas Allen. *Standing Before Kings: Work and the Work Ethic in American Drama, 1920–1970.* Unpublished Dissertation (University of Minnesota). *DAI* 41 (November 1980): 2109A.
    American drama inherits an interest in the theme of work from European dramatists and from an indigenous investment in the Protestant work ethic. Rice is the first American playwright to explore the theme, and his approach was to dramatize the fear of industrial machinery and to propose pro-labor solutions. His plays precede the more moderately pro-labor stance of Treadwell and Brewer and the New Left approach of Albee and other playwrights of the 1960s-70s. (For the published version, see S147).

S141 Palmieri, Anthony Francis. *Elmer Rice: A Playwright's Vision of America.* Rutherford: Fairleigh Dickinson Press, 1980.
    This survey of Rice's work focuses almost exclusively on the literary merit of the plays rather than their theatrical viability. Comparing Rice to other American playwrights of the period, Palmieri finds that Rice was often far ahead of his cohorts in experimental vigor and a leader in addressing important social problems in his plays. Admitting that the playwright's output was uneven, the author maintains that Rice's greatest strength—his ability to

use the stage as a platform for vigorous debate—was often responsible for his lapses. His most dated plays are those in which Rice slid too easily into propaganda and didacticism. Overall, however, Rice should assume his "rightful place among the few who in the first half of the present century brought American drama to worldwide recognition."

S142 Schulz, Von Dieter. "Elmer Rice, *Cue for Passion*; Paul Baker, Hamlet ESP" in *Anglo-Amerikanische Shakespeare-Bearbeitungen Des 20. Jahrhunderts*, ed. Horst Priessnitz. Darmstadt: Wissenschaftliche Buchgesellschaft, 1980.

While Rice's play focuses on the Freud/Jones tradition of reading *Hamlet* through the Prince's repressed psychological dynamics, Baker's play shows affinities to Artaud's conception of "total theatre." Rice's happy ending thus can be understood as a rationalist attack against the pre-rational, while Baker's implicitly valorizes the unconscious.

S143 Behringer, Fred Dayton. *The Political Theatre of Elmer Rice, 1930–1943*. Unpublished Dissertation (University of Texas-Austin). *DAI* 41 (January 1981): 2831A.

Studies Rice's most explicitly political plays (*We, the People, Judgment Day, Between Two Worlds, American Landscape, Flight to the West*, and *A New Life*) in the context of his political thought and efforts of the time. The argument is that Rice was attempting to redefine in these plays the relationship between theatre and society, but that he grew increasingly disenchanted with the results and eventually disassociated his work from his political activities after 1943.

S144 Morrden, Ethan. *The American Theatre*. New York: Oxford University Press, 1981.

The Adding Machine is an arraignment of a machine society, an intriguing blend of social criticism and theatrical experimentation. *Street Scene*, a city melodrama, has moments of life but is overwhelmed by the melodrama.

S145 Styan, J. L. *Modern Drama in Theory and Practice*. Vol. 1. Realism and Naturalism. Cambridge: Cambridge University Press, 1981.

Rice's work represents a variation on the earlier realism of Belasco. Chekov's influence is apparent in Rice's handling of dialogue.

S146 Bigsby, Christopher W. E. *A Critical Introduction to Twentieth-Century American Drama: Volume I, 1900–1940.* London: Cambridge University Press, 1982.

  Situates Rice alongside Odets as a writer whose social perceptions "never move from language to action." Rice's liberalism evinces a "nostalgia for a lost world" common to American drama, and this often pulls his plays toward the sentimental. *The Adding Machine* and *Street Scene* are the plays upon which his reputation will stand.

S147 Greenfield, Thomas Allen. *Work and the Work Ethic in American Drama, 1920–1970.* Columbia: University of Missouri Press, 1982.

  Noting that Rice will never be seen the equal of O'Neill or Wilder in the American canon, the writer nevertheless argues that Rice's social plays "are collectively among the most varied, the most thoughtful, and the most innovative American social dramas of the century." Analysis of *The Adding Machine* and *We, the People* reveals that the first play approaches the theme of work in terms of its "humanistic concerns . . . its impact on the souls and psyches of men," while the second play explores the political dimensions of working life in America. Both plays mark significant advances over the dramatic styles Rice adopted for his use, expanding the form and content of both expressionism and agit-prop. Overall, no social dramatist of the 1920s or 1930s "can rival [Rice's] intelligence or his vision."

S148 Chametzky, Jules. "Elmer Rice, Liberation, and the Great Ethnic Question." in *From Hester Street to Hollywood: The Jewish-American Stage and Screen.* Ed. Sarah Blacher Cohen. Bloomington: Indiana UP, 1983.

  Argues that although Rice often deflected interest away from questions of his Jewishness, his willingness to stand up to fascism signifies an important stage of Jewish writing in America. Even in plays like *The Adding Machine* Rice is obliquely addressing issues of mass psychology, though he does not push his critique to explore the roots of such behavior, only the symptoms. *Street Scene* also probes the anti-Semitic behavior of the anti-immigrationist Maurrant.

S149 Riedel, Walter. "Variationen der Wadlund: Gabrielle Roys Roman *Alexandre Chenevert* und die Dramen Georg Kaisers *Von morgens bis mitternachts* und Elmer Rices *The Adding Machine*." Canadian Review of Comparative Literature 11.2 (June 1984): 205-15.

All three writers express mythic versions of "the Wanderer," a character who traverses both material and metaphysical realms. These Everyman figures allow the authors to explore and critique dialectically both the psychological realities of modern life as well as the lived social experiences of the characters.

S150 Dukore, Bernard. *American Dramatists 1919–1945*. New York: Grove Press, 1984.

In "Elmer Rice," the playwright's career is summarized and readings given of his most "representative" plays, *The Adding Machine* and *Street Scene*.

S151 Bristow, Donald Gene. "A Descriptive Catalogue of the Elmer Rice Collection at the University of Texas." Unpublished Dissertation (University of Texas-Austin). *DAI* 45 (1984): 2685A.

The text catalogues Rice's manuscripts, business and personal correspondence, as well as his letters to Bertram Bloch (Rice's boyhood friend with whom he corresponded between 1922–1930) and Frank Harris (Rice's closest friend for over forty years). Bristow also records Rice's appointment books, his royalty statements, and his correspondence with the American Civil Liberties Union. Manuscripts of the plays include original drafts, revisions, acting copies and director's prompt books.

1985–1994

S152 Levine, Ira. *Left-Wing Dramatic Theory in the American Theatre*. Ann Arbor: UMI Research Press, 1985.

Daring the threat of fascism, liberal artists like Rice brought a significant reputation to left-wing theatre during the 1930s. Rice's work with the Federal Theatre helped it to absorb more radical groups, like the New Theatre League, with a more moderate reformist agenda. This reconciled the left's experimental theatre with more conventional dramatic realism.

S153 Magill, Frank N., ed. *Critical Survey of Drama: English Language Series*, Vol. 4. Englewood Cliffs, N.J.: Salem Press, 1985.

Short primary bibliography, biography, and overview of Rice's work.

S154 Brown, Russell E. "Names and Numbers in *The Adding Machine*." Journal of the American Name Society 34.3 (September 1986): 266-74.

Traces symbolic links to character of Zero.

S155 Adler, Thomas P. *Mirror On the Stage: The Pulitzer Plays as an Approach to American Drama.* West Lafayette, IN: Purdue UP, 1987.

  Street Scene represents the first important ghetto drama in American theatre. Rice explores the "relationship between environment, human action, and the quality of life" in the play, and the action is beautifully orchestrated.

S156 Murphy, Brenda. *American Realism and American Drama, 1880–1940.* Cambridge Studies in American Literature and Culture. London: Cambridge UP, 1987.

  Street Scene presents a straightforward representation of New York working-class life, and Rice's use of acoustic ambiance enhances the realism of the play. The essence of realism develops from Rice's integration of thought, structure and milieu in his plays, and he is uniquely successful at integrating melodrama and comedy into realist theatre.

S157 Smith, Wendy. *Real Life Drama: The Group Theatre and America, 1931–1940.* New York: Alfred Knopf, 1990.

  Occasional mention of Rice's affiliations with the Group Theatre. Reports that Rice had expressed interest in joining the Group before deciding to administer the Federal Theatre Project.

S158 Miller, Jordan Y. and Winifred L. Frazer. *American Drama Between the Wars: A Critical History.* Boston: Twayne Publishers, 1991.

  In "A Cry of Playwrights," Rice is treated alongside the other members of the Playwrights' Company. Close analyses of *The Adding Machine* and *Street Scene* reveal that Rice was adept at extending the expressive parameters of both expressionism and realism. A cursory review of the Depression-era plays indicates that it was Rice's lack of partisanship with either the far Right or Left in his social thinking which doomed this series of plays.

S159 Scharne, Richard. *From Class to Caste in American Drama: Political and Social Themes Since the 1930s.* Westport, CT: Greenwood Press, 1991.

  Discusses *Flight to the West* as an anti-Fascist drama and *American Landscape* as a "warning play" against fascism. Rice's affiliation with the Federal Theatre is briefly mentioned.

S160 Duffy, Susan. *The Political Left in the American Theatre of the 1930s: A Bibliographic Sourcebook.* Metuchen, N.J.: Scarecrow Press, 1992.

Bibliographic information regarding Rice's overtly political plays and other primary writings.

S161 Meseine, Walter J. *An Outline History of American Drama.* New York: Feedback Theatrebooks, 1994.

Rice is categorized as a "concerned liberal" who wrote uneven plays focusing on those victimized by society. Short plot summaries of *The Adding Machine* and *Street Scene* are included.

Productions and Credits

The following is a list of major New York and American regional productions of Rice's plays. Cast lists are provided when available, as well as additional information such as the production crews and the length of the production run. Also included are significant overseas productions. For each production listed, reviews cited in the Secondary Bibliography are indexed.

P1 *The Adding Machine*

P1.1   *The Adding Machine*. Garrick Theatre. 19 March, 1923. 72 Performances. Produced by the Theatre Guild; directed by Philip Moeller; sets by Lee Simonson; music by Deems Taylor.

           Mr. Zero — Dudley Digges
           Mrs. Zero — Helen Westley
           Daisy Diana Dorothea Devore — Margaret Wycherly
           The Boss — Irving Dillon
           Mr. One — Harry McKenna
           Mrs. One — Marcia Harris
           Mr. Two — Paul Hayes
           Mrs. Two — Theresa Stewart
           Mr. Three — Gerald Lundegard
           Mrs. Three — Georgiana Wilson
           Mr. Four — George Stehli
           Mrs. Four — Edna Burnett
           Mr. Five — William M. Griffith
           Mrs. Five — Ruby Craven
           Mr. Six — Daniel Hamilton
           Mrs. Six — Louise Sydmeth
           Policemen — Irving Dillon, Lewis Barrington

>
> Judy O'Grady — Elsie Bartlett
> Young Man — Gerald Lundegard
> Shrdlu — Edward G. Robinson
> A Head — Daniel Hamilton
> Lieutenant Charles — Louis Calvert
> Joe — William W. Griffith
>
> Reviews—R37, R38, R39, R40, R41, R42, R43, R44, R45, R46, R47, R48, R49, R50, R51, R52, R62, R64, R65, R76

P 1.2 *The Adding Machine*. London Stage Society 21 March 1924.
Reviews—R53, R54

P 1.3 *The Adding Machine*. Tributary Theatre, Stanford University October 1929. Directed by Gordon Davis; sets by Harold Helvenston.

> Zero — Burnell Gould

P1.4 *The Adding Machine*. Actor's Theatre, New York. 13 June, 1947.

P1.5 *The Adding Machine*. New York Repertory Group. December, 1948
Review—R306

P1.6 *The Adding Machine*. Phoenix Theatre, New York. February 1956. Directed by William Butler.

> Mr. Zero — Howard da Silva
> Mrs. Zero — Margaret Hamilton
> Shrdlu — Sam Jaffe
> Daisy — Ann Thomas

Reviews—R369, R370

P1.7 *The Adding Machine*. Bowling Green State University. 7 November 1962.

P1.8 *The Adding Machine*. Workshop of the Player's Art. 1970-71.

P1.9 *The Adding Machine*. Gate Theatre, New York, October 1980. Directed by Lou Stein.

> Mrs. Zero — Jenny Cryst

P1.10 *The Adding Machine*. Elsewhere Theatre, Bowling Green State University, 17 November 1993. Directed by Patrick Faherty. Scene design by Scott Gross.

> Mr. Zero — Bill Auld
> Mrs. Zero — Pam Sheehan
> Daisy — Michele Johnson
> Shrdlu — Mike Obertacz

P1.11 *The Adding Machine*. Crafton-Preyer Theatre, University of Kansas, Lawrence, Kansas. 18 April 1995. Directed by Ronald A. Willis. Virtual reality design and technology by Mark Reaney.

>Mr. Zero — Brian Paulette
>Mrs. Zero — Betsy Atkinson
>Daisy — Megan Parr
>Shrdlu — Eben Copple

P2 *American Landscape*

P2.1 *American Landscape*. Cort Theatre. 3 December, 1938. 43 Performances. Produced by the Playwrights' Company; directed by the author; sets by Aline Bernstein.

>Captain Anthony Dale — George Macready
>Betty Kutno — Patricia Palmer
>Frances Dale Spinner — Rachel Hartzell
>Gerald Spinner — Donald Cook
>Carlotta Dale — Phoebe Foster
>William Fiske — Howard Miller
>Captain Frank Dale — Charles Waldron
>Constance Dale — Sylvia Weld
>Joe Kutno — Theodore Newton
>Captain Samuel Dale — Charles Dingle
>Klaus Stillgebauer — Alfred Hesse
>Moll Flanders — Isobel Elsom
>Captain Heinrich Kleinschmitt — Con MacSunday
>Harriet Beecher Stowe — Lillian Foster
>Paul Kutno — Jules Bennett
>Abby Kutno — Ethel Intropidi
>Nils Karenson — Aage Steenshorne
>Henri Dupont — Pierre d'Ennery
>Patrick O'Brien — J. Hammon Dailey
>Reverend Jasper Washington — Emory Richardson
>Abraham Cohen — Philip Singer

Reviews—R191, R193, R194, R195, R196, R197, R198, R199, R200, R201, R202, R203, R204, R205, R206, R207, R208

P3 *Between Two Worlds*

P3.1 *Between Two Worlds*. Belasco Theatre. 25 October, 1934. 32 Performances. Produced and directed by the author; sets by Aline Bernstein.

Eleanor Massey — Nelly Malcolm
Christine Massey — Tucker Maguire
Frederick Dodd — Conway Washburne
James Roberts — Thomas Manning
Rita Dodd — Constance McKay
Vivienne Sinclair — Josephine Dunn
Rose Henneford — Osceola Archer
Richard Nielson — Lee Ellsworth
Matilda Mason — Anne Tonetti
Hilda Bowen — Diantha Pattison
Elena Mikhailovna Glitzin — Margaret Waller
Margaret Bowen — Rachel Hartzell
Louberta Allenby — Gladys Feldman
Lloyd Arthur — Maurice Wells
Henry Ferguson — James Spottswood
N. N. Kovolev — Joseph Schildkraut
Charles Holaday — Cledge Roberts
Giuseep Moretti — Frank Marino
Edward Maynard — Eric Wollencott
Junior Eddington — Lester Lonergan, 3rd
Helen Eddington — Ruth Tomlinson
Edgar Howell — Wells Richardson
Clara Roberts — Sara Peyton
Dr. David MacKnight — Elmer Brown
Daisy Copper — Sue Moore
Chester Cooper — Ralph Sanford
Harold Powers — Jack Leslie
Captain Whalley — Clyde Fillmore
Eunice Stafford — Rose Burdick
Henri Deschamps — Leonard Penn

Reviews—R171, R173, R174, R176, R177, R178, R179, R180, R181

P4 *Black Sheep*

P4.1 *Black Sheep*. Morosco Theatre. 13 October, 1932. 4 Performances. Produced and directed by the author; sets by Raymond Sovey.

Mary Thompson Porter — Jean Adair
Dorothy Woods — Helen Brooks
Elizabeth — Harriet Russell
Alfred Porter — Edward Downes
Henry Porter — Dodson Mitchell
Penelope Porter — Jane Hamilton
Thompson ("Buddy") Porter — Donald Macdonald
Kitty Lloyd — Mary Phillips
Helena Ambercrombie — Anne Shoemaker
Milton Ambercrombie — Fred Herrick
Bertha Belknap — Frederica Going

Reviews—R129, R130, R131, R132

P5 *The Blue Hawaii*

P5.1 *The Blue Hawaii* was produced in Boston late in 1924, starring Rudolph Schildkraut. It ran for 32 performances (see Hogan [S95]).

P6 *Close Harmony*
(also called *The Lady Next Door* [with Dorothy Parker])

P6.1 *Close Harmony; or, the Lady Next Door*. Gaiety Theatre. 1 December, 1924. 24 performances. Produced by Arthur Hopkins.

Harriet Graham — Georgie Drew Mendum
"Sister" Graham — Arline Blackburn
Annie — Marie Bruce
Ada Townsley — Marie Curtis
Belle Sheridan — Wanda Lyon
Ed Graham — James Spottswood
Sheridan — Robert Hudson
Bill Saunders — Paul Porter
Dr. Robbins — Frederick Burton

Reviews—R55, R56, R57, R59

P7 *Cock Robin*
(with Philip Barry)

P7.1 *Cock Robin*. Forty-Eighth Street Theatre, New York. 12 January, 1928. 100 Performances. Produced and directed by Guthrie McClintic; sets by Jo Mielziner.

McAuliffe — Edward Ellis
Dr. Grace — Wright Kramer

Julian Cleveland — Moffat Johnston
Hancock Robinson — Henry Southard
Richard Lane — Richard Stevenson
Hal Briggs — Jo Milward
Jessop — James Todd
Clarke Torrance — Howard Freeman
Mrs. Montgomery — Beatrice Harford
Helen Maxwell — Desmond Kelley
Carlotta Maxwell — Muriel Kirkland
Maria Scott — Beulah Bondi

Reviews—A07, R66, R67, R68, R69, R70

P8 *Counsellor-at-Law*

P8.1   *Counsellor-at-Law*. Plymouth Theatre. 6 November, 1931. 292 Performances. Resumed 12 September, 1932. 104 Performances. Resumed 15 May, 1933. 16 Performances. Produced and directed by the author; sets by Raymond Sovey.

Bessie Green — Constance McKay
Henry Susskind — Lester Salkow
Sarah Becker — Malka Kornstein
Zedorah Chapman — Gladys Feldman
Goldie Rindskopf — Angela Jacobs
Charles McFadden — J. Hammon dailey
John P. Tedesco — Sam Bonnell
Regina Gordon — Anna Kostant
Herbert Howard Weinberg — Marvin Kline
Arthur Sandler — Conway Washburne
Lillian Larue — Dorothy Dodge
Roy Darwin — Jack Leslie
George Simon — Paul Muni
Cora Simon — Louise Prussing
Lena Simon — Jennie Muscowitz
Peter J. Malone — T. H. Manning
David Simon — Ned Glass
Johann Breitstein — John M. Qualen
Harry Becker — Martin Wolfson
Richard Dwight, Jr. — David Vivian
Dorothy Dwight — June Cox
Francis Clark Baird — Elmer Brown

Reviews—R107, R109, R110, R113, R114, R115, R119, R121, R122, R123, R124, R127, R128, R151, R152, R154

P8.2 *Counsellor-at-Law*. Royale Theatre. 24 November, 1942. 258 Performances. Produced by John Golden; directed by the author; sets by Raymond Sovey.

    Bessie Green — Ann Thomas
    Henry Susskind — Leslie Barrett
    Sarah Becker — Clara Langsner
    Zedorah Chapman — Betty Kelly
    Goldie Rindskoff — Frieda Altman
    Charles McFadden — Jack Sheehan
    John P. Tedesco — Sam Bonnell
    Regina Gordon — Olive Deering
    Herbert Howard Weinberg — Kurt Richards
    Arthur Sandler — John McQuade
    Lillian LaRue — Frances Tannehill
    George Simon — Paul Muni
    Cora Simon — Joan Wetmore
    Lena Simon — Jennie Moscowitz
    Peter Malone — John L. Kearney
    Johann Breitstein — Barrie Wanless
    David Simon — Philip Gordon
    Harry Becker — Joseph Pevney
    Richard Dwight, Jr. — Buddy Buehler
    Dorothy Dwight — Norma Clerc
    Francis Clark Baird — Elmer Brown

Reviews—R245, R246, R247, R248, R249, R250, R251, R252, R253, R254, R255, R256, R257, R258

P8.3 *Counsellor-at-Law*. Lafayette, Indiana Little Theatre. 14 March 1954.

P8.4 *Counsellor-at-Law*. Quaigh Theatre, New York. 26 July, 1977. Resumed 6 September for 62 performances.

Review—R372

P8.5 *Counsellor-at-Law*. George Bernard Shaw Festival, Niagara-on-the-Lake, Ontario, Canada. 16 May 1992. Directed by Neil Munro. Design by Cameron Porteous.

    Bessie Green — Elizabeth Brown
    George Simon — Jim Mezeon
    Cora Simon — Sarah Orenstein
    John Tedesco — Peter Hutt
    Regina Gordon — Mary Haney
    Harry Becker — Blair Williams
    Francis Scott Baird — Craig Davidson

P9 *Cue for Passion*

P9.1 *Cue for Passion*. Henry Miller Theatre. 25 November, 1958. 39 Performances. Produced by the Playwrights' Company and Franchot Productions; directed by the author; sets by George Jenkins; costumes by Dorothy Jeakins.

> Tony Burgess — John Kerr
> Lucy Gessler — Joanna Brown
> Grace Nicholson — Diana Wynyard
> Mattie Haines — Anne Revere
> Carl Nicholson — John Kerr
> Lloyd Hilton — Robert Lansing
> Hugh Gessler — Russell Gaige

Reviews—R352, R353, R354, R355, R356, R357, R358, R359, R360, R361, R362, R363, R364, R365

P10 *A Diadem of Snow*

P10.1 *A Diadem of Snow*. White Plains, New York. 1918.

> Czar — Harry A. Overstreet

P11 *Dream Girl*

P11.1 *Dream Girl*. Coronet Theatre. 14 December, 1945. 349 Performances. Produced by the Playwrights' Company; directed by the author; sets by Jo Mielziner.

> Georgia Allerton — Betty Field
> Lucy Allerton — Evelyn Varden

> Dr. J. Gilmore Percival }
> George Allerton }
> Obstetrician }
> Judge }
> Theatre Manager }
> Justice of the Peace Billings }— William A. Lee

> Miriam Albertson Lucas }
> Arabella } — Sonya Stokowski

> Nurse — Evelyn Varden
> Jim Lucas — Kevin O'Shea
> Claire Blakeley — Helen Marcy

P11 Dream Girl

        Clark Redfield}
                Bert} — Wendell Corey

        George Hand — Edmond Ryan
     District Attorney — Keene Crockett
              Luigi — David Pressman
       Miss Delahanty — Helen Bennett
            Antonio — Don Stevens
           Salarino — Robert Fletcher

Reviews—R275, R276, R277, R279, R280, R281, R282, R283, R284, R285, R286, R287, R288, R289, R290, R291

P11.2 *Dream Girl*. New York City Center of Drama and Music. 9 May, 1951. 15 Performances. Produced by the New York City Theatre Company.

        Georgia Allerton — Judy Holliday

         Lucy Allerton }
               Nurse }— Ann Shoemaker

   Dr. J. Gilmore Percival }
        George Allerton }
          Obstetrician }
              Judge }
      Theatre Manager }
Justice of the Peace Billings }— William A. Lee

   Miriam Albertson Lucas }
             Arabella }— Marian Winters

        Jim Lucas — Walter Klavun
      Claire Blakeley — Mary Welsh
     Clark Redfield — Don DeFore

             Bert }
          Antonio }— Donald Symington

        George Hand — Edmond Ryan
    District Attorney — William LeMassena
            Luigi — Arny Freeman
      Miss Delahanty — Adrienne Moore
         Salarino — Theodore Tenley

Reviews—R319, R320, R321, R322, R323, R324, R325, R326, R327

P11.3 *Dream Girl*. University of Michigan Theatre, Ann Arbor. 8 December 1954.

P11.4 *Dream Girl*. Iowa State College. 3 November 1954.

P11.5 *Dream Girl*. Milwaukee Repertory Theatre. 24 October 1993. Directed by Kenneth Albers. Set design by Victor Becker. Choreography by Fred Weiss.

>Georgina Allerton — Catherine Lynn Davis
>Lucy Allerton — Rose Pickering
>George Allerton — James Pickering
>Miriam Allerton Lucas — Andrea Guilford
>Jim Lucas — James DeVita
>Clark Redfield — Lee E. Ernst

Reviews—R373, R374, R375

P12 *Find the Woman*
(also known as *For the Defense*)

Rice wrote *Find the Woman* sometime before 1919, but could not get it produced because he was committed to a contract to write for Goldwyn Studios in Hollywood. He gave the producer of the play, Richard Bennett, the right to revise the script. Bennett subsequently rewrote almost the entire script and retitled the piece *For the Defense*. He also copyrighted the "new" play in his own name. Rice sought legal counsel but finally allowed the play to open in Ann Arbor, MI, and later to run in New York at the Playhouse Theatre, 19 December 1919 (produced by John D. Williams), where it played to indifferent reviews for less than ten weeks. [See also *For the Defense*, P14.]

P13 *Flight to the West*

P13.1 *Flight to the West*. Guild Theatre. 30 December, 1940. 136 Performances. Produced by the Playwrights' Company; directed by the author; sets by Jo Mielziner.

>Richard Banning — Kevin McCarthy
>Thomas Hickey — Paul Mann
>August Himmelreich — Rudolf Weiss
>Edmund Dickensen — Don Nevins
>Marie Dickensen — Lydia St. Clair
>Lisette Dickensen — Helen Renee
>Louise Frayne — Constance McKay

Colonel Archibald Gage — James Seeley
Count Paul Vasilich Vronoff — Boris Marshalov
Clara Rosenthal — Eleonora Mendelssohn
Dr. Herman Walther — Paul Henried
Howard Ingraham — Arnold Moss
Hope Talcott Nathan — Betty Field
Charles Nathan — Hugh Marlowe
Captain George McNab — Karl Malden
Captain Arthur Hawkes — Grandon Rhodes

Reviews—R225, R226, R227, R228, R229, R230, R231, R232, R234, R235, R236, R237, R238, R239, R240, R242, R243, R244

P14 *For the Defense*
(also known as *Find the Woman*)

P14.1 *For the Defense*. The Playhouse. 19 December, 1919. 77 Performances. Produced by John D. Williams. [See also *Find the Woman*, P12.]

Miss Brinton — Virginia Jones
Miss Smith — Louise Closser Hale
Margaret Cameron — Frederica Going
Mrs. Reed — Louise Sydmeth
Jennie Dunn — Mary Jeffrey
Madame Petrard — Georgette Passedoit
Dr. Kasimir — John Sainpolis
Collins — Charles Coghlan
Anne Woodstock — Winifred Lenihan
Selma Thorne — Adrienne Morrison
Dr. William Lloyd — N. St. Clair Hales
Christopher Armstrong — Richard Bennett
Jane — Angela Ogden
Inspector Austin — William A. Crimans
Judge Gray — George Riddell

P15 *The Gay White Way*

The play received an amateur production in 1934 for which no records could be found.

P16 *The Grand Tour*

P16.1 *The Grand Tour*. Martin Beck Theatre. 10 December, 1951. 8 Performances. Produced by the Playwrights' Company; directed by the author; sets by Howard Bay.

Mr. Montgomery — John Rodney
A Female Traveler — Claire Justice
Nell Valentine — Beatrice Straight
A Male Traveller — Maury Tuckerman
Raymond Brinton — Richard Derr
Deck Steward — Sam Bonnell
Professor Coogan — William A. Lee
Harvey Richman — Edwin Jerome
Adele Brinton — Louisa Horton

Reviews—R328, R329, R330, R331, R332, R333, R334, R335, R336, R337, R338

P17 *The Home of the Free*

P17.1 *The Home of the Free.* The Comedy Theatre, Columbia University. 22 April, 1917. Produced by the Morningside Players. Directed by Mary Shaw.

P17.2 *The Home of the Free.* Washington Square Players. 31 October, 1917.
Reviews—R18, R20

P18 *The Iron Cross*

P18.1 *The Iron Cross.* The Comedy Theatre, Columbia University. 13 February, 1917.

Margaret Dreier — Edith Randolph
Wilhelm Dreier — Ernest Rowan
Karl Schiller — Edward Nicander
Marie — Margaret Farleigh
Captain Holbe — Bertram Hobbs
Freida — Clarice McCauley
Emma — Sylvia Wolfe
Heinrich — Gage Bennett
Rosa — Mildred Valentine

Review—R19

P19 *It Is the Law*
(adapted from the unpublished novel by Hayden Talbot)

P19.1 *It Is the Law.* Ritz Theatre. 29 November, 1922. 125 Performances. Produced by Sam Wallach.

Baker — C. W. Goodrich
Fisher — Richard Stevenson

Byron — Charles P. Bates
Yates — John F. Roche
Walker — John Burr
Johnson — Jack Thorne
Rumson — James Linhart
Dennison — Joseph de Stefani
Page — Thomas Hood
William Elliott — A. H. Van Buren
Gordon Travers — Hans Robert
Ruth — Alma Tell
Justin Victor — Ralph Kellard
Lillian — Rose Burdick
Theodore Cummings — William Ingersoll
Albert Woodruff — Arthur Hohl
"Sniffer Evans" — Alexander Onslow
James Dolan — Walter Walker
Edward Harley — Frank Westerton
Ellen — Valerie Valarie

Reviews—R34, R35, R36

P20 *Judgment Day*

P20.1 *Judgment Day*. Belasco Theatre. 12 September, 1934. 93 Performances. Produced and directed by the author; sets by Aline Bernstein.

Dr. Michael Vlora — Lee Baker
Dr. Panayot Tsankov — Raymond Bramley
Colonel Jon Sturdza — William Barwald
Professor Paul Murusi — Philip Leigh
Count Leonid Slatarski — St. Clair Bayfield
Lydia Kuman — Josephine Victor
George Khitov — Walter Greaza
Kurt Schneider — Eric Wollencott
Dr. Wolfgang Bathory — Carroll Ashburn
Malinov — Charles Durand
Dr. Stambulov — James Moore
Dr. Mensch — Horace Casselberry
Conrad Noli — Vincent Sherman
Srazhimir — Joseph Julian
Dr. Constantine Parvan — Hans Robert
Vassili Bassaraba — Mark Schweid
Marthe Teodorova — Ethel Intropidi
Sonia Kuman — Olga Druce

General Michael Rakovski — Romaine Callender
Giulia Crevelli — Fania Marinoff
Nekludov — Edward Downes
Grigori Vesnic — House Jameson
Marek — Brice Disque, Jr.

Reviews—R156, R157, R158, R159, R160, R161, R162, R163, R164, R165, R166, R167, R168, R169, R170, R172, R175

P20.2 *Judgment Day*. Swiss Cottage Theatre, London 27 May 1937. Directed by Murray McDonald.

Reviews—R188, R189, R190, R192

P21 *Life Is Real*

The play had a brief production in Munich, Germany (under the title *Wir in Amerika*) in January of 1929 and an unreviewed production on 4 June 1937 in San Francisco.

P22 *The Left Bank*

P22.1 *The Left Bank*. Little Theatre. 5 October, 1931. 242 Performances. Produced and directed by the author; sets by Raymond Sovey.

Claire Shelby — Katherine Alexander
John Shelby — Horace Braham
Alan Foster — Cledge Roberts
Claude — Alfred A. Hesse
Waldo Lynde — Donald Macdonald
Susie Lynde — Millicent Green
Lillian Garfield — Marie Maddern
Charlie Miller — Fred Herrick
Joe Klein — Murray Alper
Dorothy Miller — Rose Lerner
Gustave Jensen — A. L. Bartholot
Sonya Darachek — Tamara Nicoli
Miriam Van Diesen — Dorothy Day
Willard Simmons — Edward Downes
Mary Adams — Janet Cool

Reviews—R102, R103, R104, R105, R106, R108, R111, R112, R116, R117, R118, R120, R143

P23 *Love Among the Ruins*

P23.1 *Love Among the Ruins.* University of Rochester. March 12, 1963. Directed by Robert Hogan (cf. Hogan [S95]).
Review—R368

P24 *The Mongrel*
(adapted by Rice from the play by Herman Bahr)

P24.1 *The Mongrel.* Longacre Theatre. 15 December, 1924. 32 Performances. Produced by Warren P. Munsell; directed by Frances C. Fay; sets by Lee Simonson; translation by Frances C. Fay.

> The Justice — Maurice Colborne
> The Doctor — W. T. Clark
> Attendant — Maurice Bernard
> The Forester — Carl Anthony
> Marie — Ernita Lascelles
> Strasser — Max Montesole
> Mathias — Rudolph Schildkraut
> The Priest — Peter Lang
> Loís — John F. Hamilton
> The Aunt — Alice Bellmore Cliffe
> Kasper — George L. Fogle
> Katie — Rae Berland

P25 *A New Life*

P25.1 *A New Life.* Royale Theatre. 15 September, 1943. 70 Performances. Produced by the Playwrights' Company; directed by the author; sets by Howard Bay.

> Theodore Emery — Sanford McCauley
> Miss Hanson — Alice Thomson
> Miss Devore — Colleen Ward
> Miss Murphy — Ann Driscoll
> Miss Weatherby — Sara Peyton
> George Sheridan — Kenneth Tobey
> Lillian Sheridan — Timmie Hyler
> Esther Zuckerman — Dorothy Darling
> Mollie Kleinberger — Dora Weissman
> Edith Charles Cleghorne — Betty Field
> Olive Rapallo — Ann Tomas
> Gustave Jensen — John Ireland
> Dr. Lyman Acton — Blaine Cordner

Miss Kingsley — Frederica Going
Samuel Cleghorne — Walter Greaza
Isabelle Cleghorne — Merle Maddern
Millicent Prince — Joan Wetmore
Grover C. Charles — Arthur Griffin
Miss Swift — Terry Harris
Captain Robert Cleghorne — George Lambert
Ruth Emery — Helen Kingstead
Miss Wooley — Shirley gale
Henrietta Dunstan — Elizabeth Dewing
Herbert Dunstan — Nicholas Saunders

Reviews—R259, R260, R261, R262, R263, R264, R265, R266, R267, R268, R269, R270, R271, R272, R273, R278

P26 *Not for Children*

P26.1 *Not for Children*. The Fortune Theatre, London. 28 November 1935.
Reviews—R182, R183, R184, R185, R186, R187

P26.2 *Not for Children*. Coronet Theatre. 13 February, 1951. 7 Performances. Produced by the Playwrights' Company; directed by the author; sets by John Root; music by Robert Emmett Dolan.

Elijah Silverhammer — Keene Crockett
Clarence Orth — Alexander Clark
Timothy Forrest — J. Edward Bromberg
Ambrose Atwater — Elliot Nugent
Theodora Effington — Betty Field
Irma Orth — Natalie Core
Prudence Dearborn — Ann Thomas
Evangeline Orth — Joan Copeland
Dirby Walsh — Phil Arthur
Hugh McHugh — Fredd Wayne
Hitch Imborg — John Gerstad
Old Gentleman — Gar Moore
Pensacola Crawford — Frances Tannehill
Pianist — Bud Gregg

Reviews—R307, R308, R309, R310, R311, R313, R314, R315, R316, R317, R318

P27 On Trial

P27.1 *On Trial.* Candler Theatre, New York. 19 August, 1914. 365 Performances. Produced by Arthur Hopkins; directed by Sam Forrest.

    Robert Strickland — Frederick Perry
    Doris Strickland — Constance Wolf
    May Strickland — Mary Ryan
    Mr. Deane — Thomas Findlay
    Gerald Trask — Frederick Truesdell
    Mrs. Trask — Helene Lackaye
    Glover — Hans Robert
    District Attorney Gray — William Walcott
    Defense Counsel Arbuckle — Gardner Crane
    Judge Dinsmore — Frank Young
    Dr. Morgan — George Barr
    Russell — Lawrence Eddinger
    Jury Foreman Trumble — Howard Wall

Reviews—R01, R02, R03, R04, R05, R06, R07, R08, R09, R10, R11, R12, R13, R14, R15, R16, R17, R87

P27.2 *On Trial.* Quaigh Theatre. 20 February, 1979. 12 Performances.
Review—R267

P28 The Passing of Chow-Chow

P28.1 *The Passing of Chow-Chow.* New York University Playhouse, Washington Square. 4 January 1929. 1 Performance. Directed by George Kahn. Cast included Tamma Axel, John Koch, Morris Soroka and Anthony Surona.

P29 See Naples and Die

P29.1 *See Naples and Die.* Vanderbilt Theatre. 24 September, 1929. 62 Performances. Produced by Lewis E. Gensler; directed by the author; sets by Robert Edmond Jones.

    Small Chess Player — Gregory Dniestroff
    Bearded Chess Player — S. Sarmatoff
    Basil Rowlinson — Horace Cooper
    Angelo de'Medici — Rinaldo Schenone
    Lucy Evans — Beatrice Herford
    Hugo Von Klaus — Walter Dreher
    Charles Carroll — Roger Pryor

                    Luisa — Rose Rolanda
        Hjordis de'Medici — Margaret Arrow
        Kunegonde Wandl — Margaret Knapp Waller
        Nanette Dodge Kosoff — Claudette Colbert
          Carriage Driver — Edward Maurelli
        Ivan Ivanovitch Kosoff — Pedro de Cordoba
                    Stepan — Albert West
   Mary Elizabeth Dodge Norton — Lucille Sears
        General Jan Skulany — Marvin Kline
           Fascist Guards — Ulisse Mattioli, Joseph Pierantoni

Reviews—R90, R91, R92, R96

P29.2 *See Naples and Die.* Little Theatre, Adelphi (Britain). 1 April 1932.

                    Nanette — Olive Blakeney

Review—R126

P29.3 *See Naples and Die.* Chicago, 1937.

P30 *Skyscraper*
(musical based on Rice's *Dream Girl*)

P30.1 *Skyscraper.* 13 November 1965. 241 performances.

Rice took no part in the production of this musical.

Book: Peter Stone
Music: James Van Heusen
Lyrics: Sammy Cahn
Staging: Cy Feuer
Sets: Robert Randolph
Costumes: Theoni Aldredge
Choreography: Michael Kidd

P31 *Street Scene*

P31.1 *Street Scene.* The Playhouse, New York. 10 January, 1929. 601 Performances. Produced by William Brady; directed by the author; sets by Jo Mielziner.

            Abraham Kaplan — Leo Bulgakov
            Greta Fiorentino — Eleanor Wesselhoeft
               Emma Jones — Beulah Bondi
                Olga Olsen — Hilda Bruce
            Willie Maurrant — Russell Friffin
             Anna Maurrant — Mary Servoss

P32 Street Scene 227

Daniel Buchanan — Conway Washburne
Frank Maurrant — Robert Kelly
George Jones — T. H. Manning
Steve Sankey — Joseph Baird
Agnes Cushing — Jane Corcoran
Carl Olsen — John Qualen
Shirley Kaplan — Anna Kostant
Filippo Fiorentino — George Humbert
Alice Simpson — Emily Hamill
Laura Hildebrand — Frederica Going
Charlie Hildebrand — Alexander Lewis
Mary Hildebrand — Eileen Smith
Samuel Kaplan — Horace Braham
Rose Maurrant — Erin O'Brien-Moore
Harry Easter — Glenn Coulter
Mae Jones — Millicent Green
Dick McGann — Joseph Lee
Vincent Jones — Matthew McHugh
Dr. John Wilson — John Crump
Officer Harry Murphy — Edward Downes
Milkman — Ralph Willard
Letter-Carrier — Herbert Lindholm
Iceman — Sam Bonnell
Marshall James Henry — Ellsworth Jones

Reviews—R72, R73, R74, R75, R76, R77, R78, R79, R80, R81, R82, R83, R84, R85, R86, R87, R88, R92, R94, R95, R97, R98, R107, R114, R123

P31.2 *Street Scene*. Globe Theatre, London. 27 September 1930.

Reviews—R99, R100, R101

P31.2 *Street Scene*. American Conservatory Theatre, 1974. Directed by Edward Hastings.

P31.3 *Street Scene*. Quaigh Theatre, New York. 9 July, 1975.

P31.4 *Street Scene*. Drama Community Repertory Theatre, New York. September, 1975.

P32 *Street Scene*
(musical version)

P32.1 *Street Scene* (musical). Adelphi Theatre. 9 January 1947. 148 Performances. Produced by Dwight Deere Wiman and the Playwrights' Company; directed by Charles Friedman; music by

Kurt Weill with lyrics by Langston Hughes; sets by Jo Mielziner; costumes by Lucinda Ballard.

Abraham Kaplan — Irving Kaufman
Greta Fiorentino — Helen Arden
Emma Jones — Hope Emerson
Olga Olsen — Ellen Repp
Willie Maurrant — Peter Griffith
Anna Maurrant — Polyna Stoska
Daniel Buchanan — Remo Lota
Frank Maurrant — Norman Cordon
George Jones — David E. Thomas
Steve Sankey — Lauren Gilbert
Carl Olsen — Wilson Smith
Shirley Kaplan — Norma Chambers
Filippo Fiorentino — Sydney Rayner
Laura Hildebrand — Elen Lane
Charlie Hildebrand — Bennett Burrill
Mary Hildebrand — Juliana Gallagher
Jennie Hildebrand — Beverly Janis
Samuel Kaplan — Brian Sullivan
Rose Maurrant — Anne Jeffreys
Harry Easter — Don Saxon
Mae Jones — Sheila Bond
Dick McGann — Danny Daniels
Vincent Jones — Robert Pierson
Dr. John Wilson — Edwin G. O'Connor

Reviews—R292, R294, R295, R296, R297, R298, R299, R300, R301, R302, R303, R304.

P32.2 *Street Scene* (musical). 24 February 1966. 6 performances.
Review—R366

P33 *The Subway*

P33.1 *The Subway*. January 24, 1929. 35 Performances. Cherry Lane Theatre (New York). Produced by the Lennox Hill Players; directed by Adele Gutman Nathan; sets by Walter Walden.

Sophie Smith — Jane Hamilton
Mr. Smith — E. Brooks Descomb
Mrs. Smith — Adeline Ruby
Annie Smith — Evah Schwab
Eugene Landray — Loius John Latzer

P34 Two on an Island

    Tom Smith — Herman Bandes
    George Clark — Harry Jay Marks
    Maxwell Hurst — Ben Melson
    Robert Anderson — Peter Gwyn
 Reviews—R82, R86

P33.2 *The Subway*. Masque Theatre, New York. 1929.

    Sophie Smith — Jane Hamilton
    Mr. Smith — Jerome Seplow
    Mrs. Smith — Mary Hallett
    Annie Smith — Evah Schwab
    Tom Smith — Herman Bandes
    Eugene Landray — Edward H. Wever
    George Clark — Harry Jay Marks
    James Bradley — Edward Martin
    Maxwell Hurst — George Christie
    Robert Anderson — Louis John Latzer

P33.3 *The Subway*. Lyceum Theatre Club, London. 14 July 1929.
 Review—R89

P34 *Two on an Island*

P34.1 *Two on an Island*. Broadhurst Theatre, New York. 22 January, 1940. 96 Performances. Produced by the Playwrights' Company; directed by the author; sets by Jo Mielziner.

    William Flynn — Robert Williams
    Samuel Brodsky — Martin Ritt
    Mary Ward — Betty Field
    John Thompson — John Craven
    Clifton Ross — Earl McDonald
    Sightseeing Guide — Howard DaSilva
    Dora Levy — Dora Weissman
    Dixie Bushby — Arthur L. Sachs
    Frederic Winthrop — Whitner Bissell
    Lawrence Ormont — Luther Adler
    Martha Johnson — Terry Harris
    Heinz Kaltbart — Rudolf Weiss
    An Actor — Charles Polachek
    Dorothy Clark — Martha Hodge
    Katherine Winthrop Holmes — Joan Wetmore
    Martin Blake — Herschel Bentley
    Gracie Mullen — Ann Thomas

Helen Ormant — Harriet MacGibbon
Sonai Taranova — Eva Langbord
Mrs. Ballinger — Frederica Going
Ruth Ormant — Helen Renee
Fred — Don Shelton
Dolly — Adele Longmire
Mrs. Williams — Mary Michael

Reviews—R210, R211, R212, R213, R214, R215, R216, R217, R218, R219, R220, R221, R222, R223, R224

P34.2 *Two on an Island*. The Barter Theatre, Abingdon, VA. July, 1975. Directed by Owen Phillips.

P35 *Wake Up, Jonathan*
(with Hatcher Hughes)

P35.1 *Wake Up, Jonathan* Henry Miller's Theatre, New York. 19 January, 1921. 105 performances. Produced by Sam H. Harris; directed by Harrison Grey Fiske.

Jonathan Blake — Charles Dalton
Marion Blake — Mrs. Fiske
Helen Blake — Helen Holt
Junior Blake — Frank Hearn
Peggy Blake — Lois Bartlett
Chippy Blake — Nadia Gary
Bernard Randall — Donald Cameron
Douglas Brent — Fleming Ward
Adam West — Howard Lang
Jean Picard — Freddie Goodrow
Jennie — Edith Fitzgerald

Reviews—R25, R26, R27, R28, R29, R30, R32, R33

P36 *We, the People*

P36.1 *We, the People*. Empire Theatre. 21 January, 1933. 49 Performances. Produced and directed by the author; sets by Aline Bernstein.

Tony Volterra — Egisto Visser
Louis Volterra — Charles La Torre
Helen Davis — Eleanor Phelps
Frieda Davis — Grace Mills
Allen Davis — Herbert Rudley
William Davis — Ralph Theadore
Albert Collins — Blaine Cordner

Willard Drew — Pierre Watkins
Jack Ingersoll — Randolph Hale
James Cunningham — George Pembroke
Winifred Drew — Mildred Baker
Sarah Collins — Katherine Emmet
Thomas Williamson — William Ingersoll
Steve Clinton — Frank Wilson
Donald Collins — Fred Herrick
Larry Collins — Carol Ashburn
Fred Whipple — Gregory Deane
Mark Brookwood — Charles Davis
Leo Schwarz — Marvin Borowsky
Peter Hines — Sam Byrd
Daisy Costigan — Jane Hamilton
Mary Klobutsko — Juliana Taberna
C. Carter Sloane — Maurice Wells
Harry Gregg — George Christie
Arthur Meadwos — Howard Miller
Elbert Purdy — Thomas Tracey
Walter Applegate — Calvin Thomas
Cleveland Thomas — Walter Greaza
George Fallon — Arthur Ritchie
Luke Smith — Jean Sidney
Herman Spandau — Jules Bennett
Robert Marden — Forest Taylor
Joe Callahan — Glenn Coulter
Sam Rogers — Harry Fischer
James Moulton — House Jameson
Edna Innes — Alice John
Morris Hirschbein — David Leonard
Luther Weeks — Harry Moore
Ellis Jones — Orrin Burke
Mike Ramsay — Harry Bellaver
James Trowbridge — Burr Caruth

Reviews—R245, R246, R247, R248, R249, R250, R251, R252, R253, R254, R255, R256, R257, R258 R372

P37 *The Winner*

P37.1 *The Winner*. The Playhouse, New York. 17 February, 1954. 30 Performances. Produced by the Playwrights' Company; directed by the author; sets by Lester Polakov.

Eva Harold — Joan Tetzel
Martin Carew — Tom Helmore
David Browning — Whitfield Connor
Newscaster — P. Jay Sidney
Arnold Mahler — Lothat Rewalt
Irma Mahler — Jane Buchanan
Haggerty — Philip Puneau
Dr. Clinton Ward — Charles Cooper
Miss Dodd — Lily Brentano
Stenographer — David Balfour
Judge Samuel Addison — Frederick O'Neal
Hilde Kranzbeck — Vilma Kurer

Reviews—R339, R340, R341, R342, R343, R344, R345, R346, R347, R348, R349, R350, R367

P37.2 *The Winner*. Pembroke Theatre, Croyden (Britain). 5 October 1961.

Eva — Pauline Yates

Author Index

The following index lists all critics and scholars included in the secondary bibliography. The references are keyed to the catalogued numbers assigned to each entry.

Adler, Thomas, S155
Alexander, Leon, R179
Allen, Kelcey, R240
Allison, James A., S79
Anderson, Robert, S102
Anderson, John, R72, R193, R245
Angoff, Charles, R208
Aston, Frank, R352
Atkinson, Brooks, R66, R73, R74, R91, R102, R103, R107, R129, R133, R138, R156, R164, R171, R194, R201, R209, R211, R217, R219, R226, R239, R292, R301, R307, R319, R328, R339, R351, R353, R361, S11, S21, S25
Avery, Lawrence, S135

Barnes, Howard, R259, R274, R293
Barratt, Louise Bascom, R127
Bauland, Peter, S133
Beebe, Lucien, R108
Behringer, Fred, S143

Bellamy, F. R., R69
Benchley, Robert, R32, R44
Bigsby, Christopher W., S146
Block, Anita, S53
Bobin, Jane, S118
Bolton, Whitney, S103
Bricker, Herschel, S54
Bristow, Donald, S151
Broun, Heywood, R25, R38, R55
Broussard, Louis, S89
Brown, Jared Allen, S107
Brown, John Mason, R70, R134, R157, R195, R212, R227, R304, S13, S48 Brown, Russell, S154
Bruning, Eberhard, S137
Bungert, Hans, S121

Carb, David, R78, R112, R147
Cather, Willa, R14
Chaffe, Edmund, R145
Chametzky, Jules, S148
Chandler, Frank, S55, (with William Cordell), S62

Chapman, John, R260, R275, R294, R308, R320, R329, R340, R354
Chatfield-Taylor, Otis, R104, R109
Choudhuri, A. D., S136
Clark, Barrett, R81, R82
Coe, David Allen, R355
Coe, Kathryn (with William Cordell), S30
Coleman, Robert, R196, R309, R321, R330, R341, R356
Collins, Ralph, S73
Colum, Padraic, R83
Corbin, John, R34, S3
Cordell, William (with Kathryn Coe), S30, (with Frank Chandler), S62
Cour, Phillip, R94
Creighton, Peet, R132

Darlington, W. A., R192, S52
DeCasseres, Benjamin, R116, R148
Denlinger, Sutherland, S44
Dickinson, Thomas, S8
Dorsey, John, S139
Downer, Alan, S76
Drew, Elizabeth, S39
Driver, Tom, S138
Duffy, Susan, S160
Dukes, Ashley, S07
Dukore, Bernard, S111 (with Daniel Geroukld), S150
Durham, Frank, S114
Dusenbury, Winifred, S88

Eaton, Walter Pritchard, R13
Eder, Richard, R372
Elwood, William, S108

Farrar, John, R49, R52, S05
Fergusson, Francis, R117
Field, Louise Munsell, R122
Firkins, O. W., R30

Flanagan, Hallie, S59
Fleming, Peter, R189
Flexner, Eleanor, S49
Frazer, Winifred (with Jordan Miller), S158
Freedley, Morris, R232
Freeman, Joseph, S26

Gagey, Edmond, S70
Garland, Robert, R130, R135, R159, R261, R276, R295, R322, S28
Garlin, Sender, R162
Gassner, John, R255, R289, S47, S87, S109
Gellert, Roger, R367
Gerould, Daniel (with Bernard Dukore), S111
Gibbs, Walcott, R233, R314, R335, R346
Gilder, Rosamund, R207, R223, R244, R256, R272, R290
Goldman, Rowena, R370
Goldstein, Malcom, S125
Graves, Richard Claude, S129
Greenfield, Thomas Allen, S140, S147
Gruber, Ide, R175
Guernsey, Otis Jr., R310, R323
Gussow, Mel, R369, R371

Hamilton, Clayton, R07
Hammond, Percy, R39, R160
Hawkins, William, R296, R311, R324, R331, R342
Herron, Ima Honaker, S113
Hewes, Henry, R348
Hewitt, Bernard, S87
Himelstein, Morgan, S91
Hoffman, Frederick, S88
Hogan, Robert, S95, S98
Hughes, Charlotte, S61
Hughes, Glenn, S77
Hutchens, John, R118, R123

Isaacs, Edith, R180

Jaques, Damien R373
Jennings, Richard, R65, R100
Joslyn, Jay R374

Kaes, Anton, S130, S131
Kerr, Walter, R254, R317, R326, R332, R337, R343, R357
Kronenberger, Louis, R246, R262, R281, R299, S99
Krutch, Joseph Wood, R59, R68, R76, R88, R92, R105, R113, R139, R166, R169, R174, R203, R218, R287, S10, S17, S27, S45, S56
Kunitz, Joshua, S29

Lardner, John, R300
Laufe, Abe, S100
Lawson, John Howard, S37
Levine, Ira, S152
Lewis, Allan, S96
Lewissohn, Ludwig, R31
Littell, Robert, R84
Lockridge, Richard, R131, R136, R161, R197, R213, R228, R247
Lumley, Frederick, S83

Magill, Frank, S153
Mannes, Marya, R170, R176
Mantle, Burns, R11, R198, R214, R229, R248, S01, S14, S18, S20, S23, S31, S38, S50, S51, S63, S65
Marshall, Margaret, R234, R271
McCarthy, Mary, S84
McCarty, Barclay R153
McClain, John, R312, R333, R344, R358
McKenna, Kenneth, R155
Mathews, Jane De Hart, S105

Mendelsohn, Michael, S92
Mersand, Joseph, S57, S64, S71
Meserve, Walter, S161
Miller, Jordan (with Winifred Frazer), S158
Montrose, Moses, S09, S58
Morehouse, Ward, R263, R277, R297, S43, S74, S86
Morgan, Charles, R67, R101, R154, R184, R185, R190
Morrden, Ethan, S144
Murphy, Brenda, S156

Napieralski, Edmund, S106
Nathan, George Jean, R221, R338, S66, S67, S69, S72, S78, S80, S115
Nichols, Lewis, R249, R264, R278, R282

O'Hara, John, R237
Oppenheimer, George, S85
Ormsbee, Helen, R191, R235

Palmieri, Anthony, S124, S141
Parker, Robert Allerton, R141, R167, S04, S22
Phelan, Kappo, R270, R288
Pollack, Philip, R47
Pollack, Channing, R08
Price, William Thompson, R01

Quinn, Arthur Hobson, S40

Rabkin, Gerald, S94
Rascoe, Burton, R251, R265, R267, R279
Reid, Louis, R22, R27, R42
Rice, Vernon, S75
Riedel, Walter, S149
Roney, Edmund, S112
Ross, George, S24

Scharne, Richard, S159
Schulz, Von Dieter S142
Seidenberg, Roderick, R46
Sherriff, R. C., R97
Sievers, W. David, S82
Skinner, Richard, R61, R75, R110, R140, R165, R168
Smiley, Sam, S116
Smith, Alfred E., R149
Smith, Wendy, S157
Smith, Hugh, R186
Sobel, Bernard, S60
Soudek, Ingrid, S123, S127
Styan, J. L., S145

Taubman, Howard, S97
Taylor, William, S110
Trask, C. Hooper, R98

Usigli, Rudolfo, S119

Valgemae, Mardi, S101, S117
Vernon, Grenville, R205, R222, R238
Verschoyle, Derek, R126, R183

Waldorf, Wilela, R252, R266, R280

Watts, Richard Jr., R199, R215, R230, R298, R313, R325, R334, R345, R359
Weales, Gerald, S90
Weaver, Richard Alden, S122, S128
Weiand, Hermann, S134
Whipple, Sidney, R200, R216, R231
Williams, Jay, S126
Wilson, Edmund, R50
Wilson, Garff, S120
Woollcott, Alexander, R21, R26, R28, R40, R56, R87
Wright, Ralph, R53
Wyatt, Euphemia Van Rennselaer, R111, R124, R150, R172, R181, R206, R224, R243,
Wyatt, Euphemia Van Rennselaer (continued), R273, R291, R305, R327, R365

Young, Stark, R45, R57, R58, R77, R90, R106, R114, R143, R204, R241, R269, R286, S46

Zeller, Loren, S132

General Index

This index records page references as well as references keyed to the primary ("A") and secondary ("R" and "S") bibliographies.

Abe Lincoln in Illinois (Rice as director of), 6, A46, A48, A76, R209
According to the Evidence, 114, 124
Adding Machine, The, 6, 7, 35, 43, A04, A06, A53, R37, R38, R39, R40, R41, R42, R43, R44, R45, R46, R47, R48, R49, R50, R51, R52, R53, R54, R62, R64, R65, R76, R93, R306, R351, R369, R370, R376, S01, S02, S03, S04, S05, S06, S07, S08, S13, S19, S40, S53, S74, S76, S81, S82, S87, S89, S93, S108, S109, S11, S113, S117, S120, S121, S123, S128, S130, S131, S132, S133, S134, S136, S138, S144, S146, S147, S148, S149, S150, S154, S158, S161; characters and summary, 23-25; critical overview, 25-26; published texts, 115; manuscripts of, 124;

Adding Machine, The (continued)
production credits of, 209-211
agit-prop drama, 8, 57, S95
American Landscape, 6, A47, R191, R193, R194, R195, R196, R197, R198, R199, R200, R201, R202, R203, R204, R205, R206, R207, R208, S44, S45, S46, S47, S60, S115, S143, S159; characters and summary, 67-70; critical overview, 70; published texts of, 115-116; manuscripts of 124; production credits of, 211-212
Anderson, Maxwell, 125, S88, S135
As the Sparks Fly Upwards, 116, 124

Barry, Philip, 6, 37, A)&, 116, S45, S46, 213-214
Behrman, S. N., 125, R113, S17, S96
Belasco Theatre, 29, 60, 64, 212, 221
Between Two Worlds, 6, R171, R173, R174, R176, R177, R178,

Between Two Worlds (continued), R179, R180, R181, S143; characters and summary, 61-64; critical overview, 64; published texts of, 116; manuscripts of, 124; production credits of, 212-213

Black Sheep, R129, R130, R131, R132; characters and summary, 26-29; critical overview, 29; published texts of, 116; manuscripts of, 124; production credits of, 212-213

Blue Hawaii, The, 116, 124, 213

Chekov, Anton, S145

China, theatre of, A41

Close Harmony (also known as *The Lady Next Door*) (with Dorothy Parker), 6, R55, R56, R57, R59; characters and summary, 30-32; critical overview, 32; published texts of, 116; manuscripts of, 124; production credits of, 213

Cock Robin (with Philip Barry), 6, A07, R66, R67, R68, R69, R70, S18; characters and summary, 37-40; critical overview, 40; published texts of, 116; manuscripts of, 124; production credits of, 213-214

communism, A73, R178, S35, S115

Counsellor-at-Law, 6, 127, R107, R109, R110, R113, R114, R115, R119, R121, R122, R123, R124, R125, R127, R128, R151, R152, R154, R245, R246, R247, R248, R249, R250, R251, R252, R253, R254, R256, R257, R258, R372, S23, S24, S65, S66, S75, S125; characters

Counsellor-at-Law (continued) and summary 47-50; critical overview, 50; published texts of, 116; manuscripts of, 124; production credits of, 214-215

Cue for Passion, 7, R352, R353, R354, R355, R356, R357, R358, R359, R360, R361, R362, R363, R364, R365, S86, S96, S99, S142; characters and summary, 94-95; critical overview, 95; published texts of, 117; manuscripts of, 124; production credits of, 216

Day Dream, 117

A Defection from Grace (with Frank Harris), 5, 117, 124

Diadem of Snow, A, 6, A10, 216; characters and summary, 17-18; critical overview, 19; published texts of, 117; manuscripts of, 124; production credits of, 216

Digges, Dudley, A06, 209

Dream Girl, 7, 8, A74, R275, R276, R277, R279, R280, R282, R283, R284, R285, R286, R287, R288, R289, R290, R291, R319, R320, R321, R322, R323, R324, R325, R326, R327, R373, R374, S69, S82, S96, S226; characters and summary, 82-85; critical overview, 85; published texts of, 117; manuscripts of, 124; production credits of, 216-218

Ethiopia, S105

expressionism, 7 A04, R37, R45, R46, R48, R49, R53, R62,

General Index

expressionism (continued), R65, S02, S03, S07, SO8, S10, S81, S89, S93, S96, S108, S117, S121, S123, S131, S133, S147, S158
Exterior (part of *The Sidewalks of New York*), 37, 117

Family Affair, A, 117, 124
Federal Theatre Project, 6, A38, A48, A80, 126, S44, S50, S56, S59, S77, S126, S152, S157, S159
Field, Betty, 6, 7, 82, 85, 93, A83, R210, R211, R214, R217, R263, R269, R280, R285, R290, R307, R321, 216, 219, 223, 224, 229
Flight to the West, 6, 8, A51, A73, R225, R226, R227, R228, R229, R230, R231, R232, R234, R235, R236, R237, R238, R239, R240, R242, R243, R244, S61, S68, S143, S159' characters and summary, 74-78; critical overview, 78; published texts of, 118; manuscripts of, 124; production credits of, 218-219
Find the Woman (see also *For the Defense*), 6, 118, 218
For the Defense (see also *Find the Woman*), 6, 118, 124, R21, R22, R23, R24
Freud, 95, A77, R357, R360, R362, R363, S82, S101, S142

Gay White Way, The, 35-36, 118, 219
Good Woman, A, 118
Grand Tour, The, 7, 128, R328, R329, R330, R331, R332, R333, R334, R335, R336, R337, R338, S80; characters and summary, 86-88; critical

Grand Tour, The (continued), overview, 88; published texts of, 118; manuscripts of, 124; production credits of, 219-220
Group Theatre, The, S157

Helen and John, 118, 124
Help! Help!, 118, 124
Holliday, Judy, 85, R319, R320, R321, R322, R323, R324, R326, R327, 217
Home of the Free, The, 6, R18, R20; characters and summary, 16-17; critical overview, 17; published texts of, 118; manuscripts of, 124; production credits of, 220
Home-coming, The (with Hatcher Hughes), 118, 124
House of Archer, The, 118, 124
House in Blind Alley, The, 6, 118, 124; characters and summary, 13-16; critical overview, 16; published texts of, 116; manuscripts of, 124
Hughes, Hatcher, 6, 19, 118, 123, 124, 125, 230

Imperial City (novel), 6, A44, R220
Iron Cross, The, 5, R19; characters and summary, 12-13; critical overview, 13; published texts of, 119, manuscripts of, 124; production credits of, 220
It is the Law, 6, R34, R35, R36; characters and summary, 22-23; critical overview, 23; published texts of, 119; manuscripts of, 124; production credits of, 220-221

Japan, theatre of, A42, A43, A80
Judgment Day, 6, A33, R156, R157,

Judgment Day (continued), R158, R159, R160, R161, R162, R163, R164, R165, R166, R167, R168, R169, R170, R172, R175, R188, R189, R190, R192, S25, S26, S27, S31, S37, S50, S52, S83, S116, S143; characters and summary, 57-60; critical overview, 60-61; published texts of, 119; manuscripts of, 124; production credits of, 220-221

Kingdom of Heaven, The, 119, 124

Landscape with Figures (part of *The Sidewalks of New York*), 36-37, 119, 124
Left Bank, The, 6, R102, R103, R104, R105, R106, R108, R111, R112, R116, R117, R118, R120, R143, S20, S70, S71; characters and summary, 46; critical overview, 47; published texts of, 119; manuscripts of, 124; production credits of, 222
Levy, Hazel, 7
Life is Real (see also *Wir in Amerika*), 119, 124, 222
Living Theatre, The (critical study), 7, A28, A39, S40, A42, A43, A79, A80, A82
Love Among the Ruins, 7, R368, S95; characters and summary, 88-90; critical overview, 90; published texts of, 119; manuscripts of, 124; production credits of, 223

Marshall, Barbara, 7
Matter of Time, A, 119, 124

melodrama, 7, 12, R06, R15, R21, R23, R31, R34, R36, R53, R77, R78, R94, R140, R156, R163, R165, R167, R169, R170, R188, R232, R238, R330, R343, R344, S19, S27, S40, S56, S67, S144, S156
Mielziner, Jo, R74, R217, R241, 213, 216, 218, 226, 228, 229
Minority Report (autobiography), 7, 19, 40, 88, A65, A83, A84
Mongrel, The, 120, 124, R58, R60, R61, R63, 233
Muni, Paul, 50 R107, R109, R114, R115, R127, R128, R245, R246, R248, R249, R250, R251, R252, R253, , R254, R256, R257, S66, 214, 215
municipal theatre, A69
My Country is the World, 120, 124

naturalism, 35, R98, S10, S145
New Life, A, 7, R259, R260, R261, R262, R263, R264, R265, R266, R267, R268, R269, R270, R271, R272, R273, R278, S63, S67, S143; characters and summary, 78-82; critical overview, 82; published texts of, 120; manuscripts of, 124; production credits of, 223-224
Not for Children, 7, R182, R183, R184, R185, R186, R187, R307, R308, R309, R310, R311, R313, R314, R315, R316, R317, R318, S38, S63, S78, S80, S94; characters and summary, 64-67; critical overview, 67; published texts of, 120; manuscripts of, 124; production credits of, 224

General Index   241

O'Neill, Eugene, 5, 65, A61, R43, R61, R88, S09, S19, S82, S83, S86, S88, S89, S95, S98, S147
Odets, Clifford, S39, S47, S56, S92, S95, S146
On Trial, 5, 7, 23, A03, A67, A83, A84, R01, R02, R03, R04, R05, R06, R07, R08, R09, R10, R11, R12, R13, R14, R15, R16, R17, R18, R87, R267, S8, S40, S74, S86; characters and summary, 9-11; critical overview, 11-12; published texts of, 120; manuscripts of, 124; production credits of, 225
One Must Eat, 120, 124
Ordeal by Fire, 120

Parker, Dorothy, 6, 30, 116, 125, 213
Passing of Chow-Chow, The, 5, 36, R71, 121, 225
Playwrights' Company, 6, 8, A46, A48, A49, A64, A76, A80, A83, 125, R315, S41, S47, S158, 211
Prelude for Marionettes, 121

realism, 47, R04, R63, R75, R77, R99, R104, R105, R111, R176, R277, R304, R310, S11, S17, S19, S49, S76, S87, S104, S145, S152, S156, S158
Repertory Theatre, 8, A29, A69
Return of the Native, 121, 124
Russia, theatre of, A28, A39, A52, A54, A59, A68, A73, A80, A83, S115
Rus in Urbe (part of *The Sidewalks of New York*), 37, 121

Schildkraut, Joseph, 64, R58, R63, R180, R181, 212, 213, 223

See Naples and Die, 6, A15, R90, R91, R92, R96, R126, S50; characters and summary, 43-45; critical overview, 45; published texts of, 121, manuscripts of, 125; production credits of 225
Seventh Commandment, The, 5, 121, 125
Shaw, George Bernard, 8, A27, R182
Sherwood, Robert, 6, A76, A125, R209
Show Must Go On, The (novel), 7, A65
Sidewalks of New York, The, 36-37, 43, A12, 117, 119, 121, 125
Siege of Berlin, 121
Skyscraper (musical version of *Dream Girl*), 226
Slaves of the Lamp, 7, 121, 125
Soft Music (see *Close Harmony*)
Street Scene, 6, 7, 35, 37, 45, 50, A11, A12, A14, A23, A32, A44, A79, A128, R72, R73, R74, R75, R76, R77, R78, R79, R80, R81, R82, R83, R84, R85, R86, R87, R88, R92, R94, R95, R97, R98, R99, R100, R101, R102, R107, R111, R114, R123, S10, S11, S12, S14, S19, S28, S40, S49, S55, S56, S57, S71, S72, S74, S76, S84, S85, S87, S88, S97, S100, S104, S109, S110, S118, S125, S144, S146, S148, S150, S155, S156, S158, S161; characters and summary, 40-43; critical overview, 43; published texts of, 121-122; manuscripts of, 125; production credits of, 226-227
Street Scene (musical) R292, R294, R295, R296, R297, R298,

Street Scene (musical) (continued) R299, R300, R301, R302, R303, R304, R305, R366; characters and summary, 85-86; critical overview, 85-86; published texts of, 122; manuscripts of, 125; production credits of, 227-228

Subway, The, 6, 7, R82, R86, R89, S40, S82, S93, S101, S108, S117, S120; characters and summary, 32-35; critical overview, 35; published texts of, 122-23; manuscripts of, 125; production credits of, 228-229

Three Plays Without Words, 36, 117, 119, 121

To the Stars, 123, 125

Toller, Ernst, S53, S123, S127

Tucker's People, 123, 125

Two on an Island, 6, 7, R210, R211, R212, R213, R214, R215, R216, R217, R218, R219, R220, R221, R222, R223, R224, S63, S70, S71; characters and summary, 70-74; critical overview, 74; published texts of, 123; manuscripts of, 125; production credits of, 229-230

Voyage to Purilia, A (novel), 6, A18

Wake Up, Jonathan (with Hatcher Hughes), 6, R25, R26, R27, R28, R29, R30, R31, R32, R33, S82; characters and summary, 19-22; critical overview, 22; published texts of, 123; manuscripts of, 125; production credits of, 230

We, the People, 6, A30, A36, A44, R133, R134, R135, R136, R137, R138, R139, R140, R141, R142, R143, R144, R145, R146, R147, R148, R149, R150, R153, R155, S21, S22, S23, S26, S31, S37, S42, S48, S49, S71, S92, S125, S126, S143, S147; characters and summary, 51-56; critical overview, 56-57; published texts of, 123; manuscripts of, 125; production credits of, 230-231

Winner, The, 7, R339, R340, R341, R342, R343, R344, R345, R346, R347, R348, R349, R350, R367, S96; characters and summary, 91-93; critical overview, 93-94; published texts of, 123; manuscripts of, 125; production credits of, 231-232

About the Author

MICHAEL VANDEN HEUVEL is Associate Professor of English and Interdisciplinary Humanities at Arizona State University. He is the author of *Performing Drama/Dramatizing Performance: Alternative Theatre and the Dramatic Text* (1991), and his articles have appeared in journals such as *New Theatre Quarterly, Journal of Dramatic Theory and Criticism,* and *Theatre Journal.*

**Recent Titles in
Modern Dramatists Research and Production Sourcebooks**

Clifford Odets: A Research and Production Sourcebook
William W. Demastes

T. S. Eliot's Drama: A Research and Production Sourcebook
Randy Malamud

S. N. Behrman: A Research and Production Sourcebook
Robert F. Gross

Susan Glaspell: A Research and Production Sourcebook
Mary E. Papke

William Inge: A Research and Production Sourcebook
Richard M. Leeson

William Saroyan: A Research and Production Sourcebook
Jon Whitmore

Clare Boothe Luce: A Research and Production Sourcebook
Mark Fearnow

Rachel Crothers: A Research and Production Sourcebook
Colette Lindroth and James Lindroth

ISBN 0-313-27431-2

HARDCOVER BAR CODE